Reasonable Doubt:

A Case for LGBTQ Inclusion in the
Institutions of Marriage and Church

Author: Scott McQueen

Published by: Canyonwalker Press
Editors: Wendy Danbury & Elaine Phillips

TABLE OF CONTENTS

DEDICATION

This book is dedicated to Addison, of whom I am extremely proud. I am proud of his courage and honesty to simply be himself. I am a better person and our family is stronger because of what we have learned from him and through this experience. Thank you for who you are, son, and the Christian young man I know you to be. Your Mother, brothers, and I love you very much.

FOREWORD

I had been a pastor of a Southern Baptist church located near a conservative Christian university. Every year, students who attended our church would confide in me they were "struggling with same sex attraction". As a Southern Baptist pastor, I would counsel them towards self-control. Our church offered multiple students the funding to attend reparative therapy in hope they could overcome their unwanted attractions.

As the years went by, it became apparent no one's orientation was changing. And, every time I met with these students, I always felt like I was the bearer of bad news. To them, it meant they could never allow themselves to experience romantic love. It meant they could never allow anyone to ever come relationally close, fearing they might "stumble". Counseling sessions were creating a climate of self-loathing and self-hatred. I witnessed people leaving the church and, ultimately, their faith, altogether.

One day, one of the lesbian students I had been meeting with for over a year finally told me she could not fight her attractions any longer. She then asked me how I would feel if someone were to tell me I had to learn how to be attracted to a man. As a straight male, the idea of that was inconceivable. It dawned on me what I was asking gay, lesbian and bisexual people to do was something impossible to change.

I then met a gay man who was living with his partner. Until that time, I had never met anyone who wasn't fighting his or her same-sex attraction. As we got to know each other, I asked him the question, "As a gay man, what would someone like you want to tell a conservative pastor like me?" The question rattled him. He didn't want to answer for fear of making me uncomfortable. But I told him I was in a process of trying to understand the experiences of the gay community.

He responded by telling me during the 1980's and 1990's, when so many of his friends were suffering from HIV and AIDS, all he heard from people like me was judgment. We had told his community AIDS was a punishment sent by God. He also said he never saw anyone from my community come alongside to help or show compassion. They were left to suffer and die alone. I was stunned by his response. All I could say was, "You are right. We did cast judgment and did not come alongside you. I am so sorry." And his response to me was one of grace. This man replied, "In all my life, I never thought I'd hear an apology from someone like you. If you want to know more about who we are, I want to introduce you to my community." It was the beginning of my intentional journey in understanding the real struggles of LGBTQ people and the damage the church had inflicted.

For over five years, I also began to research what the Scriptures said regarding homosexuality. I researched primary sources on homoerotic literature from Greek and Roman antiquity. I wanted to learn how the original authors of Scripture understood homosexuality in their time. It was a long and difficult process. Eventually, I discovered my conservative reading of Scripture regarding homosexuality was deficient and my theology became one that affirmed same sex relationships.

I wish there had been more resources like this book when I began my journey. The strength of this book is Scott McQueen understands the mindset of the conservative Christian, especially those within the Southern Baptist tradition. He served as a Southern Baptist pastor for over 31 years and knows first-hand what it is like to hold a theology opposing LGBTQ identity. As a person who has taught the conservative beliefs regarding homosexuality, he knows the hurdles and questions many people struggle to better understand. And more importantly, he is able to appreciate the gravity of this conversation because he is the father of a gay son. Because of this, Scott is able to nuance what love actually looks like in real life rather than just an ideological understanding. With story telling and exegesis, McQueen makes a strong case for the Bible's affirmation of LGBTQ people.

The question Scott McQueen aims at is: How does Jesus interpret the law? Because if we claim to be followers of Jesus, we ought to interpret Scripture the way Jesus did. Through these pages, McQueen helps us to see Jesus didn't always interpret the law the way conservatives do. And in so doing, he exposes the current conservative hermeneutic as more closely aligning with the religious leaders of Jesus' day. What we find is even in the context of the law; Jesus calls us to demonstrate mercy and love. My hope is this book will help you read and apply Scripture the way Jesus did. And in so doing, you will see the beauty of Christ in the LGBTQ community.

Danny Cortez

Danny Cortez is the founding pastor of New Heart Community Church. He is a graduate of Cal State University, Long Beach (B.A.) and Talbot Theological Seminary (M. Div). He is married to Abby, has four children and lives in La Mirada.

Danny was formerly a Southern Baptist pastor.

His church website is https://www.newheart.church/

PREFACE

The air is surprisingly alive with sounds and smells. With the deepest breath you can possibly draw, you attempt to take it all in at once: the aroma of a freshly mowed lawn; the sound of a distant crop duster sweeping over a sprawling field; locusts buzzing their mesmerizing drones, reminding you summer is in full swing; back to school is weeks away. And speaking of the Alabama heat, you can literally fry an egg on the scorched concrete driveway should you so choose. Even so, you simply stand there in your own front yard enjoying the moment. "Can it get any better?" you ask yourself. Add a game of pitch and catch with your best friend, who's walking up your driveway, and now ... that's living! It's a simple freedom to play pitch and catch, enjoying the serenity of the moment. To bathe in the sounds and smells around you, even the summer sun. What a wonderful day to be alive!

That is until, from across the street, several kids walk over with bats and gloves in hand. Unbeknownst to you, they were watching from their windows and decided to join. The kid from two doors down also sees you throwing ball and decides to pick up his glove and come over, too. Before long, there is a yard full of boys talking about starting a game of baseball. It's all innocent enough or so it seems. "What are today's rules?" one asks. "What are we going to use for bases?" a second kid shouts. Another interrupts, "If you knock the ball over the fence, will we count it as a homerun or an out?" "Let's go over to the school and play on a real ball-field," one more suggests. From there, pandemonium breaks out as everything from choosing sides to whose ball will be used is argued among the crowd of would-be all-stars.

Almost as spontaneously as it materialized, the magic mood has been chased away. Replaced with teams, umpires, fences, and too many rules to remember, the simple serenity of pitch and catch has suddenly become institutionalized, even if it were just in the front yard. The sounds and smells that filled the air with joy are, in an instant, erased with bickering and the smell of sweaty armpits. What just happened? I'll tell you what happened: a child's tranquility evaporated like the morning dew.

Many years removed, I am once again finding myself similarly bombarded with rules and regulations; this time, not with child's play but, rather, by the damaging constrictions of the church. I quietly watch as dogma and denominational by-laws are swiftly and unapologetically chasing away the simplicity of loving and being loved. What's worse is I'm not alone! Growing numbers of conflicted families; Christian families, moms and dads, husbands and wives, along with their children, are being ostracized by their church homes; literally being kicked to the curb by Bible-believing, God-fearing church members who once considered those same families as brothers and sisters in Christ. Talk about serenity and tranquility evaporating before one's eyes!

But, I have grown tired of just standing still. As difficult as it is to write this book, even at the expense of being further ostracized by one-time friends and ministry peers, I can no longer stand by quietly and watch the church needlessly and inappropriately hurt a community of people and their families, basing their actions on misguided interpretations of Scripture. Anyone who has known me for any length of time would know how out of character it is for me to be an advocate for gay rights. As someone who, at one time, openly confessed my greatest prejudice has always been toward the gay and lesbian communities – and God forbid you would have gotten me started on those who are transgender. I am the last person one might expect to be writing this book! I have always held to the "Baptist Faith and Message," a document summarizing the basic beliefs and practices held by Southern Baptists. In that document there is a very clear statement condemning the practice of homosexuality.

And yet, I am evidence an incredible God can, in a single moment, stop a person dead in his tracks and cause him to reassess everything he has ever heard and believed about a specific people-group. Some readers will find this book difficult to read and process. Those who know me or have known me in the past may wonder why I would write such a book. Others who only know I am (or was) a Southern Baptist pastor may harbor ill will toward me and call me names, or believe I will now go to hell for changing my beliefs on this subject. It is also highly probable some will think of me as a traitor or a devil or a blasphemer. On the other hand, there are countless numbers of the lesbian, gay, bisexual, transgender, and queer (LGBTQ) community whose red flags of skepticism must be vigorously waving right about now simply because I was a Southern Baptist pastor. Waiting for the proverbial shoe to drop is something for which these folks are quite accustomed.

To be quite honest, I get it. I understand. Several years ago, I couldn't have been trusted to be an objective voice in favor of the LGBTQ community, much less an advocate. To the contrary, only a few years ago I, myself, would have been skeptical of any person who would have attempted to tell me the Bible does not irrefutably denounce homosexuality in any and all forms and circumstances. So, when I say, "I understand," I really mean it! In fact, I welcome your skepticism. But, what I am banking on, in fact, praying for, is each person who reads these words will honestly strive to set aside judgments until after these pages have been read.

I fully expect one's prejudices to make reading these pages an almost insurmountable challenge for some. Even so, I challenge my Christian readers to stop and pray right now God's Holy Spirit will allow your heart to, at least, attempt to listen with an unbiased ear. If I had been given this same book three years ago, I'm not sure I would have been objective or, even patient enough, to read it all. But, I so hope you will! What you will find is not a plea to overlook Scripture or to disregard God's truth. Rather, we will explore seven Bible passages that seemingly denounce any and all homosexuality. What I believe you will discover is biblical truth is never in question but, rather, the traditionally imposed interpretations that have become "infallible" among Christian conservatives and fundamentalists.

Again, please hear my heart: I am not advocating anyone be given a "pass" to sin or live in a sinful lifestyle. If it is, in fact, a sin to have same-sex attraction or to "practice same-sex behavior within the context of marriage," then we ought to call it what it is – sin – and call for true repentance.

However, if the evidence reveals otherwise, then it is the church that needs to repent of the false accusations and the prejudice from which many Christians speak and feel in their hearts!

I must also set the record straight by saying I have not changed my views on God, the Trinity, the atoning work of Jesus Christ through His shed blood on the cross, the authority of Scripture, the Church, Christ's return, Heaven and hell, or any other major doctrine.

Furthermore, I do not believe my interpretation of Scripture, as it pertains to homosexuality and same-sex marriage, is admittance God's Word is faulty in any way, shape or form. Bottom line, I believe God's Word is true! I simply contend certain scriptures have been misunderstood and erroneously taught for many years. As a pastor and a responsible Christian, I am compelled to speak out against that which contradicts the teaching of Jesus Christ. I can't live with myself trying to make everybody happy, even my Southern Baptist friends, at the expense of truth. I understand my stance on this subject will come under fire. I understand I will lose friends. I've already come under fire. I've already lost many friends. Some have even suggested what I am doing is paramount to ministry suicide. Even so, I can no longer turn a blind eye to that which has become crystal clear. You see, I have reasonable doubt. The remainder of this book is an attempt to explain why.

CHAPTER ONE
THE COURT IS NOW IN SESSION

If you are a member of the LGBTQ community, I hope you will trust me when I say I am fully aware you do not need my endorsement or anyone else's, for that matter, to be worthy of God's love or to marry the person of your choice. My goal is not to serve as the morality police or as a gatekeeper for God. I also want you to understand I no longer hold to the Prosecution's arguments I am about to share. However, I feel *all* readers should fully understand *why* it is necessary to offer a defense in the first place. While this is a polarizing debate, it is an over-step to assume everyone understands why they are either for or against LGBTQ inclusion in the institutions of Church and Marriage. Thus, the main points for the prosecution are now briefly presented. They will be followed by a more thorough defense.

The Prosecution's Case

Many conservative Christians are well indoctrinated on the talking points of homosexuality and have strong opinions, denouncing same-sex attraction on any and every level, as it concerns the institutions of Church and Marriage. I, too, having formerly served as a seminary-trained Southern Baptist pastor for 31 years, am fully aware of the conservative argument. Therefore, I will summarize the perspective from which I was taught and viewed this subject up until April 8, 2014.

The purpose of the *Baptist Faith and Message* is to identify and proclaim doctrinal beliefs and values held by those who claim to be part of the Southern Baptist Convention. In Article Fifteen of the *Baptist Faith and Message*, entitled, *The Christian and the*

Social Order, the following statement is made: "All Christians have a responsibility to try to make the will of Christ first in our own lives and in the world. The ways and methods used to improve society and to create righteousness among men can be very helpful. These changes are helpful only if they come because of the rebirth of the person by the saving grace of God in Jesus Christ. Just like Christ, Christians should be against racial discrimination, every form of greed, self-interest, and evil, and all forms of sexual wrongdoing, including adultery, homosexuality, and pornography." [1]

Southern Baptists (and most other mainstream denominations) are strictly opposed to homosexuality, viewing it as an abomination. For biblical conservatives, it is simply a matter of obeying God's plain teaching on the subject. Most denominations will argue the Bible consistently denounces homosexual activity as a sin. The seven Scriptures specifically dealing with homosexuality include Genesis 19:1-13, Leviticus 18:22, Leviticus 20:13, Judges 19:16-30, Romans 1:26-27, 1 Corinthians 6:9 and 1 Timothy 1:9-11. The prosecution argues Romans 1:26-27 clearly teaches homosexuality is a result of denying and disobeying God. When people continue in sin and unbelief, "the wrath of God is being revealed from heaven against all the godlessness and wickedness of people, who suppress the truth by their wickedness."[2] Because of turning truth into a lie, God "gives them over" to even more wicked and depraved sin in order to show them the futility and hopelessness of life apart from God. The prosecution further contends 1 Corinthians 6:9 proclaims homosexual "offenders" will not inherit the kingdom of God. Genesis 19:1-13 and Judges 19:16-30 are purported as narratives exposing the sin of homosexuality and the grave effects of committing such sins. Leviticus 18:22 and 20:13 are presented as further examples of God's displeasure in homosexuality, which He calls an abomination. Finally, the prosecution resolves 1 Timothy 1:9-11 states sodomy is considered, along with a list of other sins, as lawless, disobedient, godless, sinful, unholy and profane.

Conservative Christians insist God does not create a person with homosexual desires (orientation). Many Christians agree with author and pastor, John McArthur, who writes, as it pertains to homosexuality being unnatural: "To illustrate the degrading passions that rise out of the fallen human heart, Paul uses homosexuality, the most degrading and repulsive of all passions. In their freedom from God's truth, men turned to perversion and even inversion of the created order. In the end, their humanism resulted in the dehumanization of each of them. Perversion is the illicit and twisted expression of that which is God-given and natural. Homosexuality, on the other hand, is inversion, the expression of that which is neither God-given nor natural. When man forsakes the Author of nature, he inevitably forsakes the order of nature."[3]

Furthermore, the Bible never mentions same-sex behavior except in a negative way. In fact, every marriage relationship found in the Bible involves, specifically, male and female. Genesis 2 reveals God made Adam and Eve, not Adam and Steve, to complement each other in the bond of marriage. Human anatomy, itself, naturally reveals God's intended will, as it concerns sexuality. Thus, a foundation to human identity and to the institution of marriage can only be understood in and through a heterosexual framework. Because God did not create a person to be homosexual, then it must be understood as being a choice; a choice the Bible declares as sin. All sin is offensive to God and will be judged if not forgiven. True repentance on the part of the homosexual is the proper response. In addition, the local church has the moral responsibility to teach its congregants the whole truth of God, pointing out the sin of homosexuality, as laid out in Scripture. The church should not and cannot turn a blind eye to that which the Bible clearly denounces as sin. However, Southern Baptists (and others) will admit the Bible does not describe homosexuality as a "greater" sin than any other. "Are homosexuals to be excluded from the community of faith?" asked one gay Christian to a friend in a letter. "Certainly not," he concluded. "But anyone who joins such a community should know that it is a place of transformation, of discipline, of learning, and not merely a place to be comforted or indulged."[4] In other words, a truly repentant homosexual can and should expect, through sincere discipline and spiritual growth, to eventually revert back to God's intended design for humanity; heterosexuality.

On August 29th, 2017, no less than 150 conservative and fundamentalist Christians, comprised of spiritual leaders, scholars and pastors, endorsed a declaration that is being called the "Nashville Statement." Since that time, thousands more have signed their names in approval for which this document stands. Released by The Council on Biblical Manhood and Womanhood, the Nashville Statement serves as a guidance to churches on how to properly address issues of sexuality. This document, consisting of 14 articles of belief, rejects all forms of sexual identity and orientation not consistent with the teachings of the Bible. All lesbian, gay, bi-sexual, transgender and queer persons are actively engaging in sin as they identify outside the identity assigned to them by God. Adopting a transgender self-conception is inconsistent with God's plan and purpose for one's life and is in direct rebellion against God's design for one's life. God has made us male or female, according to His holy purposes. The male and female reproductive structures at one's birth are key to defining and understanding one's self-conception. In addition, churches and Christians are encouraged to oppose all manifestations of sexual behavior outside the biblical model of "one man and one woman." Christians who affirm or take a neutral position on this issue are also sinning by condoning those who sin. Denny Burk, President of the council, was reported as saying, "The aim of The Nashville Statement is to shine a light into the darkness-to declare the goodness of God's design in our sexuality and in creating us as male and female."5

Therefore, members of the Jury, the Prosecution charges all those who identify as lesbian, gay, bi-sexual, transgender or queer with living outside the framework of God's intended plan and design for their lives. They are living outside the will of God and are in need of forgiveness. True repentance is the only proper response to finding relationship and fellowship with God in Christ.

The Defense's Case

In a Court of Law, reasonable doubt is all a defense lawyer needs to show a jury in order for them to conclude a case should be dismissed or for a defendant to be found not guilty. If a jury of one's peers determines a reasonable doubt exists, that jury cannot, nor should they, convict the defendant. It is not necessary they find conclusive evidence the defendant be absolutely innocent; rather, it is only for the defense lawyer to show enough evidence exists to render a 'Not Guilty' verdict.

Every day across America, the LGBTQ community and, specifically, same-sex marriage (which, according to the United States Supreme Court, is simply marriage) is on trial. In October, 2014, the United States Supreme Court refused to hear cases from several states seeking to keep their marriage bans in place, thrusting this highly contested and controversial civil rights issue even further into the national spotlight. Then, on June 26, 2015, the highest court in the land ruled in a monumental decision, legalizing same-sex marriage in all fifty states. The ruling of Obergefell v. Hodges now requires a state to license a marriage between two people of the same sex and to recognize a marriage between same-sex couples who have been lawfully licensed and wed from another state.[6]

Needless to say, not everyone is in agreement with the 14th Amendment to the Constitution. Kim Davis, an elected clerk whose job is to issue marriage licenses in Rowan County, Kentucky, made international news in July 2015 when she refused to abide by the Supreme Court's ruling. Basing her refusal on religious grounds, she was even thrown into jail for a short time as a media circus erupted, making her an overnight icon for at least two conservative political Presidential candidates during the 2016 campaign, as well as the religious right.

The controversy is not going to go away any time soon as every person is his or her own judge and jury, not to mention conservative politicians who continue trying their hardest to have the landmark ruling over the new marriage laws overturned.

Needless to say, a great divide exists in our families between mothers and sons and fathers and daughters who refuse to speak to one another; congregations of churches are slow to love and quick to hate; even local and state governments who pride themselves with "justice for all" continue to demonstrate "prejudice toward some," as is the case with the Kentucky county clerk.

The court of public opinion remains in session and people's lives and futures are at stake. This book's purpose is to present biblical evidence – yes, *Biblical evidence* – challenging the traditional church's stance on same-sex attraction and marriage, in hopes a new paradigm might be embraced. United States law now recognizes all marriages as perfectly legal, regardless of a couple's sex or gender. Yet, most Christian denominations continue to renounce same-sex marriage and vehemently insist it is sin and an abomination to God, based on interpretation of Scripture. While the nation's highest court has already approved marriage for *all* U.S. citizens, it is important the church also learn to practice full inclusion. This will not be an easy task and I readily admit I don't claim to have all the answers. In fact, no one has all the answers.

As Christians, however, we do have God's Word, the Bible. I believe it to be inspired and trustworthy. Most Christians would agree. But, while we agree on the truth of God's Word, believers often disagree on its interpretation. It is for this reason there are so many denominations of Jesus Christ's church. Each denomination represents large people groups who understand God's Word as truth in their own unique way. These larger groups of people worship, study, and apply the Bible, as they understand the truth.

The real problem is confusing one's denomination's particular interpretation of truth with God's *absolute* truth. A Southern Baptist, for example, may interpret God's Word in a particular way. However, one must never assume they have completely cornered the market on interpretation over, let's say, the Methodist or the Presbyterian down the street. A person may be convinced of the validity of their denomination's interpretation of Scripture and hold it firmly with conviction in their heart; and so, they should! Nevertheless, one must guard against judging another's interpretation as inaccurate, invalid, or sub-standard to his or her own. Unfortunately, this mistake happens quite often.

The Apostle Paul, writing in Romans 14:1-5 (NIV) penned: *"Accept the one whose faith is weak, without quarreling over disputable matters. One person's faith allows them to eat anything, but another, whose faith is weak, eats only vegetables. The one who eats everything must not treat with contempt the one who does not, and the one who does not eat everything must not judge the one who does, for God has accepted them. Who are you to judge someone else's servant? To their own master, servants stand or fall. And they will stand, for the Lord is able to make them stand. One person considers one day more sacred than another; another considers every day alike. Each of them should be fully convinced in their own mind."*

Paul is clearly addressing interpretation differences between believers. There are several keys in this text to help us better understand how to manage these differences. The words, "disputable matters," "accept" and the phrase, "fully convinced in their own mind," all reveal vital components to getting along with fellow believers in the unity of Christ. Most Christians are going to agree, and so we should, on major doctrines of the Christian faith, such as those confessions found in the Apostle's Creed. While my background is Southern Baptist, who are not a creedal people, we, and most every other mainstream Christian denomination, agree with the confessions of faith found in this ancient creed:

> I believe in God the Father, Almighty, Maker of heaven and earth,
>
> And in Jesus Christ, his only begotten Son, our Lord,
>
> Who was conceived by the Holy Ghost, born of the Virgin Mary,
>
> Suffered under Pontius Pilate; was crucified, died and buried. He descended into hell.
>
> The third day he rose again from the dead.

He ascended into heaven, and sits at the right hand of God the Father Almighty.

From thence he shall come to judge the quick and the dead.

I believe in the Holy Ghost,

I believe in the holy Catholic Church, the communion of saints,

The forgiveness of sins,

The resurrection of the body,

And the life everlasting. Amen.

The Apostle's Creed consists of what virtually all-mainstream believers would confess as indisputable doctrines of the Christian faith. For believers, there is little, if any, wiggle room, so to speak. However, there are numerous other doctrines open for dispute. Paul mentioned two hot issues being heavily debated during his ministry: should or shouldn't believers continue to eat according to the Old Testament kosher laws, including avoiding meat sacrificed to idols; and should the church uphold the Fourth Commandment to meet and worship together on the Sabbath, or is it permissible to worship any day the congregation so chooses? These were and are important questions. They deal with extremely longstanding traditions. They deal with Old Testament law. They deal with one of the Ten Commandments. These are significant doctrinal issues; even so, there is room for debate. Paul said, as it concerns disputable doctrines, Christians should accept their Christian brothers and sisters, even when there are differences, and furthermore, recognize each believer must be fully persuaded in his or her own mind through faith. Modern-day examples might include the mode of baptism, consumption of alcohol, leadership of women in ministry and, dare I add, the dispute over same-sex attraction and same-sex marriage.

There is no greater lightning rod among churches today than the one surrounding the subject of homosexuality and, specifically, the acceptance of same-sex marriage. The overwhelming majority of Christians have been brought up being taught same-sex attraction is an abomination to the Lord and an undeniable and indisputable sin. However, as a former conservative, Southern Baptist pastor with over thirty-four years of ministry experience, with earned degrees from seminaries including a doctorate degree from a notable conservative institution, Luther Rice Seminary, I, myself, have found reasonable doubt: not in the Word of God, but rather, in the mainstream interpretation of Scripture, as it concerns the LGBTQ community. I admit I don't have all the answers. But I do believe the church is, at least, missing an enormous opportunity to love a people-group desperate to experience the unconditional grace of God and, at most, missing God's truth on homosexuality, altogether. I believe this to be one of the disputable matters referred to by Paul.

I am not a lawyer. I do not pretend to know the ins and outs of the judicial system. If scrutinized by a critical eye on whether I am following protocol using the correct verbiage, as it concerns law, I will fall short. Yet, because of the 2015 ruling by the highest court in our nation and because same-sex relationships continue to be engulfed in the court of public opinion, I will use the model of the courtroom to present the evidence that has been brought to my attention. I trust you will allow me the freedom to share, and further, to allow the Holy Spirit to give you an objective ear to hear. It is very tempting – and reassuring – to have already made up one's mind about this matter, even before considering, just maybe, your interpretation has been misguided. Please do not jump to a premature conclusion. Let me challenge you to:

- Listen carefully to the evidence
- Keep an open mind, without prejudice or bias
- Be fair and impartial
- Be objective
- Listen to all the evidence before reaching a verdict

After you have honestly and objectively considered the evidence and listened to Holy Spirit speak to your heart, then I trust you will decide as God has given you His discernment. That is all anyone or I could ask.

> *Lord, help us to hear from you; from your heart to ours. Help us to know how you feel about the members of the LGBTQ community. Help us to know how we should live in relation to the LGBTQ community. Give us ears to hear, eyes to see, and hearts to follow your will. In Jesus' name, Amen.*

Opening Statements

My name is Scott. I was a pastor. I was a pastor of a conservative, evangelical, Southern Baptist Church in the Bible belt state of Alabama. For 31 years I served as a pastor in some capacity at conservative, evangelical, Southern Baptist Churches in my home state of Alabama. Oh, and did I mention I have a Christian son who just happens to be gay? My name is Scott and I was a pastor; I am still actively serving as my son's dad.

We're driving down a two-lane highway and every minute we're inching closer to our destination; a small town where we are about to allow our seventeen-year-old son to visit someone he met on social media and chats with regularly on Skype. This other someone also happens to be gay. My wife and I have deeply mixed emotions. Our hearts race inside us but we do our best to remain calm. Several miles out, I decide to finally break the silence:

"Son, I know you expect this to go well. But, if when we get there and this guy is not what you expect him to be, we need a sign to let us know we need to cut it off quick and leave. You know, kind of like an escape password." My son replied,

"Cheez-its. If I say, 'I would like some Cheez-its', you'll know I'm ready to go. You'll know because I really don't like Cheez-its and I would never ask for them."

Honestly, there was a part of me praying, "God, I want to hear Cheez-its! Please, Lord God, give me some Cheez-its!"

As our GPS led us to the road where the young man lived, everyone was a little more than a bit nervous. I just kept thinking, "This is the craziest thing I've ever done! I can NOT believe I am doing this!" As we pulled up at the address we had been given, the young man, also seventeen was standing at the end of the driveway waiting. He was nicely dressed and very handsome. Our son got out of the vehicle, they embraced with a quick hug, and both got back in the vehicle. Everyone exchanged courtesies and down the road we went, taking the two of them to a shopping mall where they could walk around, talk and get to know each other better.

On the way to the mall, we engaged in small talk. Inside my head, I was strangely admitting to myself, "This isn't half as bad as I thought it would be." But then again, my mind would speak, "I pray I'm doing the right thing. I love my son and want what's best for him. I also love my God and I so truly desire to please Him, too. I just pray this is the right thing." And, there is the dilemma. "What is the *right* thing?" I've asked myself that question countless times, over and over again.

Our family embarked on a journey we never asked for on the night of April 8, 2014, when our youngest of three children calmly admitted he was gay. We were right in the middle of our Spring Revival at church and, on that fateful Tuesday evening, a conversation with our son would completely change the lives of our entire family and many others with whom we were in daily contact.

We arrived home from church, and after making our way into the house, I asked Addison to come have a seat in our bedroom. My wife closed the door behind us and the three of us all sat quietly looking at one another. I glanced at my wife Jackie, and her eyes seemed to beg, "Do we *really* have to open Pandora's box or can we somehow just pretend this isn't happening and this situation will all go away?" Taking a deep breath, knowing in my heart this wasn't going away, I began,

"I've heard some troubling news. Have you been on the internet telling some of your friends you're gay?"

Earlier in the day, one of my staff had met me at my church office door with the saddest expression on his face. When I entered the office, and sat down at my desk, he followed in behind me and sat down across from me and solemnly said,

"I'm so sorry to hear. If there's anything I can do, let me know."

"What are you talking about?" I replied.

"Oh, you haven't heard? I thought (our Student Pastor) was going to talk to you about it."

"Talk to me about what?" I asked.

And then the words were said. The words I have been dreading to hear for years were finally spoken. Like the proverbial "Shot heard around the world," my longtime friend and co-laborer in ministry spoke the taboo words I had long feared I would one day hear in context with our third child:

"Addison is gay."

I had been expecting it; waiting on it; dreading it. Strangely, I knew the day would ultimately come when the words would be uttered that our son Addison is gay. My silent prayer had always been I might somehow be wrong. But "somehow" flew right out the window when my co-worker spilled the beans. Come to find out, Addison had been on a social media website where people could ask any question and you're supposed to give an honest answer. Apparently, Addison was honest.

After making his declaration public, Addison took it a step forward and told his friends, including some of his church friends. Later, when questioned concerning what possessed him to tell his friends at church, Addison simply responded,

"I'd rather tell them myself than have those same people asking questions and gossiping about it behind my back." At any rate, after telling his friends, one of them immediately raced to our student pastor who, in turn, spoke with my pastor friend, who then met me at my office door.

The truth is, neither Jackie nor I were surprised by the news. We were saddened. We were worried for Addison. We were worried for our family. We were worried for our church family. But surprised? No. This is something neither of us ever dared discuss with one another or anyone else. However, we both knew deep down in our hearts Addison is gay. I don't know how you can know something like this when a child is so small, so young, but honestly, we knew. Our other boys knew, too. I remember discussions with Addison's older brothers and my wife on numerous occasions that would go something like this:

"Dad, you know Addison is going to be gay if you don't make him go outside and play ball."

"Dad, you've got to stop him from walking around and acting all sissy and stuff."

"Dad, my friends at school are calling Addison gay!"

"Scott, you need to do something with him outside. You need to do 'guy-things' with him."

And I would agree! And I tried! But, Addison didn't enjoy doing the typical guy-things, playing sports, or getting hot and sweaty outside. He *never* enjoyed doing those things, even as a little boy.

I coached T-ball for all three of my sons. The older two enjoyed playing and performed well. Addison hated playing and, bless his heart, he only hit the ball and reached first base one time all year. On the other hand, Addison loved wearing the uniform. He was all about dressing up and eating the sunflower seeds while sitting in the dugout. Addison couldn't care less about playing ball. He just wanted to look good in his uniform…and he did!

I bought all three of my boys' bicycles when they were small. My older two learned in a few hours. Addison still can't ride a bike. My older boys go in the woods and hunt or fish or camp. Addison

25

has never wanted to experience any of these activities. Even when we forced him to participate, he was always miserable and constantly complaining. The point is Addison has *always* been different. I clearly understand everybody is unique and different in some ways. I also understand despising outdoor life and "guy" stuff is not necessarily a prerequisite for being gay. But, with Addison, it went deeper. The differences between him and his brothers were light years apart. I saw it. Jackie saw it. His brothers saw it. Addison saw it. Nobody dared claim to see it.

A Story about Saul

His name was Saul. He was just the most up and coming Pharisee of his day. Highly trained and well versed in Scripture, Saul loved the Word of God and was dedicated to keeping the letter of God's law. In addition, Saul was on a mission to see everyone else equally loved God's law and followed it precisely as Saul and others like him prescribed. Saul had no problem confronting sin or sinners who didn't advocate the same values and principles held by the majority. In fact, Saul reveled in the idea he was considered worthy to persecute Christians. He had zero patience for them and wanted to see them pay, even die, for their sins.

One day, while he was on his way to inflict harm on some people in a neighboring city, something extraordinary happened. Luke shares with us the written account: *"As he neared Damascus on his journey, suddenly a light from heaven flashed around him. He fell to the ground and heard a voice say to him, 'Saul, Saul, why do you persecute Me?' 'Who are you, Lord?' Saul asked. 'I am Jesus, whom you are persecuting,' He replied."*[7]

At that precise moment, a new and different life opened like a door for Saul of Tarsus. It was such a radical and life-changing moment even Saul's name was changed to Paul, demonstrating an entirely new person was emerging from the wreckage of what had taken place in this undeniable encounter with the Divine. Saul had thought he was on his way to pleasing God by shutting down some riff-raff with crazy beliefs that went against God's teachings. Instead, God, Himself, met him on a dusty road, and claimed to be part of that very riff-raff!

It is not surprising Saul would be shocked. After all, no one was any more sincere in his faith than Saul. Sincerity, however, is not, nor has it ever been, the litmus test for truth. One can be sincere and sincerely wrong, simultaneously. Such was the case for Saul. Such has been the case for many others, before and since. Such was the case for me. The night I confronted my son about his "sin" of homosexuality, I was altogether convinced I held the high road. I couldn't explain how he grew up so different from his brothers. I couldn't explain how his mother and I sensed this day would surely come. There were so many facets of his life, which hovered over us as a mystery, but nevertheless, I was convinced I was right and he was wrong. Little did I know, like an episode of the Twilight Zone, I was about to step into a different dimension; I was about to walk my own dusty road.

I grew up attending a Southern Baptist church for as long as I can remember. And, while I certainly couldn't boast of a resume anywhere close to the likes of the Apostle Paul, I did believe I was solidly grounded in what I considered to be ironclad truth, doctrinally speaking. Well educated in some of the finest and most respected Southern Baptist universities and seminaries, I had absolutely no doubts I had the biblical answers and insights needed to adequately speak out against homosexuality. And, speak out, I did! It was commonplace for me to preach from Romans, Chapter One and about Sodom and Gomorrah, as found in the Old Testament book of Genesis. I was quick to voice my disapproval of homosexuality and was intolerant in my spirit of the LGBTQ community. And, while I couldn't help but notice my own son's demeanor and actions, I refused to budge on my beliefs. It is for this very reason I am all the more amazed at the change that has been wrought in my own life and in that of my wife, Jackie. As I will describe in greater detail in the following chapters, God began to convict our hearts and expose our prejudices.

The Heavenly Father also allowed, first Jackie and then me, to begin meeting LGBTQ Christian friends through the Gay Christian Network. This is an online website designed for members of the

LGBTQ community to find Christian encouragement, support, education and more. I was surprised to discover the spiritual depth we found evident in the daily conversation and lives of these newfound friends. Furthermore, we began meeting literally hundreds of Christian couples just like ourselves, who were on the same journey to find truthful answers about our sons and daughters. Most we met online. Some we met in person. Either way, we learned there are many moms and dads, just like us, who know in their hearts their children didn't "choose" a lifestyle.

I committed myself to re-examining every Bible passage pertaining to homosexuality. I dusted off my Greek and Hebrew Bibles from seminary. I began combing through the pages of my personal copy of *Vines Expository Dictionary of Old and New Testament Words.* In addition, I began educating myself by reading books; books not found at the mainstream Christian bookstores. Rather, I began reading volumes like the one you now hold in your hand. While there were many that spoke to my heart, two books that really caused me to think are, *Bible, Gender, Sexuality* by James V. Brownson and *Walking the Bridgeless Canyon* by Kathy Baldock. At the end of this book, I will share with you a more complete list of books and other resources Jackie and I have found helpful in our journey.

Finally, more than anything else, Jackie and I both committed ourselves to prayer. We sought the Lord daily searching His heart… and ours. Our sincere prayer has been, as it still is today, to find and remain in the will of our Heavenly Father. Our commitment and worship is solely directed to and for an audience of One and we are only concerned with pleasing Him with our lives. For this reason, we are on this journey. We did not know the dusty road on which we traveled would lead us to where we now stand. Again, I am amazed at what God has wrought. The Lord, Himself, has removed the scales from our eyes to see we were, in so many ways, among the goats.

Jesus once shared a story with His disciples about some goats…and some sheep. Matthew 25:31-46 records the words Jesus used:

"When the Son of Man comes in His glory, and all the angels with Him, He will sit on His glorious throne. All the nations will be gathered before Him, and He will separate the people one from another as a shepherd separates the sheep from the goats. He will put the sheep on His right and the goats on His left. Then the King will say to those on His right, 'Come, you who are blessed by My Father; take your inheritance, the kingdom prepared for you since the creation of the world. For I was hungry and you gave Me something to eat, I was thirsty and you gave Me something to drink, I was a stranger and you invited Me in, I needed clothes and you clothed Me, I was sick and you looked after Me, I was in prison and you came to visit Me.'

"Then the righteous will answer Him, 'Lord, when did we see You hungry and feed You, or thirsty and give You something to drink? When did we see You a stranger and invite You in, or needing clothes and clothe You? When did we see You sick or in prison and go to visit You?' The King will reply, 'Truly I tell you, whatever you did for the least *of these brothers and sisters of mine, you did for Me.' Then He will say to those on His left, 'Depart from Me, you who are cursed, into the eternal fire prepared for the devil and his angels. For I was hungry and you gave Me nothing to eat, I was thirsty and you gave Me nothing to drink, I was a stranger and you did not invite Me in, I needed clothes and you did not clothe Me, I was sick and in prison and you did not look after Me.'*

> **It is only in and through the lives of those who have received the grace of Christ that God's grace can, in turn, be shared with others.**

"They will also answer, 'Lord, when did we see You hungry or thirsty or a stranger or needing clothes or sick or in prison, and did not help You?' 'He will reply, "Truly I tell you, whatever you did not do for one of the least of these, you did not do for Me.' Then they will go away to eternal punishment, but the righteous to eternal life."

29

Just as in the case with Saul and the people of Damascus, Jesus identifies, once again, with the marginalized, persecuted and outcast. This time, when speaking with His disciples, Jesus cautions them to demonstrate love and compassion to complete strangers who have little, if any, identifiable connections with His followers.

As an illustration, consider for a moment this biblical example: "For even when we were with you, we gave you this rule: 'The one who is unwilling to work shall not eat.'" [8] The rule is easy to understand: A person shouldn't be lazy and expect a handout. God's Word clearly encourages people to work and earn their way. Yet, in the earlier passage we read, Jesus was clearly encouraging His followers to feed the hungry. Jesus doesn't qualify or quantify. He simply says feed the hungry. So, what we see then, are two truths playing out in parallel. One truth is from the law, a rule, so to speak; work for your living. Earn your food with hard and honest work. You might say it is a godly standard. But, we also see another truth; grace. Grace is unmerited favor. Grace is receiving something for which you did not work to earn. Jesus told His disciples to feed the hungry; period. This is a pattern we find throughout the Bible. In fact, it is best portrayed in the death, burial and resurrection of Jesus Christ, Himself.

Throughout God's Word, we see people living their lives in an attempt to keep the Law of God. God has filled His Holy Word with standards concerning practically every area of life. The most well known are described as The Ten Commandments. You might think they are given so mankind can work to earn their keep, to pay their own way, to eat from that which they have earned. The Bible, however, is plain to state humans cannot earn their way to God. Humans cannot keep God's standard! Romans 6:23 reads: *"For the wages of sin is death, but the gift of God is eternal life in Christ Jesus our Lord."*

I would like to think Jesus' call for His disciples to feed the hungry is an exercise to better understand and participate in the grace of God. It is only in and through the lives of those who have received the grace of Christ that God's grace can, in turn, be shared with others. That is precisely why those who have fed the hungry and thirsty, clothed the naked, and assisted the stranger, the sick, and the prisoner are considered sheep belonging to the Master. It is because they, themselves, have experienced the grace of God that now, woven into the very fabric of their lives, is an understanding as to how to share it with others. While those who understand God's grace can share it, those who are fixed on God's law can only understand and work within the constraints of the law. Jesus said it this way:

"No good tree bears bad fruit, nor does a bad tree bear good fruit. Each tree is recognized by its own fruit. People do not pick figs from thorn bushes, or grapes from briers. A good man brings good things out of the good stored up in his heart, and an evil man brings evil things out of the evil stored up in his heart. For the mouth speaks what the heart is full of. Why do you call Me, 'Lord, Lord,' and do not do what I say?"[9]

After reading this scripture, I find there is a problem. The specific problem this passage raises is precisely this question: In Jesus' eyes, what constitutes "good" and what constitutes "evil?" The answer will help us identify exactly the difference between law and grace. And there, we will find a basis to establish reasonable doubt. Without further ado, let me introduce Exhibit A.

Chapter One Notes

1. The Baptist Faith and Message, Article XV: The Christian and the Social Order, Executive Committee of the Southern Baptist Convention, 1999 – 2001
2. Romans 1:18 (NIV)
3. John McArthur, The McArthur New Testament Commentary, Romans 1-8 (Chicago: Moody Press, 1991), pages 104-105
4. Richard B. Hays, The Moral Vision of the NT (San Francisco: Harper San Francisco, 1996), page 401
5. Samantha Schmidt, Evangelicals' 'Nashville Statement'

denouncing same-sex marriage is rebuked by city's mayor:
The Washington Post, August 30

6. Melissa Murray, Obergefell v. Hodges and Nonmarriage
   Inequality: 104 California Law Review 1207, 2016

7. Acts 9:3-5 (NIV)

8. 2 Thessalonians 3:10 (NIV)

9. Luke 6:43-46 (NIV)

CHAPTER TWO
EXHIBIT A: GOOD AND EVIL

"One Sabbath Jesus was going through the grain fields, and his disciples began to pick some heads of grain, rub them in their hands and eat the kernels. Some of the Pharisees asked,

"Why are you doing what is unlawful on the Sabbath?" Jesus answered them,

"Have you never read what David did when he and his companions were hungry? He entered the house of God, and taking the consecrated bread, he ate what is lawful only for priests to eat. And he also gave some to his companions." Then Jesus said to them, "The Son of Man is Lord of the Sabbath."

On another Sabbath he went into the synagogue and was teaching, and a man was there whose right hand was shriveled. The Pharisees and the teachers of the law were looking for a reason to accuse Jesus, so they watched him closely to see if he would heal on the Sabbath. But Jesus knew what they were thinking and said to the man with the shriveled hand,

"Get up and stand in front of everyone." So he got up and stood there. Then Jesus said to them, "I ask you, which is lawful on the Sabbath: to do good or to do evil, to save life or to destroy it?" He looked around at them all, and then said to the man,

"Stretch out your hand." He did so, and his hand was completely restored. But the Pharisees and the teachers of the law were furious and began to discuss with one another what they might do to Jesus. One of those days Jesus went out to a mountainside to pray, and spent the night praying to God. When morning came, he called his disciples to him and chose twelve of them, whom he also designated apostles: Simon (whom he named Peter), his brother Andrew, James, John, Philip, Bartholomew, Matthew, Thomas, James son of Alphaeus, Simon who was called the Zealot, Judas son of James, and Judas Iscariot, who became a traitor. He went down with them and stood on a level place.

A large crowd of his disciples was there and a great number of people from all over Judea, from Jerusalem, and from the coastal region around Tyre and Sidon, who had come to hear him and to be healed of their diseases. Those troubled by impure spirits were cured, and the people all tried to touch him, because power was coming from him and healing them all. Looking at his disciples, he said:

"Blessed are you who are poor, for yours is the kingdom of God. Blessed are you who hunger now, for you will be satisfied. Blessed are you who weep now, for you will laugh. Blessed are you when people hate you, when they exclude you and insult you and reject your name as evil, because of the Son of Man.

"Rejoice in that day and leap for joy, because great is your reward in heaven. For that is how their ancestors treated the prophets. But woe to you who are rich, for you have already received your comfort. Woe to you who are well fed now, for you will go hungry. Woe to you who laugh now, for you

will mourn and weep. Woe to you when everyone speaks well of you, for that is how their ancestors treated the false prophets. But to you who are listening I say: Love your enemies, do good to those who hate you, bless those who curse you, pray for those who mistreat you. If someone slaps you on one cheek, turn to them the other also. If someone takes your coat, do not withhold your shirt from them. Give to everyone who asks you, and if anyone takes what belongs to you, do not demand it back. Do to others as you would have them do to you.

"If you love those who love you, what credit is that to you? Even sinners love those who love them. And if you do good to those who are good to you, what credit is that to you? Even sinners do that. And if you lend to those from whom you expect repayment, what credit is that to you? Even sinners lend to sinners, expecting to be repaid in full. But love your enemies, do good to them, and lend to them without expecting to get anything back. Then your reward will be great, and you will be children of the Most High, because he is kind to the ungrateful and wicked. Be merciful, just as your Father is merciful.

"Do not judge, and you will not be judged. Do not condemn, and you will not be condemned. Forgive, and you will be forgiven. Give, and it will be given to you. A good measure, pressed down, shaken together and running over, will be poured into your lap. For with the measure you use, it will be measured to you." He also told them this parable:

"Can the blind lead the blind? Will they not both fall into a pit? The student is not above the teacher, but everyone who is fully trained will be like their teacher.

"Why do you look at the speck of sawdust in your

*brother's eye and pay no attention to the plank in
your own eye? How can you say to your brother,
'Brother, let me take the speck out of your eye,'
when you yourself fail to see the plank in your own
eye? You hypocrite, first take the plank out of your
eye, and then you will see clearly to remove the
speck from your brother's eye. No good tree bears
bad fruit, nor does a bad tree bear good fruit. Each
tree is recognized by its own fruit. People do not
pick figs from thorn bushes, or grapes from briers.
A good man brings good things out of the good
stored up in his heart, and an evil man brings evil
things out of the evil stored up in his heart. For the
mouth speaks what the heart is full of.*

*"Why do you call me, 'Lord, Lord,' and do not do
what I say? As for everyone who comes to me and
hears my words and puts them into practice, I will
show you what they are like. They are like a man
building a house, who dug down deep and laid the
foundation on rock. When a flood came, the torrent
struck that house but could not shake it, because it
was well built. But the one who hears my words and
does not put them into practice is like a man who
built a house on the ground without a foundation.
The moment the torrent struck that house, it
collapsed and its destruction was complete."* [1]

You just read the entire sixth chapter of the Gospel of Luke. The
question raised is an obvious testament many of those hearing
Jesus speak assumed they were His followers but, in fact, were not.
Many called Him "Lord" but their actions simply did not
demonstrate Jesus was, in fact, Lord of their lives. You might say
they were evil trees because they were producing evil fruit.

So here is, once again, the problematic question raised in the
previous chapter: According to Jesus, what constitutes "good" and
what constitutes "evil?" What makes the tree "evil?" I believe the
answer can be found in the previous passages, as contained in

Luke, Chapter 6. As Chapter 6 begins, Jesus is portrayed as hungry and tired. His disciples, too, are tired from their journey and ready to stop and eat.

So, they eat. But, there's an issue; it is against the Law of God to do any work on the Sabbath. That even includes reaching out, taking grain into your hand, rubbing off the chaff, and putting it in your mouth. No kidding! The law, as found in the Old Testament, clearly condemns any act constituting work on the Sabbath. In addition, the Jews wrote the Talmud, a commentary spelling out the interpretation of the law and how it was to be kept. The 39 Melakhot, as found in the Jewish Talmud, are categories which describe the specific illegal activities on the Sabbath. One of those categories includes 'winnowing' which is the separating of chaff from the grain. In the Talmud, winnowing would consist of any separation of intermixed materials, which render edible that which was inedible. So, when the disciples rubbed the grain in their palms to separate the seed from the chaff they were, by law, sinning because this act occurred on the Sabbath. The Pharisees, according to Jewish law, were technically right to accuse Jesus and His disciples of committing an act, which constituted evil! However, Jesus did not recognize the act as evil, but good.

Later in the same chapter, we read about a second incident occurring on a different Sabbath: Jesus heals a man with a shriveled hand. Once again, we see Jesus acting in a manner deemed illegal, and thus, evil in the eyes of the Pharisees and teachers of the law. There is no debate concerning the letter of the law. The law is clear: do no work on the Sabbath. That includes helping hurting people. Technically, the lawyers were right. Technically, the law was broken when Jesus healed the man's hand.

> **Grace is when undeserving people receive an undeserved gift; and that is exactly what entered the scene of humanity when Jesus arrived!**

But, notice again the question Jesus posed to the religious law-keepers: *"I ask you, which is lawful on the Sabbath: to do good or to do evil, to save life or to destroy it?"*

In this case, in Jesus' eyes, "good" was breaking the law and "evil" was keeping it. This can be confusing unless we understand grace always trumps the law. While the law gives us a standard of perfection, grace presents us with unmerited favor. So, the hungry are fed even though the law states their stomachs should still be rumbling. That is grace! The man's hand is healed even though he should have left that building just the way he arrived: crippled. That, too, is grace. Grace is when undeserving people receive an undeserved gift; and that is exactly what entered the scene of humanity when Jesus arrived!

Continuing in Luke, Chapter 6, we move ahead to see Jesus selecting His twelve disciples. Then we find ourselves reading what is commonly known in Christian circles as Luke's version of the Beatitudes. In verse 20-26, Jesus, looking at His disciples, proclaims: *"Blessed are you who are poor, for yours is the kingdom of God. Blessed are you who hunger now, for you will be satisfied. Blessed are you who weep now, for you will laugh. Blessed are you when people hate you, when they exclude you and insult you and reject your name as evil, because of the Son of Man. Rejoice in that day and leap for joy, because great is your reward in heaven. For that is how their ancestors treated the prophets. But woe to you who are rich, for you have already received your comfort. Woe to you who are well fed now, for you will go hungry. Woe to you who laugh now, for you will mourn and weep. Woe to you when everyone speaks well of you, for that is how their ancestors treated the false prophets."*

It is clear Jesus is contrasting those who know and appreciate grace from those who are immersed in the law and in the keeping of the same. Grace is offered to all those who are marginalized and on the fringe, all those who are incapable of helping themselves, all those who are beaten down and trampled on by others. Grace is given to those without anything to bring to the table. I am reminded of a passage found in Isaiah 55:1:

"Come, all you who are thirsty, come to the waters; and you who have no money, come buy and eat!"

We are invited to come to the Lord, even empty handed. Blessed are all who call on the Lord and accept His grace. In fact, grace can only be enjoyed as one is freed from the shackles of the law. Grace can only be imparted upon those who recognize their works are inadequate. The irony of it, however, is those who claim to be the godliest are most often those chained to the strict regimen of the law. Jesus knew this and offered a warning to His disciples not to be sucked in to believing dutifully following the standard was, in itself, a sign of godliness. In fact, it was not even considered "good." Behavior modification does not, nor can it ever, produce righteousness. It is only as we trust Christ and accept His grace, that real and lasting internal change takes place. In Christ, the law is fulfilled.[2] You see, Jesus accomplished the standard the law required. As we place our faith in Him, there is, for us, no more law. Grace trumps the law because Jesus trumps sin!

"So the law was our guardian until Christ came that we might be justified by faith. Now that this faith has come, we are no longer under a guardian. So in Christ Jesus you are all children of God through faith, for all of you who were baptized into Christ have clothed yourselves with Christ. There is neither Jew nor Gentile, neither slave nor free, nor is there male and female, for you are all one in Christ Jesus. If you belong to Christ, then you are Abraham's seed, and heirs according to the promise."[3] Grace is the great equalizer.

Now, back to the question at hand: according to Jesus, what constitutes "good" and what constitutes "evil?" In verses 27-36, Jesus discusses love and hate. It was well known the law demanded a follower of God love his neighbor. However, Jesus threw a wrinkle into the mix when He said, as recorded in Luke 6:27-28:

"Love your enemies, do good to those who hate you, bless those who curse you, pray for those who mistreat you." These words

were not what the law demanded. These words were not even contained in the law. Yet, Jesus is clarifying the intent of the law rather than simply focusing on the letter of the law. The Pharisees would have said doing the letter of the law constitutes "good." Jesus, on the other hand, says, in effect, doing good is not about keeping the letter of the law but, rather, loving your neighbor and, through an act of grace, your enemy, as well.

We are all too familiar with the story of the Good Samaritan (Just in case you are not, you will find the story recorded in Luke 10:25-37. You'll love it.) and how the religious people were too busy being religious to do "good" on behalf of an injured man. It was the Samaritan who demonstrated goodness by offering grace to the injured traveler. In the eyes of the religious elites, this Samaritan was nothing more than an unclean, mixed-bred, sinning low-life! However, it was this same "low-life" who demonstrated goodness through grace! Do you see a pattern here? Grace cannot be contained by the parameters of the law!

A final thought before we move on from Exhibit A concerning "good" and "evil:" throughout this chapter, Jesus intentionally exposes the religious law-keeping people as being judgmental. He strongly warns against judging and condemning others by ultimately sharing an illustration about a large plank of wood and a small flake of sawdust. Jesus said,

"Why do you look at the speck of sawdust in your brother's eye and pay no attention to the plank in your own eye? How can you say to your brother, 'Brother, let me take the speck out of your eye,' when you yourself fail to see the plank in your own eye? You hypocrite, first take the plank out of your own eye, and then you will see clearly to remove the speck from your brother's eye." [5]

Once again, Jesus is contrasting those who follow the letter of the law against those who indulge in grace.

The keepers of the law will always find fault in the sinner. It is very easy to spot and call out their "sin." The law-keepers become a kind of referee watching to blow the whistle on any and every foul or infraction that occurs. The law-keepers want to manage everyone else. They are interested in everyone modifying their behavior to meet *their* specific criteria, *their* definition of right and wrong and thus, *their* agenda.

The law-keepers are also quick to remind us, "We love the sinner; we hate the sin! It is only for your own good that we're watching over you!" Well, I don't think it's for our own good at all. I don't even think it is good, period. In fact, by Jesus' definition, I believe it to be evil.

Colossians 2:16-17 reads this way:

"Therefore, do not let anyone judge you by what you eat or drink; or with regard to a religious festival, a new moon celebration or a Sabbath day. These are a shadow of the things that were to come; the reality, however, is found in Christ."

You see, the person of Jesus is the fulfillment of God's standard! And with Jesus comes grace. Now, that is what I call *good.*

Chapter Two Notes

1. Holy Bible, New International Version®, NIV® Copyright © 1973, 1978, 1984, 2011 by Biblica, Inc.® Used by permission. All rights reserved worldwide.
2. See Matthew 5:17
3. Luke 6:1-5
4. Galatians 2:24-29
5. Luke 6:41-42

CHAPTER THREE
EXHIBIT B: LAW AND GRACE

If we were in a true court of law, I would move that my client be immediately acquitted of all charges, based solely on the fact there are no unbiased judges or juries worthy to try this or any other spiritual case. The only wise Judge is God, Himself, and each and every one of us must stand before Him as sinners, either saved by His grace or lost in our sin. Not any one person or denomination of people is vested to judge in His place. However, I am well aware societies are going to make judgment calls on homosexuality and any number of other issues. Therefore, I will continue, under protest, to argue this case in an effort to shed light to anyone who has ears to hear. Unfortunately, a sad truth is many people are not listening to gain understanding but, rather, listening to prepare a rebuttal.

Thus far, I have attempted to share with this jury sincerity to follow God's truth is not a litmus test for truth. Like Saul of Tarsus, one can sincerely believe something is true but be sincerely wrong, even when that belief has been handed down for generations as God's truth.

I have also sought to introduce evidence Jesus and the "law-keepers" have different definitions of "good" and "evil." If one listened to and trusted the testimony of the Pharisees (the law-keepers), Jesus would, in fact, be guilty of breaking numerous laws of God. In addition, Jesus would be considered an accessory to crimes for also allowing His disciples to participate in breaking laws. Indeed, those same law-keepers did try and execute Jesus for His alleged crimes. Furthermore, I have endeavored to illustrate "evil" is attempting to live by the letter of the law and to manipulate others to do likewise. "Good," on the other hand, is living in the grace of Christ Jesus and demonstrating that same grace toward others. So, now let us, once and for all, define both law and grace.

James 2:8-13 reads like this:

"If you really keep the royal law found in Scripture, 'Love your neighbor as yourself,' you are doing right. But if you show favoritism, you sin and are convicted by the law as lawbreakers. For whoever keeps the whole law and yet stumbles at just one point is guilty of breaking all of it. For he who said, 'You shall not commit adultery,' also said, 'You shall not murder.' If you do not commit adultery but do commit murder, you have become a lawbreaker. Speak and act as those who are going to be judged by the law that gives freedom, because judgment without mercy will be shown to anyone who has not been merciful. Mercy triumphs over judgment."

I remember well the day one of our pastors stepped in my office to tell me about a recent beach trip our youth had made to Florida. What I discovered from the ensuing conversation was Addison had openly shared with a couple of church kids I had driven him to meet and visit with his new "friend." Well, I can only imagine how fast they burned the soles of their shoes running to this pastor and the other chaperones to share what they had been told. So, in our conversation about the trip, I asked, "So, how did things go with Addison? Were there any problems on the trip with him or anyone else?" The pastor said everything went well, *"But..."* My heart sank.

"So, what happened? Just tell me," I asked.

He said, "I heard you took Addison to meet that boy he's been talking to on the Internet. I just don't understand that. I don't know if I agree with that."

I responded, "It's not for you to understand; I'm his Dad and I did what was in his best interest. But since you brought it up, I'll try to explain my actions by asking you some questions. Would you rather me call you to come over to our house and help me clean his brains off the ceiling because he took my 9mm pistol and blew his head off? Or, would you rather me call you in the middle of the night to tell you he has run away from home to go see this guy? Or, that he and the boy have run away together and they're down in Mexico?"

The fellow pastor quickly responded "Of course not! I guess I understand what you mean."

Then I simply stated, "Honestly, I don't care if you understand or not; I'm his Dad and I will do what is in his best interest; period."

How quickly even the most well meaning of people, even close friends, will judge another's actions. I am reminded of the writer of Ecclesiastes who tells us there is nothing new under the sun. In other words, this kind of judgmental attitude has been around virtually forever. It was certainly prevalent, even among Christians, during the time James penned his letter. But judgment comes. It makes its way through people's hearts and out from their mouths to all those believed to be breaking the law. I broke the law. It's just that simple. I broke it when I took my son to see another boy. A pastor escorting his gay son to visit with another gay boy must be law breaking. After all, my minister friend thought so; the chaperones thought so. All the other people with whom they discussed it thought so, too. But, perhaps we need to investigate a little deeper concerning law and grace and identify, exactly, what God *really* thinks before we make our final judgment.

In the above-mentioned passage, the apostle James shares a sobering reminder it is God, and not the law, itself, that demands we live according to His standard. It is not the law we are attempting to please. Rather, it is God who demands we must not steal. It is the very same God, with the very same standard, who demands we not murder. So, in reality, the emphasis is not, nor should it ever be, on our behavior or the command we are attempting to keep, so as not to commit sin.

The emphasis is, and should always be, on the holiness and perfection of Almighty God, Himself. The Law, first and foremost, identifies God and His holiness. Furthermore, we are equally reminded by the law we are *not* God; it is simply impossible to keep. Any faltering on our part to keep God's law, in effect, makes us altogether guilty, regardless of what particular sin we committed or omitted. We can argue specific sins all we want but, in fact, sin is sin. In God's way of looking at things, He wouldn't say, "Well, you are a thief, but at least you are not a murderer." Instead, God simply acknowledges, "You are a sinner." Even more important is we accept that acknowledgment about ourselves.

Years ago, the Apostle Paul penned a letter to the Romans thoroughly discussing the Law of God and the miracle of grace. Paul's letter to the Romans is unique in two ways:

First, As Paul introduces his argument for grace, he does so in a teaching style common in his day. Paul baits his audience, causing them to nod in affirmation with everything he is saying. Then, just when they are in total agreement, Paul turns the tables and exposes their own flaws. We see this style of teaching several places throughout the Bible. For example, when confronting King David with his sin of adultery and murder, Nathan the Priest informed the King about a wealthy man who owned many sheep but still chose to come and steal a poor man's only lamb. This made King David angry and he shouted, *"As surely as the Lord lives, the man who did this must die! He must pay for that lamb four times over, because he did such a thing and had no pity."* Then Nathan said to David, *"You are the man!"*[1]

In the book of Amos, beginning in the first two chapters, we find the prophet speaking out against the many sins of Israel's enemies. Amos cries out against Damascus, against Gaza, against Tyre, against Edom, against Ammon, against Moab, and even against Judah. The phrasing Amos used is, *"For three sins of"*...and then he would name the country... *"even for four, I will not relent."* At that point, Amos would rattle off a list of sins committed by that particular nation.

As Amos spoke, the Israelites were celebrating. They were nodding in affirmation. They were cheering on the hammer of God as it slammed down upon Israel's enemies. They were in total agreement God needed to punish those neighboring nations for all of their despicable sins. But, then, just as the Israelites were being whipped into a frothy lather, Amos shifted gears when he said, as recorded in Amos 2:6, *"This is what the Lord says: For three sins of Israel, even for four, I will not relent."* At once, the Israelites came to realize whatever else God needed to say to the other nations, the real message was for them. In Amos 3:1, Amos continued, *"Hear this Word, people of Israel, the Word of the Lord has spoken against you—against the whole family I brought up out of Egypt."*

While it was true the other nations were being judged by God, the message wasn't directed toward any of them. The real point was being made to the listening audience: the Israelites, themselves.

Fast-forward to Paul speaking to both Jewish and Gentile Christians in Rome, as recorded in Romans 1:18-32:

> *"The wrath of God is revealed from heaven against all the godlessness and wickedness of people, who suppress the truth by their wickedness, since what may be known about God is plain to them, because God has made it plain to them. For since the creation of the world God's invisible qualities—His eternal power and divine nature—have been clearly seen, being understood from what has been made, so that people are without excuse. For although they knew God, they neither glorified Him as God nor gave thanks to Him, but their thinking became futile and their foolish hearts were darkened. Although they claimed to be wise, they became fools and exchanged the glory of the immortal God for images made to look like a mortal human being and birds and animals and reptiles. Therefore God gave them over in the sinful desires of their hearts to sexual impurity for the degrading of their bodies*

*with one another. They exchanged the truth about
God for a lie, and worshiped and served created
things rather than the Creator—who is forever
praised. Amen. Because of this, God gave them over
to shameful lusts. Even their women exchanged
natural sexual relations for unnatural ones. In the
same way the men also abandoned natural relations
with women and were inflamed with lust for one
another. Men committed shameful acts with other
men, and received in themselves the due penalty for
their error. Furthermore, just as they did not think
it worthwhile to retain the knowledge of God, so
God gave them over to a depraved mind, so that
they do what ought not to be done. They have
become filled with every kind of wickedness, evil,
greed, and depravity. They are full of envy, murder,
strife, deceit, and malice. They are gossips,
slanderers, God-haters, insolent, arrogant, and
boastful; they invent ways of doing evil; they
disobey their parents; they have no understanding,
no fidelity, no love, no mercy. Although they know
God's righteous decree that those who do such
things deserve death, they not only continue to do
these things but also approve those who practice
them."*

The first to read this letter was the church in Rome, comprised of both Jews and Gentiles, who were accepting a new message of hope in faith in Christ Jesus. The church was located in the heart of Rome, surrounded by rampant and unabashed sin, ruled by men who were known to commit some of the most ungodly atrocities imaginable. These new church attendees, no doubt, lived amidst the horrors forced upon them by Roman citizenry. It is in this backdrop Paul writes his letter. He begins by describing what so many godly Christians and Jews were witnessing right before their eyes: not just the sins of Rome's people but, more specifically, the sins of Rome's Caesars! Throughout the lifetime of the recipients of Paul's letter, they were exposed to the very worst examples of leadership that could possibly be imagined. Caesars Gaius (Caligula), Claudius, and Nero openly and flagrantly lived out inconceivable lives in all of Italy and encouraged the same of its citizens.

Imagine how the Church at Rome must have held their leaders in contempt. Paul is calling out those very leaders he hopes and prays to confront when he arrives in Rome...and the church is being whipped into the same frothy lather, just as Amos did to Israel years earlier. Paul has the Romans nodding in the affirmative, probably saying amen to every word the Apostle is using to describe the depths to which Rome had plummeted under the current regime.

Furthermore, Paul is preaching wrath and judgment on those very same people. And, don't think for a moment it goes unnoticed. The Christians in Rome are hated and despised. The Jews in Rome are looked down upon, as well. There is a clear dividing line between Roman citizens and everybody else. So, when Paul writes in Romans 1:18 (NIV) of the wrath of God *"being revealed from heaven against all the godlessness and wickedness of people, who suppress the truth by their wickedness,"* the Roman church must be saying "Avenge us quickly, Lord Jesus!"

But, just when the readers are in full agreement with Paul's condemnations, Paul turns the tables. He soberly declares, *"You, therefore, have no excuse, you who pass judgment on someone else, for at whatever point you judge another, you are condemning yourself, because you who pass judgment do the same things."*[2] Notice how many times Paul uses the pronoun, "you." Five times Paul directs the attention back to his readers. And, did you catch that last part, "You who pass judgment do the same things"? It is obvious Paul is comparing the Christian church with "another" group everyone would eagerly consider worthy of judgment and condemnation. I argue the Caesars, along with their corrupt citizens, fit that bill.

Secondly, Paul's letter to the Romans is unique in that Paul had not yet visited Rome at the time it was penned. His entire ministry had

Paul traveling in many parts of the world. Paul invested himself in the lives of all kinds of people planting churches everywhere he went. After moving on to the next city and beyond, Paul would write back to those new churches providing further direction and encouragement. But, Romans is different. It is the only letter written to a church and its community which Paul has yet to visit. In Romans 1:8, Paul states:

"First, I thank my God through Jesus Christ for all of you, because your faith is being reported all over the world."

Paul had heard snippets about the upstart church in Rome. He was excited for them and desperately desired to make his way to Rome and share in and through the church. In fact, I believe Paul wanted to see Rome so he might preach the gospel, not only to the Roman people but, also, to the Caesar, himself. After all, if the absolute leader of the known world converts to Christianity the trickle-down effect would, no doubt, be enormous. I believe Paul was pre-occupied with carrying his message to the very top and, for that reason, insisted on meeting Caesar when the opportunity finally presented itself.

According to Acts, Chapters 21-28, we read about the accusations made against Paul: that he was somehow attempting to cause rioting among Jews and Romans, alike. The passage details Paul's arrest in Jerusalem and the subsequent events surrounding his incarceration. While the matter surrounding his arrest could have been handled rather quickly, Paul chose to force the issue so he might be taken to Rome and stand in Caesar's court to be judged. Jesus, as recorded in Acts 23:11 appeared to Paul with the mandate:

"Take courage! As you have testified about Me in Jerusalem, so you must also testify in Rome."

With this in mind, Paul demanded, as a Roman citizen, to be tried in Rome and not in Jerusalem. To that, we see the following verdict from the presiding Roman judge in Jerusalem, as stated in Acts 25:12: *"After Festus had conferred with his council, he*

declared: 'You have appealed to Caesar. To Caesar you will go!'"
And, with that, Paul was on his way. He would soon be brought to
Rome, the city that was home to the church he had written just a
short time earlier. In fact, Paul will be executed in Rome for
preaching his revolutionary message of grace. But, make no
mistake; The Apostle knew exactly what he would find when
encountering Rome. So, what would Paul encounter?

To understand the Roman world in Paul's day, one needs to look
no further than August 24th, 79 AD. On this date, one of the most
horrific natural disasters ever inflicted on mankind took place in
the city of Pompeii and several smaller villages in Southern Italy.
It was there a massive volcanic eruption from Mount Vesuvius
completely covered and destroyed the city of Pompeii and the
surrounding communities. And, from that day forward, it was as if
the city and villages never existed. That is, until approximately
1,700 years later when archeologists found the buried civilization.
Uncovered were people and animals alike, encased in calcified
layers of ash. Also found were relics and numerous works of art,
reflecting the culture of that day. It was as if the civilization that
was the Roman Empire had been encapsulated and frozen in time.
What was uncovered was shocking.

Archeologists discovered Pompeii was home to some of the
wealthiest people in the Roman world as evidenced by the
architecture of the municipal buildings and their homes. Pompeii
also reflected their love and worship of the gods and goddesses of
the Roman world, as evidenced by the temples and the remaining
religious relics. What was shocking, however, was Pompeii
additionally exposed the Romans' infatuation with sex. The
architecture and especially, the artwork, portrayed erotic scenes
found in virtually every home in the city. Statues and paintings
evidenced the Roman world was fixated with all manner of sexual
experience, but especially the male genitalia. Erotic scenes and
statues featuring the male genitalia were found throughout the city.

David Loth writes, "Among the ancients, sex was unashamedly
joyous, in reading as in practice. The subjects carried no more
taboos than food or sports, family quarrels or international wars." [3]

Yet, those who unearthed the statues and artwork some 1,700 years later were appalled at their scandalous findings. So much so, in fact, the Victorians who excavated Pompeii, took the newfound artwork and statues to the Naples Archeological Museum where, for many years, it was locked away because of its obscene nature. Only in recent years has this secret chamber, containing hundreds of paintings and statues been made available for public viewing within the confines of the museum.

What is so pertinent about this discovery is we are able to pull the curtain back and gain an accurate candid glimpse of the social and cultural norms of Roman life during the First Century. When Paul, the Apostle was writing his letter to the Romans, these same erotic overtones were already prevalent in Rome, and beyond. This was the backdrop to which Paul was preaching throughout the entire Roman world.

It also needs to be explained Roman society was basically comprised of two social statuses: citizens and everyone else. Paul, for example, as previously stated, was a citizen of the Roman Empire. Therefore, Paul was a person of status. Paul enjoyed certain privileges not afforded to all who lived within the empire. This is the very reason Paul was able to be granted a day in court before Caesar, himself.

Many, who lived in Rome and the surrounding cities, on the other hand, were people without status. The non-citizens lived in dishonor, in stark contrast to those who were esteemed citizens of the state. These non-citizens had few, if any, rights. These people might include gladiators, prostitutes, orphans and most certainly anyone not of Roman origin. In addition, Roman status was signified by, of all things, the male genitalia. This strange idea, however, did not originate with the Romans, but rather, was intergraded into their own culture from the Ancient Greeks and worship practices as they had borrowed the gods from Greece and renamed them as their own.

The Ancient Greeks were fascinated by male genitalia and incorporated it into their worship rituals. Athens was the largest and most powerful city in the entire Grecian world. There, just outside its main gate stood a grand statue of Hermes with a big, erect penis, signifying Greeks had not only an open-minded attitude toward sex but also belief in the power and dignity of the erect penis. The erect penis symbolized male power in ancient Greece.[4] "During a festival in Alexandria in 275 BC, there was a procession hauling a gigantic 180-foot-long phallus through the city as part of the celebration of Dionysus, the Greek god of mystery, wine and intoxication. People sang to it and recited poems."[5]   Also, Priapus, the Greek fertility god and protector of male genitalia, had a penis of oversized and permanent erection, from which the medical term, "priapism" is derived." [6] The Greek way of linking the penis to strength and power was simply continued in the Roman culture.

One way Roman men would exert their power and status, as well as find sexual gratification without loss of masculinity or status, was through penetration; that is, engaging in sex as a sign of dominance over another human being. Roman men took wives in order to pass on their name and wealth through childbearing. But, in addition, Roman men often exercised their status and rights by engaging in sex. The other person could be either male or female. That person could be adult or adolescent. One key factor, however, was the one who penetrated (dominant role) had to be a citizen with status and the one who was being penetrated (submissive role) had to be a non-citizen, thus, without status. This kind of barbaric behavior where people of status were controlling those with little or no status was quite common in Rome. This was behavior exemplified by their gods. It was also being lived out in front of all Rome by their leadership, the Caesars, who considered themselves "gods in the flesh."

With minimal investigation, one finds overwhelming evidence the Caesars, who were considered as living gods, lavished themselves in every kind of debauchery imaginable. The three Caesars who lived and reigned during Paul's ministry were Gaius (Caligula), Claudius and Nero.

According to the Roman historian Seutonius, Caesar Gaius

(Caligula), who reigned from A.D. 37 to 41, was a raving emperor, regularly dining on the excesses of cruelty, murder, hedonism and multiple and peculiar sexual escapades.[7] "He had not the slightest regard for chastity, either his own or others', and was accused of homosexual relations, both active and passive, with Marcus Lepidus, also with Mnester the actor, and various foreign hostages; moreover, a young man of consular family, Valerius Catullus, revealed publicly he had enjoyed the Emperor and they quite wore one another out in the process."[8] This kind of open and irresponsible behavior would be on the forefront of the minds and hearts of God's people. They would cringe at the very thought of Gaius and the unimaginable acts in which he participated.

Caesar Claudius, who reigned from A.D. 41 to 54, was not known to participate in same-sex behavior, but he wasn't very good at choosing his brides. Claudius was married four times. His third wife, Messalina, was very beautiful and very promiscuous. She had many men, including her last known affair with a nobleman by the name of Gaius Silius.[9] Claudius had Silius killed and Messalina quickly left the palace.

Not long after leaving, Messalina also died, paving the way for Claudius to marry his niece, Agrippina. The daughter of Caesar Germanicus and sister of Caligula, Agrippina's own thirst for power began a chain of events that would ultimately cost Claudius his life. Dio Cassius, a noted historian on Roman history, described how first, Agrippina had Claudius bring a previously exiled philosopher named Seneca to the palace to mentor her son, Nero, who had been born to her by her previous husband. Next, she had Claudius disown his own son, Brittanicus, who was his child by Messalina. Finally, Agrippina shared a plate of mushrooms, one of them poisoned, with her husband. By morning, Claudius was dead and Nero was Caesar.[10]

Caesar Nero began his reign in A.D. 54 and would rule the Roman Empire until his death in A.D. 68. Nero, who sat on the throne when Paul was brought to Rome, was well documented as having numerous homoerotic encounters. Seutonius, the Roman historian, writes:

"Besides the abuse of free-born lads, and the debauch of married women, he committed a rape upon Rubria, a Vestal Virgin. He was upon the point of marrying Acte, his freedwoman, having suborned some men of consular rank to swear that she was of royal descent."

"He gelded the boy Sporus, and endeavored to transform him into a woman. He even went so far as to marry him, with all the usual formalities of a marriage settlement, the rose-colored nuptial veil, and a numerous company at the wedding. When the ceremony was over, he had him conducted like a bride to his own house, and treated him as his wife. It was jocularly observed by some person, 'that it would have been well for mankind, had such a wife fallen to the lot of his father Domitius.' This Sporus he carried about with him in a litter round the solemn assemblies and fairs of Greece and afterwards, at Rome through the Sigillaria, dressed in the rich attire of an empress; kissing him from time to time as they rode together."[11]

We also find similar documentation from the Roman historian, Dio Cassius:

"Now Nero called Sporus, 'Sabina' not merely because, owing to his resemblance to her he had been made a eunuch, but because the boy, like the mistress, had been solemnly married to him in Greece, Tigellinus giving the bride away, as the law ordained. All the Greeks held a celebration in honor of their marriage, uttering all the customary good wishes, even to the extent of praying legitimate children might be born to them.

After that, Nero had two bedfellows at once, Pythagoras to play the role of husband to him, and Sporus that of wife. The latter, in addition to other forms of address, was termed "lady," "queen," and "mistress." Yet why should one wonder at this, seeing Nero would fasten naked boys and girls to stakes and then, putting on the hide of a wild beast, would attack them and satisfy his brutal lust under the appearance of devouring parts of their bodies? Such were the indecencies of Nero."[12]

In light of a greater understanding of the Greco-Roman world in the day of Paul; in light of its social and cultural norms, its religious practices and overtones, along with its rulers and citizens superiority over those without status, please re-read Romans 1:18-32:

> *"The wrath of God is revealed from heaven against all the godlessness and wickedness of people, who suppress the truth by their wickedness, since what may be known about God is plain to them, because God has made it plain to them. For since the creation of the world God's invisible qualities—His eternal power and divine nature—have been clearly seen, being understood from what has been made, so that people are without excuse. For although they knew God, they neither glorified Him as God nor gave thanks to Him, but their thinking became futile and their foolish hearts were darkened. Although they claimed to be wise, they became fools and exchanged the glory of the immortal God for images made to look like a mortal human being and birds and animals and reptiles.*
>
> *Therefore God gave them over in the sinful desires of their hearts to sexual impurity for the degrading of their bodies with one another. They exchanged the truth about God for a lie, and worshiped and served created things rather than the Creator—who is forever praised. Amen. Because of this, God gave them over to shameful lusts. Even their women exchanged natural sexual relations for unnatural ones. In the same way the men also abandoned natural relations with women and were inflamed with lust for one another. Men committed shameful acts with other men, and received in themselves the due penalty for their error.*
>
> *Furthermore, just as they did not think it worthwhile to retain the knowledge of God, so God gave them over to a depraved mind, so that they do what ought not to be done.*

*They have become filled with every kind of
wickedness, evil, greed, and depravity. They are full
of envy, murder, strife, deceit, and malice. They are
gossips, slanderers, God-haters, insolent, arrogant,
and boastful; they invent ways of doing evil; they
disobey their parents; they have no understanding,
no fidelity, no love, and no mercy. Although they
know God's righteous decree that those who do
such things deserve death, they not only continue to
do these things but also approve those who practice
them."*

Contrary to popular opinion, Romans 1:18-32 is not a passage
specifically targeting homosexuality and it is certainly not a
passage meant for attacking monogamous relationships of any
kind; straight or gay. Rather, the Caesars were practicing all of the
above-mentioned sins. And, if that is not bad enough, the citizens
of Rome were following their lead. They were engaging in every
kind of sexual experience the mind could conjure. They were
living wild and careless lives. But, most of all, they were abusing
other human beings, dominating and mistreating them with no
regard.

Can't you see how this would prove to be the very leverage needed
for the Apostle Paul to expose his Christian audience to the fact
they, too, were sinners and deserving of judgment? Their extreme
disdain for these ungodly leaders and their vile behavior, along
with the citizens of the Roman Empire would be the catalyst
through which Paul would teach the principles of grace. How else
would these Christians ever grasp the power of grace without first
manifesting a judgmental spirit the law invokes from deep in one's
soul?

While this passage does speak against same-sex acts, Romans
1:18-25 describes specific, lavish and immoral acts of the Caesars
and their citizens of status, meant to be understood within its own
historical context, rather than used as a blanket statement against
homosexuality, altogether.

An excellent example is one I heard from Danny Cortez, pastor of New Heart Community Church, in La Mirada, California, who led his Southern Baptist congregation to become more accepting and welcoming of the LGBTQ communities in May 2014. The congregation was dis-fellowshipped from the SBC in September 2014.

> **Romans 1:18-32 describes specific lavish and immoral acts of the Caesars and their citizens of status, meant to be understood within its own historical context, rather than used as a blanket statement against homosexuality.**

Imagine it is the 1990's and a newspaper publishes that an American president had sexual relations with his intern, bringing embarrassment to the entire nation. Everyone would know exactly to whom the paper was referring. Everyone would immediately recognize the story and connect it with the names of both a specific president and his intern. In addition, congregations of God's people might be inclined to respond negatively toward that specific president and harbor judgmental feelings toward him for his explicit actions. However, two thousand years from now, with an entirely different government and an entirely different value system, people may no longer know or care an American president had sex with his intern. They might even be inclined to misconstrue the words from the newspaper to mean that *all* sex with interns is wrong.

I believe this is precisely what the traditional church is doing today by misinterpreting Paul's references to the Caesars as an edict against all same-sex behavior, regardless of context.

As you can well see, the extreme lifestyles being detailed by Paul, as recorded in Romans 1:18-32, are characteristic of the Roman Caesars and the elitist company they kept. It is obvious Paul is describing the numerous and well-known sins being daily lived out by Rome's citizens of status. They were guilty of comparing themselves to God, even to the point of making themselves out to be gods, they were greedy, they were full of envy, they were murderers, they were filled with strife, they were deceitful, and, they were acting in malicious ways toward anyone and everyone who were not people of status. Paul says they were gossips, slanderers, God-haters, insolent, arrogant, and boastful; they invented ways of doing evil; they disobeyed their parents; they had no understanding, no fidelity, no love and no mercy.

In the historical context of this passage of Scripture, Paul is not attacking same-sex marriage any more than he is attacking gossip or arrogance. In fact, he is not attacking the Caesars, either. He is, if anything, attacking the judgmental Christians and Jews who cannot see their own sinfulness because they are too busy judging someone else's. They are so swallowed up by the law they are missing out on that very truth Paul is desperate to bring to their attention: the miracle of grace.

Chapter Three Notes

1. 2 Samuel 12: 5-7
2. Romans 2:1
3. David Loth, The Erotic in Literature: a historical survey of pornography as delightful as it is indiscreet. (New York: Dorset Press, 1994.)
4. Won We Kim, History and Cultural Perspective, Penile Augmentation. (Springer-Verlag: Heidelberg, Berlin, New York, 2016.), page 15
5. Ibid.
6. Ibid
7. Suetonius, *The Lives of the Caesars.* Loeb Classics Library, 1913. Online Life of Caligula (Suetonius; English translation and Latin original) Retrieved September 18, 2008.
8. Suetonius, *The Twelve Caesars*, #36, Translated by Robert

Graves, 1957.

9. The Roman Empire in the First Century, Claudius, Devillier Donegan Enterprises, 2006

10. Cary E, ed., Dio Cassius: Roman History. London: Heinemann, 1925

11. Suetonius, *The Twelve Caesars*, Nero, XXVIII.

12. Cassius Dio,_*Roman History*, LXII, 13.

CHAPTER FOUR
EXHIBIT C: US AND THEM

To hear it from some Christians, same-sex attraction is the absolute worst plague ever to hit planet Earth. In fact, many place blame of one specific plague, AIDS, entirely on the shoulders of the LGBTQ community. Suffice it to say, homosexuality is loathed by most conservatives and fundamentalists and merely tolerated by an even larger number of moderate evangelicals.

For example, I scrolled across a post on Facebook stating The Burger King Corporation, in recognition of Gay Pride Month, decided to use an outer wrapper for their hamburgers that displayed a rainbow and the word "PRIDE." I never would have known about the fast food chain doing this if a Facebook friend hadn't posted it on his wall. But, he did. He not only posted the article but also made some distasteful and derogatory comments. They, in turn, were followed by more and more and even more negative comments. Finally, there was one fellow, who braved the shark-infested waters, and spoke about Christ's love and how Christians shouldn't speak with such venom toward anyone, regardless of their personal beliefs. But, do you think his comments made a difference? Oh, you better believe his comments made a difference, all right. It caused the shark frenzy to become an even more bloodthirsty swarm toward the compassionate man, the restaurant chain and the LGBTQ people, in general. The Christians went mad like man-eaters in chummed waters.

When it comes to LGBTQ people, a large majority of churches force their membership to make a choice. It's US or THEM. There is no middle ground. If you are gay, you must either repent and be celebrated as a poster child for the (now-defunct) ex-gay agenda or continue what you're doing and keep the hell away! If you support gay rights in any way, shape or form, you must cease and desist or be blackballed until you're shamed out of the fellowship.

With so much animosity and aggressiveness displayed you would think the Bible must be jam-packed with words condemning homosexuality. But quite the opposite is true. David Lose, from HuffPost, blogs: "There are only seven passages in the Bible that refer directly to homosexual behavior, and none of them are associated with Jesus. Compare that to the more than 250 verses on the proper use of wealth or the more than 300 on our responsibility to care for the poor and work for justice, and you appreciate quickly that homosexuality was not exactly a major theme of the Bible."[1]

But, don't tell that to conservative and fundamentalist Christians. Don't tell that to me a few years ago, because I was not buying it. Those Christians who pride themselves on being "Bible-believing" have their marching orders and are on the attack. I am reminded of a song by the iconic band, Pink Floyd, entitled, *Us and Them*. An excerpt of the lyrics goes this way:

> *Us and them and after all we're only ordinary men.*
> *Me and you; God only knows it's not what we would choose to do.*
> *'Forward' he cried from the rear and the front rank died.*
> *And, the general sat and the lines on the map moved from side to side.*
> *Black and blue and who knows which is which and who is who.*
> *Up and down; but in the end it's only round and round."[2]*

It appears to me it is, in fact, round and round we go and "where it ends, nobody knows."

What we do know, however, is countless people are being stirred by their denominational "generals" to "hate the sin of homosexuals" and, unfortunately, that far too often translates into, "hate the homosexuals who sin." And, it's not just the church leaders. Former Alabama Supreme Court Justice, Roy S. Moore, famous for his fight to keep a wooden Ten Commandments plaque visible in his Alabama courtroom, made the following announcement on the eve of which same-sex marriage licenses were to be issued in the conservative southern state: "Effective immediately, no Probate Judge of the State of Alabama nor any agent or employee of any Alabama Probate Judge shall issue or recognize a marriage license that is inconsistent with Article 1, Section 36.03, of the Alabama Constitution or § 30-1-19, Ala. Code 1975."[3]

Moore, once again, defied a federal judge's order. On November 13, 2003, the Alabama Court of the Judiciary unanimously removed Moore from his post as Chief Justice for his refusal to remove from the Alabama Judicial Building a monument of the Ten Commandments he commissioned in 2001 despite orders to do so from a federal judge. However, in 2012, Moore was re-elected by the majority of Alabamians to reclaim his position as Chief Justice. Conservative, Bible-belt Alabamians view Moore as a religious patriot who stands with God promoting their particular brand of Christianity. Nevertheless, Moore was, once again, suspended from his position and ordered to vacate his chair a second time for not recognizing same-sex marriage laws. But no matter; a large majority of Alabama constituents are in Judge Moore's corner as he makes his conservative stand on behalf of God and the Alabama voters. Even now, Moore is making a strong bid for the open Alabama U.S. Senate seat vacated by the now U.S. Attorney General, Jeff Sessions. Moore recently won the Republican primary and is a strong favorite to be elected in December.

Moore's insubordination is reminiscent of then Governor George C. Wallace who, on June 11, 1963, stood in defiance of federal law, preventing Vivian Malone and James Hood, two African-American students, from entering into Fosters Auditorium to enroll in classes at the all-white University of Alabama.[4] In a stand of resistance, Wallace endeared himself to conservative, white segregationists who viewed integration with the same kind of hostility and disgust as conservative and fundamentalist Christians now do with same-sex marriage.

With the Supreme Court's ruling in June of 2015, and with a Presidential election that loomed in 2016, a majority of GOP candidates were extremely vocal against the high court's ruling. Some candidates called for nothing short of revolution. In an interview, just after the SCOTUS ruling, Fox News analyst, Megyn Kelly, spoke with GOP candidate, Mike Huckabee, asking for his reaction to the ruling. The former Arkansas Governor and television host said, "'I will not acquiesce to an imperial court any more than our Founders acquiesced to an imperial British monarch. We must resist and reject judicial tyranny, not retreat.' 'What does that mean?' the Fox host asked Huckabee. 'You have to accept this ruling, right? I mean, are you planning on not accepting this ruling in a way?' 'How do we accept something that, on its face, is unconstitutional?' Huckabee replied as Kelly gave him a bemused look and said, 'How do you not accept it? It's the Supreme Court's job to interpret the Constitution and tell us what it means,' Kelly patiently explained to Huckabee."[5]

I, myself, have held similar sentiments in times past. I, myself, have encouraged and have been encouraged to stand rigid against all appearances of anything "gay." I've seen sweet old ladies and nice old grandpas come unglued at the thoughts of homosexuals stepping foot in the church house. I've witnessed moms and dads who love their children but have openly stated, *if* they ever discovered one or more of their children to be gay, that child would no longer be welcomed in their homes. It is unimaginable how churches full of Christian people can be such breeding grounds for homophobic prejudices and hate and yet, that is precisely what continues to take root, not just in the South but nationwide. Even more bizarre is how all of it swirls around only a small handful of Bible passages used (or better, misused) to leverage the church to harbor such a condemning spirit against the

LGBTQ community. I have already examined and attempted to clarify one of those passages, Romans 1:18-32, in the previous chapter. In this chapter, I will introduce two more passages I will refer to as Exhibit C.

Both passages are found in the Old Testament Book of Leviticus and are a part of what is often referred to as the Holiness Code. The first reads, *"You shall not lie with a male as with a woman; it is an abomination."*[6] The second passage is blunter: *"If a man lies with a male as with a woman, both of them have committed an abomination; they shall be put to death; their blood is upon them."*[7] The Holiness Code of Leviticus, spanning chapters 17-26, is a set of rules and regulations intended to set Israel apart from the Egyptians they fled and the Canaanites with whom they were now living. God demanded His chosen people of Israel be distinguishable from all other tribes and nations. There is no doubt God meant business; He sanctioned death for anyone who disobeyed.

However, there are some valid questions we need to ask before applying these verses. First: Are these two passages referring to all same-sex relationships or are they referring to the cultic practices and/or the promiscuous sexual practices of Israel's neighbors and adversaries? A second question is simply: Are these regulations given to establish universal and everlasting sexual norms or are they given because of the specific challenges and situations the Israelites faced at that time? And finally: Are these regulations, specifically intended for law abiding Israelites of that day, binding for grace-receiving Christians today?

> **If the Bible wasn't referring to faithful, committed and monogamous same-sex relationships then, Scripture surely can't be referring to faithful, committed and monogamous same-sex relationships today!**

Let's begin with the first question: Are these two passages

referring to all same-sex relationships or are they referring to the cultic practices and/or the promiscuous sexual practices of Israel's neighbors and adversaries? To answer the question, we must preface the response by reminding ourselves historical context means everything when it concerns good exegesis. For example, it is virtually impossible to correctly interpret the passage from Leviticus 18:22 without also understanding verses 3 and 21 from the same book and chapter. Likewise, attempting to understand Leviticus 20:13 without the framework of verses 2-5 and verse 23 make interpretation shaky, at best.

After careful deliberation, I would argue both of these passages are carefully placed in context to Moloch and Ashtoreth worship, both considered an abomination to God. Being fertility-focused, Canaanite idol worship frequently entailed both female and male temple prostitution. No wonder, then, God forbids his people from practicing these rituals, as noted in Deuteronomy 23:17: *"No Israelite man or woman is to become a shrine prostitute."* The historical context of these passages specifically centers on idol worship practices not homosexual practices. Although the worship of these idols included homoerotic acts, there is absolutely no evidence God was making a blanket statement about same-sex attraction. As an illustration, take the Old Testament food laws, for example. Concerning meat sacrificed to idols, the Old Testament Jews would have never partaken. That is not to say, however, they were opposed to eating. They were only opposed to eating food connected to idolatry.

Likewise, it was not homosexuality that was forbidden here but, rather, temple prostitution. It is the church, not God, who has attempted to connect these dots! But, in historical context, God was simply forbidding the Israelites from carrying out anything remotely resembling the profane idol worship of these foreign gods and goddesses. The bottom line is precisely this: God, who spoke through Moses, was referring to pagan practices and same-sex practices of worshipers of the Canaanite god and goddess, and not homosexuality, in general. The issue wasn't same-sex marriage. The real issue was spiritual adultery by worshiping foreign gods.

This fact greatly affects the interpretation of this passage and cannot be ignored. If the Bible wasn't referring to faithful, committed and monogamous same-sex relationships then, Scripture surely can't be referring to faithful, committed and monogamous same-sex relationships today. As conservative, Bible-believing Christians, we have always stressed context. So, why is it we completely disregard context in this case and blindly forge ahead with homophobic rhetoric?

The second question we need to address is this: Are these regulations given to establish universal and everlasting sexual norms or are they given because of the specific challenges and situations the Israelites faced at that time? It is a fact God forbad His people from participating in the cultic rituals associated with idols in the day and time in which the Holiness Code was given. Those rituals included sexual relations with both men and women. However, God did not outlaw sexual relations altogether but, rather, only those sexual relations connected with the worship of foreign gods and goddesses.

Consider for a moment the Hebrew word "qadosh" meaning "sacred" or "holy."[8] You might be surprised to discover the Hebrew word for a male temple prostitute is "qadesh," meaning, "a sacred person."[9] A "qadesh" was considered holy and sacred to all those who worshiped the fertility gods. If a man, for example, desired a large yield from his crops or to be blessed with healthy cattle, he would appeal to the fertility gods. For this, he would approach the temple of that god and engage in sexual intercourse with a temple prostitute. Most of these prostitutes were men. They were a type of minister who, through intercourse, were believed to bring about a communion between a man and his god. However strange as this seems, the practice was a normal part of everyday life and was, in fact, widespread throughout Egyptian, Mesopotamian and Babylonian cultures.

These practices would later creep into Greek and Roman cultures, as well. What is even worse, these cultic practices also found their way into the worship of Yahweh. Throughout the Old Testament, God condemns the foreign gods who were being worshiped in

Israel. God called it spiritual adultery. During the time of the judges, which was prior to Israel having kings, the Jews adopted many sinful practices being lived out by the fertility cults. Judges 8:33 describes, *"No sooner had Gideon died than the Israelites again prostituted themselves to the Baals. They set up Baal-Berith as their god."* Leviticus 18:21 condemned child sacrifice, also a cultic ritual.

Later, during the time of Israel's kings, the prophets Ezekiel (16:20-22; 23:37) and Isaiah (57:5) speak out against these same kinds of practices. Under King Rehoboam, there were male temple prostitutes associated with the hill shrines (1 Kings 14:23-24) and King Ahab similarly established Baal worship, which included prostitution (2 Chronicles 33:3). Not everyone participated in the worship of pagan fertility gods, but everyone would have been aware of its significant presence (1 Kings 15:9-14; 22:46; 2 Kings 23:4-15; Ezekiel 16:5-58). Fertility-focused worship and its associated practices remained common in the known world up through the time of Jesus and Paul. Even today, Easter, named after the fertility goddess Ashtoreth, highlights bunny rabbits and eggs (both symbolizing fertility).

It is ironic many of the same conservative and fundamentalist Christians who despise homosexuality and quote Leviticus as a proof-text are, in fact, breaking the spirit of the law by hosting Easter egg hunts at their churches and pretending with their children a giant bunny brings candy on the day our Savior arose from the dead. Perhaps, in this case, we need to re-evaluate who is actually being biblical and who is simply wanting to justify their own agendas?

Returning to the Hebrew word earlier introduced into evidence, it's important to know the word "qadesh," which literally means "a sacred person," is mistranslated in some versions of the Bible as "sodomite." The Authorized King James Version, first translated in 1611, popularized the term. This conjures a completely different mental picture from how this word is actually used and what this word even means. "Sodomite" is a term that should be used to describe someone who lived in the biblical city of Sodom. The word, however, has become a negative, slang term used to describe the gay community. We will look at the supposed reasoning for this misuse of the term in the next chapter when we investigate Sodom and Gomorrah. But, for now, let it be simply noted "sodomite" is *not* the term used in Hebrew Old Testament verses to describe *anyone*. The passages in question are actually describing temple prostitutes. In fact, the translators of The New International Version caught this misinterpretation and corrected it in their version of the Bible.

Temple prostitutes were representatives of their fertility gods. It is for this reason Yahweh declares this kind of sexual practice an abomination. Therefore, to answer the second question, we must objectively conclude these regulations are not given to establish universal and everlasting sexual norms for either heterosexuality or homosexuality. Instead, the Holiness Code, as it concerns sexuality in Leviticus 18:22 and 20:13, speaks to the specific issue of fertility god worship among the Jewish nation.

The third and final question we need to answer is this: Are the regulations specifically intended for law-abiding Israelites of that day currently binding for grace-receiving Christians today? In all honesty, I believe this question has already been answered; yet I will make a further argument. While I believe the entire Bible is totally authoritative for the believer, the fulfillment of the law is in Christ Jesus. Practicing Christians, conservative or otherwise, accept very little of the Old Testament Levitical Holiness Code as applicable to their personal lives today.

Here are some examples of Levitical laws most Christians no longer adhere to as believers: Leviticus 19:27 reads, *"Do not cut the hair at the sides of your head or clip off the edges of your beard."* If you promote this law as authoritative then, technically, all short-haired guys with cropped or no beards are committing sin. Leviticus 11:7-8 reads, *"And the pig, though it has a split hoof completely divided, does not chew the cud; it is unclean for you. You must not eat their meat or touch their carcasses; they are unclean for you."* That basically means you cannot tailgate with Bar-B-Q pork at a football game. For that matter, you can't play with a football (pigskin) either. It would be a sin. Here in Alabama in the heart of South Eastern Conference football country, I suspect over 95 percent of our state is sinning every Saturday during the Fall of each and every year.

Leviticus 19:31 states, *"Do not turn to mediums or seek out spiritists, for you will be defiled by them. I am the Lord your God."* Granted, most Christians aren't going to the palm reader's house for their fortune but many do read their horoscope in the newspaper or crack open their fortune cookie after a meal. This, too, would be considered sin by the Holiness Code. Do you have any tattoos? If so, you've broken the Holiness Code. Leviticus 19:28 reads, *"Do not cut your bodies for the dead or put tattoo marks on yourselves, I am the Lord."* Strictly speaking, that would include butterflies, hearts, girlfriends' or boyfriends' names and yes, even crosses and Jesus' face. Leviticus 19:19 really gets interesting. It reads, *"Keep my decrees. Do not mate different kinds of animals. Do not plant your field with two kinds of seed. Do not wear clothing woven of two kinds of material."* Picture this: A farmer planting soybean and cotton in the same field, plowing with a mule, bred from his horse and donkey, while wearing a cotton-polyester blend shirt. That is not only a weird scene to imagine; it is also a sin, three times over.

Leviticus 19:26 states, *"Do not eat any meat with the blood still in it."* If you were thinking about ordering your next T-bone steak medium-rare, you better think again! And, if you decide, no problem, I'll just order shrimp; think again, *again*. Leviticus 11:10 reads, *"But all creatures of the seas or streams that do not have fins and scales—whether among all the swarming things or among all the other creatures in the water—you are to detest. And since you are to detest them, you must not eat their meat and you must detest their carcasses."* Lobster, shrimp, clam chowder and oysters are off the menu. Ironically, you can order crickets. Leviticus 11:21-22 says, *"There are, however, some winged creatures that walk on all fours that you may eat: those that have jointed legs for hopping on the ground. Of these you may eat any kind of locust, katydid, cricket or grasshopper."* Yum.

As a final note on this last question, I realize these verses come from the Old Testament, which Christianity doesn't necessarily adhere to as law. And that is my very point: If you're going to ignore the entire section of Leviticus banning pork, shellfish, short haircuts, beardless men, tattoos, fortune cookies, polyester, mules, mixed crops, medium rare T-bone steaks and football, how can you possibly cite and support Leviticus 18:22 and 20:13 as a binding law and "proof texts" in an attempt to bolster arguments against same-sex inclusion and marriage? You can't have it both ways!

Chapter Four Notes

1. Lose, David, HuffPost Blog, 10/10/11
2. Pink Floyd, The Dark Side of the Moon, Roger Water, 1973
3. Fox News Post, AL Chief Justice orders halt to same-sex marriage licensing, WAAF.com Staff, February 9, 2015; 4:58 AM CST
4. Elliot, Debbie. Wallace in the Schoolhouse Door. NPR. June 11, 2003. Accessed February 19, 2009.
5. Fox News Live, Megyn Kelly Interview with Mike Huckabee, June 26, 2015 8:05 PM
6. Leviticus 18:22 (NIV)
7. Leviticus 20:13 (NIV)
8. #6918 qadosh, Vine's Complete Expository Dictionary of Old and New Testament Words, W.E.Vines, Merrill F. Unger, William White, Jr., Thomas Nelson Publishing, 1985, pg.113
9. The New Strong's Exhaustive Concordance of the Bible, James Strong, LL.D., S.T.D. Thomas Nelson Publishers, 1984. #6945 qadesh, pg. 102

CHAPTER FIVE
EXHIBIT D: JUSTICE AND INJUSTICE

*C*hurch Family, I want and need to share some information with you. I place a high value on integrity and honesty. Therefore, it is important for you, as a congregation, to know something about our family. Our seventeen-year-old son, Addison, has struggled with a secret his whole life. Recently, he broke his silence by sharing honestly with our family he is gay. We were not surprised by his admission and we, as an entire family, have reassured Addison of our unconditional love.

After Addison shared this with our family, I met that same week with our Personnel Team's chairman and, not long after, I met with our active deacon body. I wanted to be open and honest with them, just as I want to be with you today. I can assure each one of you we have talked with Addison and he assures me he has no desire to cause confusion and will be mindful and respectful to his fellow members and Christian brothers and sisters on the property of xxxxxxxxx Baptist Church, not intentionally doing anything to promote homosexuality in regard to any other person.

*Having said this I will, however, admit my family's situation has certainly raised many questions. I must also admit I am objectively exploring the Scriptures in an attempt to bring greater understanding and an affirmation to my long-held beliefs. But, let me assure you **if** I should ever change my beliefs on this, or for that matter, any teaching that would conflict with our Southern Baptist doctrine and/or polity, you can rest assured the deacons and, then you will be the very first ones to know. I would trust you know me to be a person of integrity and I will never do anything to confuse or teach anything but Southern Baptist doctrine as long as*

I pastor xxxxxxxx Baptist Church.

Please keep our family and our church in your prayers. Because we have asked Addison to show you courtesy and refrain from discussing his personal life at church, I would also like to ask each one of you extend the same courtesy to my family by not allowing yourself to discuss Addison's personal life, either. If my explanation today does not satisfy your concerns, I welcome you to please come directly to me and I will do my best to set your minds at ease. My door is always open to you about this or any matter. We love you. We have served alongside you for 10 years. We hope God will allow us many more years together in ministry. I trust you will continue to be confident I will do my very best to lead xxxxxxxx Baptist Church forward in Kingdom work.

E. Scott McQueen

After much discussion with the deacons and personnel director of the church, I was told to pen a letter and be prepared to make a statement to our congregation. The letter you just read is an exact copy of the one I was prepared to share with our church body. On Wednesday evening prior to the Sunday I was to read this to our membership, the deacons determined, because very little was being discussed by the congregation, I should not read the letter at all. The thought was, by reading it, even greater concerns might be stirred. I strongly agreed; after all, I didn't want to make a statement, anyway. The deacon body had originally told me I only had two options: tell the church I was still a dyed-in-the-wool Southern Baptist and my son would not spread homosexuality among the church members, or resign. For the record and to their credit, they did not want me to resign. I agreed to write the letter as long as I could add to the statement I didn't think it was right for people to continue discussing Addison's life if he, himself, couldn't discuss it publicly. And, secondly, I was struggling with this issue theologically and I was going to continue to pursue the truth. While they were okay with the part about Addison, they were less eager for me to keep searching the Scriptures. In fact, one person came to me privately and suggested I omit that part of the statement, altogether, because he didn't want to see me "lose your ministry." After much prayer, I refused to edit the letter and they, in turn, decided we would remain silent to the church membership, for now.

On that night, we left the meeting on two separate planets. I am fully aware the deacons sincerely meant well. These guys had been my friends for years and I had absolutely zero animosity against any of them or their families. They compassionately prayed for my family and me before we left the room that evening. But, even so, I couldn't help but think how it was such an injustice to enforce a "gag" order on a seventeen-year-old and, for that matter, on us all. Every other teenager in our church could talk about their boyfriends and girlfriends; they were allowed to discuss dating; they could express their feelings and their fears; they could ask questions about relationships and nobody cared. On the other hand, Addison was forced to keep these same kinds of thoughts and feelings bottled up inside. He wasn't allowed to discuss his emotions; he wasn't allowed to show a picture of his boyfriend to others (even if they asked); he wasn't allowed to answer any questions about why he is gay or the struggles of being gay or anything, for that matter, remotely appearing to be gay.

No one in the meeting considered maybe being gay could bring on all kinds of anxiety or loneliness or depression. No one in the room wondered if talking about his orientation might not only help him but, also, help someone else dealing with the same struggles. That is an injustice. My wife, who has fought through a wide range of emotions, couldn't openly discuss her son who is gay. She couldn't share her feelings or her pain or her fears or her joys. That, too, is an injustice. Our other sons, likewise, had no one to turn to in the church for support. Even I, myself, had no one who understood or wanted to objectively listen. For the longest time, each and every time I entered a conversation with someone, whether another staff person or deacon or personnel member, it seemed the conversation couldn't end unless the other person expressly made the point in one way or the other: "Homosexuality is a sin." Early on, when we first needed to talk to friends about Addison's revelation, we called upon those we felt the closest and trusted the most. We needed to cry. We needed to vent. We needed to be loved. We needed all these things but what we received from one was, "Does Addison think he can still be a Christian if he's gay?" and from another, "Well, you know that's a sin, don't you?" That is an injustice!

Yes. I left the meeting that night feeling our family was on a different planet. The deacons, on the other hand, left the meeting believing justice was served. I'm sure they thought and several probably went so far as to vocalize, "We're doing the right thing by retaining our pastor, believing only his son and not the pastor, himself, sinned." I'm sure they felt as if they had taken the high road in this entire ordeal, truly believing by enforcing the "don't ask, don't tell" rule, they were protecting the church from my son. I only wish protecting my son and my family from the church had been equally weighed.

As we remain on the subject of injustices, let me now introduce Exhibit D; two passages of Scripture referring to homosexual behavior set in larger narratives. While both passages are found in the Old Testament, neither passage is part of a legal or moral code. Each story deals with the threat of same-sex rape. The more famous of the two stories is found in Genesis 19:1-11. Sodom and Gomorrah is the setting where Lot, Abraham's nephew, lives with his family. Two angels who appear to be men visit Lot. As it becomes evening, the men from the city of Sodom come to Lot's house and demand they be allowed to have sex with Lot's guests. Lot refuses and when he is threatened by the townspeople, the angels he has hosted protect him by blinding the city dwellers.

A similar story occurs, as found in Judges 19:16-30. In this story, a stranger passing through town is invited to stay inside a neighborly man's home for the night as opposed to sleeping in the city square. In the middle of the night, the Bible says wicked men came and beat on the door, insisting the homeowner put the stranger out into the street so they might have sex with him. The homeowner begs the townspeople to go home but they insist on the man being sent outside. The homeowner, not knowing what to do, sends the stranger's concubine out to the men instead of the stranger. The townspeople rape and abuse the woman all night until she dies.

The stranger takes his deceased concubine home the next day, chops her into twelve separate pieces and distributes her body parts to the heads of the twelve tribes of Israel, demanding justice.

These two stories are often cited as proof texts against homosexuality. While both of these stories do, in fact, speak of homoerotic acts, we can clearly see the context of these stories is not centered on a loving relationship between monogamous partners but, rather, it is focused on gang rape. In both of these scenes, a host is attempting to protect his guest from severe humiliation and despicable injustice. We see a group of men, in both scenarios, desirous to rape a stranger who has entered their village. While it is altogether possible some of these men were gay, it is more probable they were heterosexual. Consider an excerpt from Simon Garfield's news feature entitled "When Man Rapes Man":

> "WHAT KIND of man does this? Male rape shares something with female rape: it is not about sex, but about power and degradation, about violence in which sex is the weapon. Psychologists identify several causes: a desire for conquest and control; revenge and retaliation; and what is called 'conflict and counteraction,' in which a rapist may punish his victim as a way of dealing with confusion about his own sexuality.
>
> Because sexual gratification is not the main objective, a rapist may be 'gender blind,' able to act either on a male or a female victim. An offender often pays little attention to his choice of victim, or his age or physical condition."[1]

The suggestion the rapist may be "gender blind" certainly rings true in the story, as found in Judges 19. The men in the story, who act more like ravenous wolves, rape the woman and abuse her throughout the night. If they were simply gay men looking for male sex partners, they would not have given her the time of day. But that was not their motive. Neither was it the motive of the men in Sodom to simply have sex with the two angels, appearing to be male. No, their motive, too, was rape, control, and conquest. A passage of Scripture you may be unfamiliar with from the prophet Ezekiel reads this way: *"Now this was the sin of your sister Sodom: She and her daughters were arrogant, overfed and unconcerned; they did not help the poor and needy."[2]* Ezekiel does not speak of Sodom in terms of sexual immorality but in terms of arrogance and injustices upon their fellow man.

Now, look at the prophet Jeremiah and hear the Lord's words through him: *"And among the prophets of Jerusalem I have seen something horrible: They commit adultery and live a lie. They strengthen the hands of evildoers, so that no one turns from his wickedness. They are like Sodom to Me; the people of Jerusalem are like Gomorrah."[3]* As in the case with the previous prophet, Jeremiah does not mention sexual practices or preferences as the issue among Jerusalem's inhabitants. The adultery he is speaking of is not of a sexual nature but of a spiritual. At any rate, same-sex attraction is not even mentioned in connection with Sodom; injustice, on the other hand, is at the core of Jerusalem's problem. The statement, *"They strengthen the hand of evildoers"* is a spotlight on the injustices being served by the Judean people.

Finally, hear the words of the Lord spoken by the prophet Isaiah: *"Ah, sinful nation, a people loaded with guilt, a brood of evildoers, children given to corruption! They have forsaken the Lord; they have spurned the Holy One of Israel and turned their backs on Him...Your country is desolate, your cities burned with fire; your fields are being stripped by foreigners right before you, laid waste as when overthrown by strangers. The Daughter of Zion is left like a shelter in a vineyard, like a hut in a field of melons, like a city under siege. Unless the Lord Almighty had left us some survivors, we would have become like Sodom, we would have been like Gomorrah. Hear the word of the Lord, you rulers of Sodom; listen to the law of our God, you people of Gomorrah! The multitude of your sacrifices—what are they to Me? Says the Lord...Stop bringing meaningless offerings! Your incense is detestable to Me. New moons, Sabbaths and convocations—I cannot bear your evil assemblies...Wash and make yourselves clean. Take your evil deeds out of My sight! Stop doing wrong, learn to do right! Seek justice, encourage the oppressed. Defend the cause of the fatherless, plead the case of the widow. 'Come now, let us reason together,' says the Lord."*[4]

Did you catch that last part; "Seek justice?" When comparing Sodom and Gomorrah to Israel, Isaiah doesn't mention homosexuality but he does mention the injustices Israel has committed. Isaiah even goes so far as to list the ways Israel, in turn, might repent and demonstrate justice so God will be pleased. Yet, according to most Christians, homosexuality *must* be the main consideration of these passages. After all, that is what tradition dictates. But think about this for just a moment. The text of the story concerning Sodom reads, *"the men from every part of the city of Sodom—both young and old—surrounded the house"* and demanded Lot's guests be brought out to them.[5]

It is significant to note *every* man in the entire city, young and old, was at the door. If the traditional view is correct, that means every single male in the city was gay. Think about this realistically. "Washington D.C. has been named the gayest city in the United States by the LGBT-interest magazine, The Advocate, in its annual ranking of queer-friendly cities."[6] Yet a 2012 Gallop poll revealed, while Washington D.C. does house the greatest number of gay residents, that number is only at 10% of total residents.[7] If this text had read, "certain men, young and old, of the city" or "some of the men, young and old, of the city" were gathered at Lot's door, this might strengthen the argument. But to suggest every single male in the city was gay just doesn't make any sense. In addition, where were the "young" coming from, if every man in the city was gay? How were more children being born, if every male was gay? Let me also remind you both of Lot's daughters were engaged to men of Sodom when this event took place. How can that be *if* every man in the city was gay? Logically, to suggest every man, young and old, in the city was gay is simply not plausible.

To add credence to this thought process, consider Lot was willing to send his two virgin daughters out the door to the men. Lot does an awful thing by offering the females of the house to the men. Yet, as with the story in Judges, this makes no sense if this is a story simply about homosexual men seeking gratification. If that were the case, it would be worthless to send out the daughters. One would not even consider such an option if, in fact, it was a given every man in the city was gay. Again, this is not about same-sex relationships and certainly not about monogamous relationships between two married adults.

Adding to this argument, let me call to the stand the most famous of all Jewish historians; Josephus Flavius, who once served as a Jewish military officer and, later, as a Pharisee. In his Book One of The Antiquities of the Jews, Chapter 11: From the Creation to the Death of Isaac, Josephus recorded:

> "1. About this time the Sodomites grew proud, on account of their riches and great wealth; they became unjust towards men, and impious towards God, insomuch that they did not call to mind the advantages they received from him: they hated strangers, and abused themselves with Sodomitical practices. God was therefore much displeased at them, and determined to punish them for their pride, and to overthrow their city, and to lay waste their country, until there should neither plant nor fruit grow out of it.

> 2. When God had thus resolved concerning the Sodomites, Abraham, as he sat by the oak of Mambre, at the door of his tent, saw three angels; and thinking them to be strangers, he rose up, and saluted them, and desired they would accept of an entertainment, and abide with him; to which, when they agreed, he ordered cakes of meal to be made presently; and when he had slain a calf, he roasted it, and brought it to them, as they sat under the oak. Now they made a show of eating; and besides, they

asked him about his wife Sarah, where she was; and when he said she was within, they said they would come again hereafter, and find her become a mother. Upon which the woman laughed, and said that it was impossible she should bear children, since she was ninety years of age, and her husband was a hundred. Then they concealed themselves no longer, but declared that they were angels of God; and that one of them was sent to inform them about the child, and two of the overthrow of Sodom.

3. When Abraham heard this, he was grieved for the Sodomites; and he rose up, and besought God for them, and entreated him that he would not destroy the righteous with the wicked. And when God had replied that there was no good man among the Sodomites; for if there were but ten such men among them, he would not punish any of them for their sins, Abraham held his peace. And the angels came to the city of the Sodomites, and Lot entreated them to accept a lodging with him; for he was a very generous and hospitable man, and one that had learned to imitate the goodness of Abraham. Now when the Sodomites saw the young men to be of beautiful countenances, and this to an extraordinary degree, and that they took up their lodgings with Lot, they resolved themselves to enjoy these beautiful boys by force and violence; and when Lot exhorted them to sobriety, and not to offer any thing immodest to the strangers, but to have regard to their lodging in his house; and promised that if their inclinations could not be governed, he would expose his daughters to their lust, instead of these strangers; neither thus were they made ashamed.

4. But God was much displeased at their impudent behavior, so that he both smote those men with blindness, and condemned the Sodomites to

universal destruction..."[8]

When Josephus used the term "Sodomite," he was referring to those people who lived in Sodom, unlike the way the term is used today to describe anyone with a same-sex attraction. Don't allow the term Josephus uses to misdirect your attention from the content of his historical account of this incident. It is also obvious Josephus understands the context of this story plot to be about the inhospitable spirit of the citizens of Sodom. Unlike the other inhabitants of Sodom, Lot demonstrated the same "goodness of Abraham" in the way he treated the strangers. Granted, men in the city came to Lot's house for the purpose of humiliating the strangers and showing their dominance. The practice of humiliation via rape was not about sexual gratification; it was about showing the out-of-towners how unwelcome they were in Sodom. Had these angels appeared as women rather than men, we would be no less appalled the men of the city gathered at the door demanding sex with the inhabitants of the house. We would clearly recognize this as inappropriate, regardless of whether they were straight or gay, because of the way these men attempted to force themselves on the strangers. Apparently, this was not the first time the men of Sodom had behaved this way. I believe this is what Josephus is referring to when he states the city's people "abused themselves with Sodomitical practices."

Josephus, who lived from AD 33-AD 100, compiled Jewish history well received by his peers and the Jewish people, in general. Long before any other commentaries were written on this subject matter, the historical account of Josephus was welcomed and respected. Commentaries today, however, paint an entirely different picture. And, for that matter, they seldom, if ever, reference Josephus on this topic. That is, unless they refer to his work in Book Two: *Against Apion,* 38:27: "And why do not the Lacedemonians think of abolishing that form of their government which suffers them not to associate with any others, as well as their contempt of matrimony? And why do not the Eleians and Thebans abolish that unnatural and impudent lust, which makes them lie with males?" [9]

It appears Josephus is, in this entry, condemning same-sex attraction in any and every form. However, upon closer examination, we see the references concerning homoerotic activities are being made about a specific people group known as the Eleians and the Thebans. Xenophon, a Greek historian and student of Socrates wrote the following about both, the Eleian and Theban armies in contrast to the Spartans: "They sleep with their loved ones, yet station them next to themselves in battle ... with them, it's a custom, with us a disgrace."[10] It is not that Xenophon necessarily viewed same-sex attraction as a disgrace but, rather, military leaders would intentionally pair male lovers together so as to intensify the desire to fight for the person by one's side. The Sacred Band of Thebes was the most well-known troop of picked soldiers, consisting of 150 pairs of male lovers which formed the elite force of the Theban army in the 4th century BC.[11] Furthermore, these were not just *any* homosexual pairs of males. Walter Ludwig writes the Sacred Band of Thebes practiced pederasty, which consisted of an older male and a much younger male apprentice.[12] While this practice will be discussed in much greater detail in the next chapter, understand pederasty is tantamount to molestation; at least by today's definition. So, in other words, Josephus was not addressing a loving and committed relationship between two consenting adults.

Before we move to the next piece of evidence, I want to re-address something I mentioned in an earlier chapter. The Hebrew word, "qadesh," literally means "a sacred person." It is translated in the New International Version of the Bible as "male shrine prostitute" and so it should be rightly translated. However, some versions of the Bible including The Authorized King James Version, mistranslates the word as "sodomite." Also, just for the record, the Hebrew word interpreted "whore," as found in Deuteronomy 23:17 of The Authorized King James Version is "qedesha," which literally means female devotee or prostitute.[13] Both the male and female shrine prostitutes were considered "sacred" to their pagan followers, as their Hebrew names suggest. Both terms, "qadesh" and "qedesha" are derived from the root word, "qadosh," meaning "holy" or "sacred." The table below lists scripture passages comparing The Authorized King James Version to the New International Version as it concerns sodomites versus shrine temple priests.

Reference / Passage	Authorized King James Version	New International Version
Deuteronomy 23:17	There shall be no whore of the daughters of Israel, nor a sodomite of the sons of Israel.	No Israelite man or woman is to become a shrine prostitute.
1 Kings 14:24	And there were also sodomites in the land: and they did according to all the abominations of the nations which the LORD cast out before the children of Israel.	There were even male shrine prostitutes in the land; the people engaged in all the detestable practices of the nations the LORD had driven out before the Israelites.
1 Kings 15:12	And he took away the sodomites out of the land, and removed all the idols that his father had made.	He expelled the male shrine prostitutes from the land and got rid of all the idols his father had made.
1 Kings 22:46	And the remnant of the sodomites, which remained in the days of his father Asa, he took out of the land.	He rid the land of the rest of the male shrine prostitutes who remained there even after the reign of his father Asa.

Reference / Passage	Authorized King James Version	New International Version
1 Kings 23:7	And he brake down the houses of the sodomites, that were by the house of the LORD, where the women wove hangings for the grove.	He also tore down the quarters of the male shrine prostitutes, which were in the temple of the LORD and where women did weaving for Asherah.

By using the term "sodomite," this immediately and wrongly connects the immoral cultic practices discussed in the previous chapter and, as identified in the above stated Old Testament passages, to the city and the inhabitants of Sodom. The translators attempted to connect the dots by linking the homoerotic activity of pagan temple priests to the gang rape intentions of the Sodomite people, citing homosexuality as the

> This mismanagement in interpreting God's Word has, in effect, caused a prejudice to form and grow from passages not even close to resembling their original context or intent, or one another. That is a true injustice; not to mention, terrible exegesis.

common denominator. This mismanagement in interpreting God's Word has, in effect, caused a prejudice to form and grow from passages not even close to resembling their original context or intent, or one another. That is a true injustice; not to mention, terrible exegesis.

Chapter Five Notes

1. The Independent, July 10, 2014, Inside Story: When man rapes man, Simon Garfield, Original story printed December 6, 1992

2. Ezekiel 16:49

3. Jeremiah 23:14

4. Isaiah 1:4, 7-11, 13, 16-18

5. Genesis 19:4

6. And the Gayest City Is, The Advocate, Alexandria Sifferlin, January 6, 2014

7. LGBT by state, 2012, Gallop Poll, February 15, 2013

8. Josephus Flavious, Book I of The Antiquities of the Jews, Chapter 11; *From the Creation to the Death of Isaac*

9. Josephus Flavious, Book Two: *Against Apion,* 38:27

10. Xenophon, Plato's Symposium, 8:32-5

11. History Today, Volume:44 Issue:11, 1994; "An Army of Lovers"-The Sacred Band of Thebes, Louis Compton

12. Paul Walter Ludwig (2002). *Eros and Polis: Desire and Community in Greek Political Theory*. Cambridge University Press. ISBN 9780521810654.

13. The New Strong's Exhaustive Concordance of the Bible, James Strong, LL.D., S.T.D. Thomas Nelson Publishers, 1984. #6948 qedesha, pg. 102

CHAPTER SIX
EXHIBIT E: BOYS AND MEN

In rural Alabama, where I grew up, men were always trying to be macho. They hunt, fish, play sports, and eat beef jerky; you know...guy stuff. They want their boys to be macho, too. That's why men often prefer to dress their "little men" in jerseys and ball caps to bring them home from the hospital. That's why men often sign them up for t-ball when they're barely old enough to hold a baseball bat. Never mind the ball might hit them; in fact, they think that will only make them tougher.

I remember those days all too well. If one of our boys lay on the ground whimpering because they fell or because they were tackled or because a ball hit them in the shin or because they toppled over with their bike, as a good dad, I would say, "Shake it off, boy! Get up and quit that crying!" "It's not making blood!" "Rub some dirt on it!" I'm sure most of the other dads that made up our church body felt just the same way toward their boys, too. In the South (and I suppose many other places), men want their boys tough as nails and their girls soft as a flower. Maybe that's one of the reasons it is so terribly hard for a man in the South (and, perhaps, elsewhere) to come to grips with his son being "effeminate."

Speaking of the term, "effeminate," the word is found in 1 Corinthians 6:9-10. The Scripture reads, *"Know ye not that the unrighteous shall not inherit the kingdom of God? Be not deceived: neither fornicators, nor idolaters, nor adulterers, nor effeminate, nor abusers of themselves with mankind, nor thieves, nor covetous, nor drunkards, no revilers, nor extortioners, shall inherit the kingdom of God."*[1] In all my years of ministry, I have always been taught and, in turn, have taught the term "effeminate" was synonymous with "gay." Other newer Bible versions use similarly meaning terms such as perverts[2] or homosexuals.[3]

Yet, according to the KJV New Testament Greek Lexicon, the word translated "effeminate" comes from the Greek word "malakos," meaning: "1. soft, soft to the touch 2. metaph. in bad sense – a. effeminate – 1. of a catamite – 2. of a boy kept for homosexual relations with a man – 3. of a male who submits his body for unnatural lewdness – 4. of a male prostitute."[4] Just for good measure, I double-checked a second lexicon and it also stated the word literally means "soft."[5] But, what exactly does that mean? This common Greek word had so many different connotations depending on the context in which it was used. In regards to morality, "effeminate" might be used to describe laziness, decadence, or lack of courage.[6] The word could also be describing delicate or expensive clothing worn by rich men. Men who pampered themselves or liked expensive things would have likely been considered soft. But, whatever the word does mean, what "malakos", that is, "effeminate" certainly does not mean is "gay." At least in the way the traditional church teaches; in the way I taught. In fact, the concept of sexual orientation was not defined until the late 1800s; before that, same-sex behavior was seen as an excess of lust or an abuse of power.

What does jump out at me is the expression "catamite" which I discovered in my lexicon search. The term refers to boys or young men who were kept for purposes of sexually pleasuring older men. While we would call this molestation today, the practice was not uncommon in the Greco-Roman world. In fact, it was popularized in Greek mythology with the story of Ganymede, whose Latin name was Catamitus. Ganymede, who became the "cupbearer of the gods," was the son of Tros, king of Troy. Because of his youthful beauty, he caught the eye of Zeus, who, disguised as an eagle, swooped down from Mount Olympus and carried him off. In compensation, Zeus gave Ganymede's father a stud of immortal horses.[7]

Also called pederasty, the practice of sexual relations between grown men and adolescent boys was prevalent in the Greco-

Roman world and, therefore, certainly during the time in which Paul would have written the Corinthian letter. In the previous chapter, I pointed out Josephus Flavius reported pederasty was common among the Eleians and the Thebans. The Sacred Band of Thebes was an elite army comprised of 150 grown men, each with his own catamite apprentice. With this historical backdrop in mind, I am convinced the Apostle, as recorded in 1 Corinthians 6:9-10, is speaking out against this very practice.

To strengthen the argument, Paul immediately follows the term "malakos" with another Greek term, "arsenokoitai," which in The Authorized King James Version is translated, "abusers of themselves with mankind." However, the Greek word, while extremely rare and used only twice in the New Testament, comes from two words: "arsen" meaning man and, "koite," meaning bed (in a crude, sexual context).[8] The imagery is of a grown man who is in bed, ready for sex. While there is debate on the interpretation of this rare expression, the fact remains these two words are literally side-by-side in the scriptures and there is no doubt this practice, while commonplace, would be considered highly unacceptable in the church. For grown men to take young boys and use them as sex objects is deplorable. Yet, because these terms are linked together, strategically placed as

> **It is much more plausible to accept pederasty as the commonsense interpretation than to try and force these terms to somehow mean same-sex attraction between consenting adults in a loving marriage relationship.**

they are in the body of the letter, we find solid evidence to argue this, in fact, is the very practice Paul is strongly rebuking. It is much more plausible to accept pederasty as the commonsense interpretation than to try and force these terms to somehow mean same-sex attraction between consenting adults in a loving marriage relationship.

A second passage exists also containing the word, "arsenokoitai." The Authorized King James Version of the Bible interprets 1 Timothy 1:9-11 in this fashion: *"knowing this, that the law is not made for a righteous man, but for the lawless and disobedient, for the ungodly and for sinners, for unholy and profane, for murderers of fathers and murderers of mothers, for manslayers, for whoremongers, for them that defile themselves with mankind, for men-stealers, for liars, for perjured persons, and if there be any other thing that is contrary to sound doctrine; according to the glorious gospel of the blessed God, which was committed to my trust."*

In this passage, the Greek word is translated in the New King James Version as "Sodomites." The New International Version reads, "those practicing homosexuality," and the New American Standard simply reads, "homosexuals." But, make no mistake, the Greek word is the very same as that one found in 1 Corinthians 6:9-10 being translated, *"abusers of themselves with mankind."* While in this instance the term, "malakos" is not mentioned, two other interesting words are strategically placed on either side of this rare expression. On one side of "arsenokoitai" is the Greek term, "pornos," which is translated as "whoremongers" in The Authorized King James Version. The word, also often translated as fornicators, is always used in reference to illicit sexual intercourse outside of a monogamous marriage relationship.[9] If "pornos" sounds familiar, it should; the English word pornography is derived from this very term.

On the other side of "arsenokoitai" is another Greek term, "Andrapodistes," interpreted in the New International Version as, "slave trader." However, the word is not referring to a typical slave trader of that day and time. I remind you during Paul's day, slavery was not considered illegal or immoral. In fact, the New Testament Book, Philemon, centers on a runaway slave who is encouraged by the Apostle Paul to return to his master with his new-found faith. No, this term, "andrapodistes," is referring to a much darker side of slave trade. In fact, this term literally means, "men-stealer."[10] The Authorized King James Version incorporates this interpretation while the Revised Standard Version uses the term, "kidnapper." Today, we, too, would describe "andrapodistes" as kidnapping. Apparently, kidnapping associated with slave trade was quite common. In addition, it often occurred in connection with the prostitution of young males.

Pliny the Elder, a very well-known First Century Roman philosopher, produced what is considered the first encyclopedic work, Naturalis Historica (Natural History). In this collection, Pliny the Elder describes the preparation of sex slaves for retail sale with the slave trader acting much like a modern-day pimp. Not only Christians, but also pagan moralists, attacked this kind of industry, which fueled homoerotic prostitution.[11] These slave dealers were known to do cosmetic makeovers of their slaves. Pliny the Elder writes "Salpe the midwife touched-up slave boys for market" by removing superfluous hair in order to make them more effeminate, and so, attractive to high paying buyers.[12] "The value slave dealers (and their customers) placed on effeminacy in youth compounded their vice in the eyes of Roman moralists and helps explain the juxtaposition of "slave traders" with pornos and arsenokoitai in the moralizing of 1 Timothy 1:10."[13]

In light of the proper understanding of these Greek terms, we can surmise with a high degree of confidence neither of these two verses apply to a monogamous relationship in any shape or fashion. They certainly are not intended to attack same-sex marriage. Rather, in its original context, Paul is speaking out in both instances against the despicable practice of pederasty. Paul, who would have surely known of this practice of kidnapping and selling adolescents for the purpose of sexual pleasure by grown men, would not only be disgusted by these actions but, would also associate this sin with those preventing someone from entering the kingdom of God.

So, why do conservative and fundamentalist believers refuse to honestly investigate these Scriptures? I can't speak for anyone else but I can tell you my excuse was I sincerely thought it was a "slam-dunk" issue. Given the fact, in our culture, there are no fertility gods with their temple prostitutes, nor are there any pederasty practices that are open, accepted and considered normal, I had never thought the Bible passages in question might be speaking of something other than what I had always been taught. In short, I had no reason to question. The Bible seemed clear enough in regards to the practice of homosexuality. Never once did I think to question that, perhaps, words were being mistranslated. I never had a reason to look any further than what the English text appeared to make obvious. Couple that with my own prejudices and what emerged is a very pious and overconfident Christian who found it easy to believe the traditional take on these Scriptures, without question. That kind of blind arrogance can be deadly.

I am reminded of the R.M.S. Titanic, the supposedly invincible ocean liner which struck an iceberg in the North Atlantic Ocean at 11:40 p.m. on the evening of April 14, 1912 and sank approximately two and a half hours later. The arrogance that led to at least 1,721 people's death was founded on the premise the ship simply could not sink. That kind of pride led the ship builders to insufficiently equip the vessel with lifeboats. Even more importantly, they failed to make the bulkheads tall enough, because the upper class passengers on the upper decks would have been inconvenienced by too many stairways to get from one end of the ship to the other.

Their over-confidence caused them to skip necessary life-saving drills. Their conceit even waved off iceberg warnings wired to the crew earlier in the evening from a nearby vessel, the S.S. Californian. In the eyes of Captain E.J. Smith and his crewmen, there was nothing to worry about. The massive ship sailed "full steam ahead" while the captain slept. In a recorded account of the placidity with which practically everyone had toward the initial crash, "it is related that Pierre Marechal, son of the vice-admiral of the French navy, Lucien Smith, Paul Chevre, a French sculptor, and A.F. Orment, a cotton broker, were in the Café Parisien playing bridge. The four calmly got up from the table and after walking on deck and looking over the rail returned to their game. One of them had left his cigar on the card table and, while the three others were gazing out on the sea, he remarked he couldn't afford to lose his smoke, returned for his cigar and came out again. They remained for only a few moments on deck and then resumed their game under the impression the ship had stopped for reasons best known to the captain and not involving any danger to her."[14]

While those in the upper decks/classes felt no immediate effect from the impact, the poor, unwashed masses locked below were already starting to drown. That cold evening in April, is in many ways, a metaphoric mirror of macabre, reflecting upon our own Christian society's misappropriated ideas of sexual status and superiority. While the majority of Americans never consider their sexuality as a liability, the LGBTQ community struggles to earn a proper living unless they conform to society's expectations. Gay Christian teens often find themselves abruptly kicked out of their own homes, forced to survive the mean streets with no prior history of foster care or street savvy. Suddenly, exposed to a hostile and homeless world, numerous gay, lesbian, bi-sexual and transgender young men and women are forced to leave their soft, warm and safe Christian homes. "The least of these" are forced below to suffer while the comfortable Christians are clueless about what's happening below their church's decks down in Steerage.

It is with that same kind of arrogance pastors, teachers, and church members alike, steam "full speed ahead" with no regard to the thought just *maybe* someone, somewhere has misinterpreted scripture as it pertains to the LGBTQ population and that a teaching has been erroneously passed down as concrete, unsinkable truth. For me, at least, I held to just this kind of zealous overconfidence. You would have never convinced me otherwise. It wasn't that I had scholarly investigated these scripture passages. No, I didn't need to nor desire to dig any deeper into word studies on this subject matter. First, the whole idea of homosexuality conjured mental pictures in my mind's eye I, quite frankly, didn't want to entertain. To someone who has been so submerged in anti-gay doctrine and rhetoric, even the topic itself, is enough to cause one to be uncomfortable.

My first exposure to homosexuality came from listening to a vinyl record in my own home. I still remember as a small child asking my brother, who is ten years older than me, "What is a faggot?" The year was 1971 and I was all of seven years old. He quickly hushed me up so mother wouldn't hear me, which made me know something wasn't right with saying the word.

"Where did you hear that word?" he asked.

"I heard it on the record you have of that TV family; you know, the Bunkers."

Somewhere, my brother had obtained a recording of an episode of "All in the Family" on a 45rpm record, and I had heard Edith Bunker ask her husband Archie about a particular man, "Is that a faggot?"

"You don't need to know what that is," my brother quickly replied, somewhat upset but simultaneously laughing. He never told me. I figured it out, just the same, from a school bathroom wall not long afterwards. My other exposure came approximately a year later, when, on one evening while sitting in front of our black and white television, I was watching the CBS evening news with Walter Cronkite with my dad. Somewhere between the war talk of Vietnam and who knows what else, I suddenly recognized who I thought was a big-time celebrity; Anita Bryant. Anita Bryant had been named First runner-up in the Miss America Pageant a few years earlier, but I knew her as the lady who loved Florida orange juice. She was on commercials all the time. So, when Anita Bryant was on the news that evening, talking about homosexuality, I remember turning to Daddy and asking,

"What's homosexuality?" Dad who hadn't been paying attention because he had been busy reading his newspaper, peered over the "funny papers" and asked,

"What did you say?"

"What's homosexuality?" I asked again. "Anita Bryant is saying something about it."

I can't remember all Daddy did say but I do remember him saying something about God, the Bible and I didn't need to know about that right now. For whatever I didn't know about "that" right then, I did know it wasn't good. Years later, I would discover Anita Bryant was actually a Southern Baptist who often spoke at Billy Graham crusades and served as a crusader against the LGBTQ community. In fact, Bryant wrote a book in 1977 entitled, *The Anita Bryant Story: The Survival of our Nation's Families and the Threat of Militant Homosexuality.* Among other topics, Bryant's book hammered her platform suggesting all LGBTQ people were actively attempting to "recruit" America's children to becoming gay.

The truth is; a systematic and concerted effort in the areas of business, psychology, religion and politics was initiated much earlier in the 20th Century to conjure negative and, even repulsive thoughts, toward anyone even hinting they might be attracted to someone of the same sex. I strongly recommend the book, *Walking the Bridgeless Canyon: Repairing the Breach Between the Church and the LGBT Community,* by Kathy Baldock. Like myself, Kathy Baldock is a Christian, straight and a one-time fundamentalist whose views were not unlike my own. In her book, she writes:

> "I believed marriage was reserved by God for a man and a woman. I'm one of those nice people; I'm not mean-spirited. I wouldn't intentionally harm another person, but my beliefs were the truth because they were based on verses directly from the Bible. I had a death-grip on the viewpoint that 'you can't be a practicing gay person *and* a Christian.' I thought *maybe* I *might* see some gay people in heaven but *only if* they had already been Christian when they became gay, were no longer 'practicing homosexuals' when they died, and had committed to a life of celibacy. I never considered examining these 'long-established truths.' That would have been akin to questioning God Himself. Besides, I had no reason to invest study time in the issue—I wasn't gay, my kids weren't gay, and none of my friends were gay. I didn't even have extended family members who were gay. I existed in a cocoon."[15]

These were MY sentiments, exactly. So, no, I did not desire to research or dig any deeper on the topic. After all, I surmised, someone more equipped to do the research had already made the effort. Someone else had already invested the hours needed to confirm what everyone around me believed: Homosexuality is clearly a sin and an abomination before God. Besides, the whole idea the Southern Baptist Convention's theology; in fact, mainstream Christianity's theology; *my* theology could be wrong on same-sex behavior would be about as likely as, let's say, the sinking of the Titanic.

But, the great ocean liner *did* sink. And with her went numerous lives who carried to their watery graves their hopes and dreams; their skills and ingenuity; their intellect, their monies, their talents and their potential. Some of the world's richest and best-known personalities went down that fateful evening. Colonel John Jacob Astor, one of the world's wealthiest men, had been to Egypt on a trip with his wife. Benjamin Guggenheim, also one of the wealthiest men in the world, was aboard the ship. Also sailing were Isidor Straus, a wealthy merchant and banker; George D. Widener, a famous entrepreneur and financier; Washington Roebling, the builder of the Brooklyn Bridge; Charles M. Hays, a railroad president; Francis D. Millet, one of the best-known American painters of his day.[16]   The list goes on and on. These were extremely wealthy and important people, in their day. These were some of the most intelligent moneymakers and executives in our nation. These people didn't attain their positions in life by chance; they were privileged and powerful, some by birth and some by their own effort. These individuals were leaders in their respected fields. Yet, they climbed aboard a ship believing they had absolutely no reason to fear anything, whatsoever. They assumed they and their families were safe. They assumed someone had done their research; someone had all of the bases covered. Otherwise, they would have made inquiries as to why there were too few lifeboats and why safety measures were not in place in the event an accident might occur. In short, they believed the newsprint that proclaimed the Titanic an unsinkable ship, and they went aboard, no questions asked.

Let's not forget, also lost that fateful evening, were so many numerous men, women and children who were simply immigrating to America. We will never know the vast potential and countless contributions these hundreds of unwashed, under-educated, but hopeful, worker bees and families might have made to our great country. When the ship sank, those in the lower decks were literally locked into their fates and a watery grave.

As I look across my desk at the shelves along the wall, in front of me are bound pages bearing the names of famous and popular Christian authors. If I were to call their names, you would immediately recognize those to whom I am referring. On all these pages are words that have exhausted practically every theological subject matter imaginable; except on the subject of homosexuality. And, what little is found by most conservative authors is more of a rant or a sermonizing that simply echoes the rants and sermonizing that came before them. One will find very little information presented other than the typical, "It's a sin "because God said so" rhetoric.

Personally speaking, I never once engaged in any of my undergraduate or seminary studies in an in-depth research on same-sex behavior. I remind you I majored in Religion in my undergraduate degree. I majored in biblical studies in both my master's and doctorate degrees. I never once engaged in Greek and Hebrew word study on terms that have been interpreted in the Bible as "homosexual," "sodomite," "effeminate" or the like. Furthermore, as I have more recently attempted to read in those volumes of books collected over the years and filling my shelves, I find very little, if any, *research* to substantiate arguments longstanding in the conservative and fundamentalist churches. In a sense, I feel akin to all those intelligent, wealthy, influential people who went down with the ship on that fateful April night back in 1912. They climbed aboard a ship believing it was unsinkable simply because they had been told it was so. It never even entered their heads maybe, just maybe, they were a part of a deadly over-step that would cost them more than any of them could pay.

I am also reminded my son, and many other sons and daughters, are like those below deck, the hundreds more who also sank, without any chance of surviving. They were trusting someone would bring their families to the American shore in safety. They were abandoned and forced to fend for themselves. Sadly, LGBTQ families are being abandoned every day. As Christians, we have enjoyed the sights and sounds of "First Class" while the LGBTQ community has been tucked away, "out of sight; out of mind." But, don't look now; the ship is sinking.

As we prepare to move to yet another piece of evidence, surely you must acknowledge a legitimate reasonable doubt has been established. Full steam ahead.

Chapter Six Notes

1. 1 Corinthians 6:9-10, Holy Bible, The Authorized King James Version, Oxford University Press, 1984, pg. 1216
2. Revised Standard Version, Holy Bible
3. New King James Version
4. The KJV New Testament Greek Lexicon, malakos, Strong's #3120
5. William Arndt, A Greek-English Lexicon of the New Testament and Other Early Christian Literature (University of Chicago Press, Chicago, 1979, pg. 489.
6. Alexander Jones, ed., The Jerusalem Bible. Garden City, New York; London: Doubleday; Darton, Longman & Todd, 1966.
7. Ganymede, Encyclopedia Britannica, 2014.
8. Dale B. Martin, Arsenokoitês and Malakos: Meaning and Consequences (Source: Biblical Ethics and Homosexuality: Listening to Scripture edited by Robert L. Brawley; Westminster John Knox Press, Louisville Kentucky, 1996), page 124.
9. The New Strong's Exhaustive Concordance of the Bible, James Strong, LL.D., S.T.D. Thomas Nelson Publishers, 1984. #4205 pornos, pg. 252

10. The New Strong's Exhaustive Concordance of the Bible, James Strong, LL.D., S.T.D. Thomas Nelson Publishers, 1984. #441 andrapodistes, pg. 403

11. Slaves In The New Testament, James Albert Hamill, 2006, pg. 24

12. Pliny The Elder, Naturalis Historia, 32.47.135

13. Slaves In The New Testament, James Albert Hamill, 2006, pg.132

14. "The Sinking Titanic and Great Sea Disasters," Logan Marshall, Ed. , L.T. Myers Publishing, 1912, pg.50-51

15. Kathy Baldock, Walking the Bridgeless Canyon: Repairing the Breach Between the Church and the LGBT Community, Canyonwalker Press, Reno, NV, 2014, pg.1-2

16. "The Sinking Titanic and Great Sea Disasters, pg.37-45

CHAPTER 7
EXHIBIT G: MAN AND WOMAN

As I prepare to enter Exhibit G into evidence, let me pause long enough to bring to our attention that *all* seven of the Scripture passages specifically mentioning homosexuality have now been addressed. Credible, biblical evidence has been introduced, which I strongly believe presents, at the very least, reasonable doubt and grounds for a "Not Guilty" verdict. Even so, I am aware a hovering cloud exists in many people's minds: *the* issue for many that seems to underlie all the other issues; the human anatomy. The traditional stance is simple: God created man and woman to complement each other in the institution of marriage. This is natural and foundational to human identity. Any variation from the biblical model presented in Genesis 2 is considered against the will of God and, therefore, sin. Robert Gagnon, who authored The Bible and Homosexual Practice, argues: "Same-sex intercourse represents a suppression of the visible evidence in nature regarding male-female anatomical and procreative complementarity.[1]

Before moving forward, allow me to point out the word, "complementarity" will be often used in this chapter. The term may or may not be familiar. To be honest, in all my years of ministry, I can't ever remember using the word, myself. And, in those rare occasions I did come across its usage, the term was being used as an argument for keeping women desiring to be in ministry in their place (which meant out of the pulpit.) But, now, I'm hearing the word used again, and much more often. It now also serves the evil purpose of devaluing relationships that do not lead to procreation.

In November 2014, at an interfaith conference held at the Vatican,

Gagnon, along with other evangelical Christians, joined ranks with Roman Catholics to discuss same-sex marriage. In the wake of the conference, a statement was released stating, "We must say as clearly as possible that same sex unions, even when sanctioned by the state, are not marriages...Christians who wish to remain faithful to the Scriptures and Christian tradition cannot embrace this falsification of reality, irrespective of its status in law."[2]

Dr. Timothy George, dean of Samford University's Beeson Divinity School and the only Southern Baptist represented at the conference as part of the *Evangelicals and Catholics Together* (ECT), said, that while Catholics and evangelicals disagree on many issues, he "felt the complementarity of man and woman in marriage under God was an issue on which evangelicals and Catholics could present a united witness."[3] The ECT released a formal statement concluding, "Marriage is a unique and privileged sign of the union of Christ with His people and of God with His creation--and it can only serve as that sign when a man and a woman are solemnly joined together in a permanent union."[4]

So, there you have it! If we're to buy into this line of thinking, we will embrace the worn-out adage, simply agreeing "God created Adam and Eve, not Adam and Steve." But, is this really the case? Is complementarity what God had in mind as His primary goal when creating man and woman? Can the union of Christ with His church **only** be symbolized through the permanent union between a man and a woman? Should we embrace this line of thinking? Let's take a closer look!

"The Lord God formed the man from the dust of the ground and breathed into his nostrils the breath of life, and the man became a living being...The Lord God said, 'It isn't good for the man to be alone. I will make a helper suitable for him.' Now the Lord God had formed out of the ground all the beasts of the field and all the birds of the air. He brought them to the man to see what he would name them; and whatever the man called each living creature, that was its name. So, the man gave names to all the livestock, the birds of the air and all living beasts of the field. But for Adam no suitable helper was found. So, the Lord God caused the man to fall

into a deep sleep; and while he was sleeping, he took one of the man's ribs and closed up the place with flesh. Then the Lord God made a woman from the rib he had taken out of the man, and He brought her to the man. The man said, *'this is now bone of my bones and flesh of my flesh; she shall be called "woman," for she was taken out of man.' For this reason, a man will leave his father and mother and be united to his wife, and they will become one flesh."*[5]

Initially, there are several incontestable truths: In the beginning, God created man and woman; God created man and woman for each other; and, in addition, God created man and woman to reproduce. Genesis 1:28 (NIV) reads, *"God blessed them and said to them, 'Be fruitful and increase in number; fill the earth and subdue it.'"* Again, these three truths are undeniable. There is no debate. However, do these truths, in and of themselves, automatically disallow God can create, accept and, even, bless monogamous, same-sex relationships? For one to be true, must the other be false? Do not be quick to respond before we look at the evidence.

Going back and more closely examining the passage in Genesis 2, there are several concerns I would like to introduce into evidence as Exhibit G. First, let's examine the point God created man and woman. Of this fact, there is no doubt. But, do you believe God made woman to complete the man? Do you hold to the belief the anatomy of the man and woman suggest by their becoming "one flesh" in sexual intercourse they are, in fact, completing one another in a way same-sex partners cannot accomplish? If so, you are not alone. The theory has been the longstanding consensus of Christianity for hundreds of years. However, the idea isn't clearly articulated in either the Old or New Testaments. Rather, the belief was actually introduced and popularized by Plato's Symposium. Aristophanes, one of several Greek philosophers debating the origin of love, offered a theory which he shared in the form of a myth:

"This creation myth places humans of all three genders

(androgynous, male, and female) in a primeval state of eternal bliss. However, we grew insolent in our blissful state and refused to properly honor the gods (and even tried to pursue them in their mountainous home). As punishment, we were split in two. Those with a "male" nature (the Children of the Sun) became homosexual men; those with a "female" nature (the Children of the Earth) became homosexual women; and the androgynous (Children of the Moon) became heterosexuals. These creatures were very powerful and vigorous and made threatening attacks on the gods. The gods did not want to destroy them because they would then forfeit the sacrifices humans made to them, so Zeus decided to cut each person in two. This is the origin of our instinctive desire for other human beings. Those who are interested in members of the opposite sex are halves of formerly androgynous people, while men who like men and women who like women are halves of what were formerly whole males and females. Given that we are all separate, when we find our other half, we are lost in an amazement of love that cannot be accounted for by a simple desire for sex. Love is the name that we give to our desire for wholeness, to be restored to our original nature."[6]

The belief one can find a soul mate, one that literally completes them, is not so much a biblical truth as it is a Greek philosophical concept. Yet, many conservative and fundamentalist Christians maintain God created Adam as an androgynous being (neither specifically feminine nor masculine) prior to God's removing his rib to form Eve. The terms I am using may be unfamiliar to the average Christian layperson, but the idea of finding one's "better half" or "soul mate" is a very common thought. It is often argued the difference in the man's and the woman's sex organs validate God's design is for the man and woman to naturally fit together in a complementary, sexual way as "one flesh." The problem with this theory, however, is it is simply not scriptural, according to the biblical language and its meaning. Rather, tradition has handed down an interpretation of Scripture, mixed with Greek philosophy, which most Christians embrace, even now.

The Hebrew word for "flesh" is *"basar,"* literally meaning the meaty part of the body.[7] It is also used, as seen in Genesis 29:14 and Genesis 37:27 to mean "blood relative," showing kinship. In the New Testament, Jesus referenced the Genesis 2 passage when He said concerning marriage, *"And the two will become one flesh. So they are no longer two, but one flesh."[8]* Jesus, like the Old Testament writer before Him, was not teaching a complementarity theology but, rather, simply stating a new family unit was forming with the union of the two separate parties. A new kinship bond is established in marriage. Sons are to leave their fathers and mothers and begin a new family unit with their spouses. That doesn't mean the son and his spouse must leave the state, city, or even the house in which he was raised. Consider that in the Old Testament times, sons were, in fact, encouraged to live on the family property and work and function in community with the larger family unit. We don't see the sons moving off away from their parents (take Jacob and his children, for example). However, we do see the sons and their wives beginning new kinship or family units.

The term "one flesh" does not suggest, through sexual intercourse, the man and the woman are spiritually reuniting as a "whole." That is a poor interpretation of Scripture and simply not biblical. Consider for just a moment the full scope of this erroneous theory; to maintain a consistent complementarity argument, one would, in essence, diminish the spiritual wholeness of many biblical characters, including Jesus and the Apostle Paul. It is as if to say, "A person can't be spiritually complete unless they are married." If man and woman are, in fact, anatomically designed to complement one another, it would be nothing short of sin for them not to find an adjoining, opposite-sexed mate. No matter how godly they might

> If God's design is to bring a helper alongside man so that man would not be alone, then it is also arguable that God's intention for marriage is a shared experience of life between two people; not solely a catalyst for the purpose of procreation.

live their lives as singles, one would have to conclude a person is somehow missing out on God's intended plan for their lives if complementarity were, in truth, God's objective in our anatomical design. I strongly argue nothing could be further from the truth. Paul, in 1 Corinthians 7:7-8 (NIV) states, *"Now to the unmarried and the widows I say: It is good for them to stay unmarried, as I do. But if they cannot control themselves, then they should marry, for it is better to marry than to burn with passion."*

If God created man and woman as complementary beings, every unmarried, divorced and widowed person is incomplete. It also means Jesus is incomplete – surely not! While it was Jesus who spoke about "one flesh," He, Himself lived a celibate life as a single man, dislodging the false assumption marriage is the only way for humans to live a complete and fulfilled life. So, regardless of any pre-conceived notions, the Bible does not mean by "one flesh," specifically, one man and one woman, based on their anatomical design. What the Bible does mean is a new "kinship" or family unit. Marriage, then, is not a solution for incompleteness but, rather, a solution for a person's loneliness. Just read the text of Genesis 2:18 (NIV): *"The Lord God said, 'It is not good for the man to be alone. I will make a helper suitable for him."* How much more clearly does the text need to be to see that complementarity is not what Scripture implies?

Yet, I continue to be amazed at statements like the one made by Rick Lance, executive director of the Alabama Baptist State Board of Missions, who wrote on his website and was documented in the state's Baptist newspaper: "As Alabama Baptists we will continue to stand for marriage as defined by Scripture."[9] Shouldn't he have more accurately stated, "As Alabama Baptists we will continue to stand for marriage as *we define* what *we believe* the Scripture teaches?" One expects a person to have strong convictions about that which they believe. However, the self-righteous assumption there is but one interpretation *and* that a particular denomination or denominations have secured the *only correct* interpretation is at best, an over-step and, at worst, borders on being cult-like.

It is not just the Baptist elite who hold these sentiments, either. Rank and file Southern Baptists are very quick to parrot their leadership, whether or not they have personally invested much, if any, significant study of scripture on this topic. Upon hearing the news about our son being gay, a pastor friend sent me a warm e-mail reassuring our friendship and even went so far as to share he has "two close friends who are openly gay" with whom he continues to have "an occasional visit over lunch." Even so, he went on to say, "I can only side with Scripture regarding those who practice the homosexual lifestyle." I held my tongue because I used to parrot the same patented sound bites. In fact, I'm certain he has heard me in the past tell him those exact same words. But, the truth is evident; conservative, evangelical Christians envision only one possible correct interpretation; theirs! Any other possible scenario is, well, unimaginable.

This prompts me to introduce a second concern. If marriage is about a solution to a person's aloneness, then is it an absolute necessity the partner who fills the void of aloneness be one of the opposite sex? Tradition says, "Absolutely!" But, does God's Word expressly echo the same? While there is no doubt God created the first man and first woman for each other, there is no conclusive scriptural evidence mandating, through the example of Adam and Eve, God was setting a concrete absolute forbidding man's loneliness from being remedied by a person of the same sex. Conservatives and fundamentalists point back to the few misunderstood "homosexual" passages we've already addressed in previous chapters as proof texts. However, growing evidence prevents us from using these passages, in their original intent, to refute monogamous, same-sex relationships, unless we take these verses out of context. Conservatives and fundamentalists also point to the fact every example given of married couples in the Bible was only between men and women. While I must admit this is a compelling argument and have in times past used it myself; the fact remains what we're dealing with here is circumstantial evidence at best.

While the first created couple was obviously a man and a woman, and we see men and women together as couples in the Bible, there is, nevertheless, not a thread of biblical evidence, apart from the misinterpreted "homosexual" passages, disqualifying God from creating two same-sex individuals to provide real fulfillment to man's need for companionship. If God's design is to bring a helper alongside man so man would not be alone, then it is also arguable God's intention for marriage is a shared experience of life between two people; not solely a catalyst for the purpose of procreation. Granted, God first began with Adam and Eve. There is no debate God created the first humans with the ability to procreate. In fact, God commanded the first couple to *"be fruitful and increase in number; fill the earth and subdue it."*[10] It is obvious God wanted man to populate His creation. But to argue procreation is still the primary purpose of marriage suggests couples who choose not to have children are, in fact, sinning. Couples who use birth control to prevent pregnancies until they are ready for children would also be sinning. So then, if we argue homosexuality is wrong based on the inability for same-sex marriages to procreate, we must maintain the same argument to include all relationships that do not specifically lead to procreation. But, if it isn't sinful for heterosexual couples to ignore the passage from Genesis 1:28, then it cannot be deemed sinful for same-sex couples to be together, based on the argument of their inability to procreate. We can't have it both ways.

In my research, I did not have to look far to find same-sex couples who seem to be, not only happy in a monogamous marriage but also strong in their Christian walk. Listen with your heart as you read a couple of their stories. What you'll find are intelligent, thoughtful and kind people who just happen to be committed followers of Jesus Christ.

Chris and Mark's Story:

I first met Mark through an online support group called The Gay Christian Network, a community of people who identify as LGBTQ. Both of us had been married and divorced and we both had kids. We had come looking for answers to who and what we were, wanting to know if it was possible to be both gay and

Christian. Within this website we found the understanding and hope we had been desperate to find and what followed was an unlikely series of events leading to a whirlwind romance that attached us heart and soul and finished with our own version of happily ever after.

To better understand the importance of what we went through and to fully appreciate how our story ended, it is important to understand both Mark and I spent most of our adult lives in what is known as a Mixed Orientation Marriage, a marriage where one partner is gay and the other is straight. For seventeen years I tried desperately to live the straight life; Mark spent twenty-five years doing the same thing. Both of us prayed daily God would make us straight and we desperately strove to love our wives the way we believed we should. But no matter how hard we tried, there was always something missing in our respective marriages and so, in 2013, Mark and I, separated by 2,752 miles, and without knowing each other, ended up divorced from our wives, and started our own journeys toward accepting who we were. As I searched for help via podcasts, I found the book, *Torn*, and GCN; as Mark searched for help via Amazon, he found the same book and GCN, and it was there we met.

I think I met Mark on December 16th, though that date isn't firmly fixed in my mind. Mark posted in the "My name is ..." forum and I responded, welcoming him to the site and encouraging him to get involved and to meet people. A few weeks later, he posted in the "Help, Prayer and Support" forum, asking for prayer. He had only been divorced for about two months and he was struggling with how to communicate with his ex-wife and how to deal with her anger. I quickly responded, letting him know I had just gone through my own divorce, I had six kids, I was making it, and, if he needed a friend, I was there for him and would love to hear his story. Not long after posting that, Mark took me up on my offer and sent me a message to which I quickly responded.

That first message led to eight private messages that first day. I found out so much about him and I was shocked to see exactly how much we had in common: both educators; both married for a number of years; recently divorced; children. Our stories had so much in common and I found my excitement growing as I read message after message. We UNDERSTOOD each other in a way no one else had. The connection was immediate and deep as was the friendship that followed. The only problem was the 2,752 miles separating us and so we resigned ourselves to being good friends, with the hope, one day, we might meet face to face. However, private messages were difficult as we had to log into the network each time to check if the other had written so we moved our conversations to personal email in order to communicate easier. As I was sitting in my chair watching TV with my kids, I was also on my phone getting to know my new best friend. But even that seemed too time consuming so within two or three days we exchanged phone numbers and resumed our conversation via text though we still sent more bulky messages via email daily.

I suddenly found I was as giddy as a teenager. I finally found someone I could connect with, someone who understood me and I was excited because I had never, ever felt this way before. I began looking forward to his texts and soon enough we were texting all day, asking questions, learning about each other and just enjoying having that special someone in our lives whom we could trust. At the same time Mark and I were developing our friendship, I had been trying to meet people in my state for dating purposes and had had several failed Skype dates. I remember telling my friend whom I worked with I wished I could meet someone like Mark in person. My friend just smiled at me.

On January 28th, I woke up to a long email from Mark. He was hurting because he didn't know what to do anymore. His ex was hurting and he wondered if he had made a mistake; should he just suppress his sexuality and go back to her, sacrifice himself to make others happy, like he had done his entire life? I quickly texted him, told him I had read his email and I would get back to him but to wait the day out. If I was going to respond, I wanted to make sure I did it justice and so all day I wrote while I was at work. Taking five minutes here and ten minutes there, telling him how I felt. Three pages of typing, and eight hours later, I was happy with my message to him and so I sent it to him and quickly followed with a text telling him I had sent it off. A few minutes later, he texted me and told me he had read the message, he appreciated it, he was so lucky to have a friend who loved him as much as I did and that's when it hit me. I did love him. Not as a friend, not as a brother in Christ, but as a man. I realized HE was the one I was looking for, and so, jumping off the proverbial ledge I sent him a text and told him, "Mark, I think I'm falling for you" to which he replied, "I know the feeling."

What happened next was insane. We spent four hours on the phone that night and the next day we started Skyping. Within a week, we had a pattern. We would text all day, and when I got home after work, as he was three hours ahead of me, we would Skype till he went to bed. On days when I didn't have my kids, we were Skyping five hours a day after school. On weekends where I didn't have my kids, we were Skyping eight to ten hours. We didn't just spend time talking, we did things together. We dated. We fixed meals together. We ate together. We cried together. We laughed together. We shared stories and fears. We prayed together. And we decided we had spent too much of our lives doing what others wanted us to do and it was time for us to experience what we believed God had created us to do. So we hatched a plot. We were too old to mess around anymore. He was 44 and I was 40. We both knew what we wanted in life and we thought it was each other. The problem was the 2,752 miles separating us so we decided it was time to meet. Mark bought a ticket and flew out to meet me on March 10th. The few people who knew about me and knew I was interested in Mark asked me if I was nervous and I found I wasn't. We had logged almost 150 hours on Skype in just five weeks. I knew he was sweet and gentle. I knew he cared for me. And I knew the worst-case scenario would be I would just solidify a really good friendship and we would go back to our lives.

But when I met him in person, all doubts fled. I still remember how I felt when he took me into his arms and hugged me. And as I sit here and remember that feeling, the tears fill my eyes because the only word to describe that moment is "beautiful". We sat on the couch together, just him and me, our hands intertwined, hearing each other, finally touching each other, breathing each other in and I knew this is where I wanted to be; with him; for the rest of my life. That night was the most magical night of my life. We dressed up and had our very first meal in person together. It was a candlelit dinner, pot roast I had started cooking that morning. And everything felt perfect. I had been married for 17 years and never had I once felt this way.

Two days later, on March 12th, we exchanged rings and committed ourselves to each other for the rest of our lives. The only problem was the fact he still lived in West Virginia and I still lived in Oregon and so, two days later, my husband got on a plane and headed back to his apartment. Along the way, he opened our first joint checking account and started applying for jobs. One month later, I flew out to West Virginia to spend 48 hours with him. One month after that, he moved here permanently, and the rest is history.

Mark and I are husband and husband and live as such and it is safe to say I FINALLY get it. As emotionally intelligent as I have always been, I never understood what it was like to be truly mated with someone. When I was married and wanted to spend time with my friends, I could never understand why they were always talking about wanting to be with their wives. So many times I heard pastors standing on stage, talking about how much they loved their wives and how they couldn't make it through without their wife as their God-given help mate, and, honestly, I just didn't get it. Part of me felt that was a nice thing to say, and, sure, I appreciated my wife but it just didn't resound in me. Now, though, I get it. I understand what it's like to be completely in love with someone. Mark and I fight just like every other married couple out there. We make up. We go grocery shopping. We talk about our kids. We make plans for the future. We pay bills. We talk about work and complain about our bosses. We enjoy lazy Saturday mornings and we love watching Survivor and The Amazing Race. We despise cutting the grass and doing the dishes. We take vacations together and with the kids. We cry over the things that hurt and laugh about the funny things in life. We text all day long. We whisper "I love you" at night. And we are equally happy God has brought us together.

You see, I understand now. I understand what it is like to be with the man with whom God created me to be. I know what it's like to need to have that other person around. When I crawl into bed at night and I feel his arms around me, I feel so safe and loved. When I wake up in the morning and feel his arms wrap around me again, and hear him whisper, "Good morning, sweetheart," I am truly happy. I have no doubt God created us to be with each other. Once, when I was on the GCN boards, someone asked why God made us gay and this crossed my mind: God, in all His benevolent wisdom created Chris and He created Mark. And when He was done, He looked down at these two amazing men He had created and thought to Himself, "Hmmm ... they would be great together," and so He made them gay.

I don't know everything that future has in store for Mark and me. Like every other couple, we live day by day, looking together toward the future, facing the same way. When we crash, we pick the other up; when we cry, we hold the other; when we laugh, we laugh together. I just know no matter what life throws our way, we will face it hand in hand; the way God intended it to be.

Sandy and Lia's Story

HI! We are Sandy and Lia Bostian. We have been together for 9 ½ years and married for the last 4 ½ . We are pretty much like any other married couple – we go to work, fix up our house, pay our bills, go to church, have friends over, etc. We think of ourselves as an equal partnership of two people who share the roles and decisions necessary in any family. We feel our relationship reflects the words of Jesus when he tells his disciples to "love one another." Neither of us needs to be "in charge" because, with love and respect, we both want what is best for one another.

We don't have any set assignment of roles, but we share responsibilities based on strengths, interest, and availability. For example, Sandy has a much longer commute and goes to school two evenings a week, so Lia does most of the everyday cooking and cleanup. But Sandy likes to try new recipes, so she often cooks for holidays or when we have guests. The tasks stereotypically more "masculine" or "feminine" are again divided by strength, interest, and availability – not by who is the "male" or who is the "female" in the relationship. For example, Sandy enjoys fixing things around the house, like installing a ceiling fan or a garbage disposal. Some might think of that as a more "male" role. But if she runs into a spider when she is under the sink installing the disposal, she steps away and yells and Lia has to come to the rescue to kill the spider.

Neither of us gets the last word when it comes to making decisions. If we have a difference of opinion, we talk it out and try to give and take until we arrive at a solution we both can live with. We both dislike conflict and so we used to give in too easily and then feel upset with the result. We have learned we have to speak our minds, even when it results in some initial conflict, in order to avoid a bigger problem up the road. We recently did some home renovations and got lots of practice at dealing with differences – especially when it came to money. Like we said before, we are just like any other couple, regardless of gender(s) involved. But we try to respect the fact people see things differently and we don't both have to agree on everything. We just keep trying to find ways of living that honor both of our perspectives. In this way, we feel our relationship reflects the diversity of Creation and the love of the Creator.

These two couples are "regular" people and examples of thousands more just like them. They have no agenda. They are not communists. They are not attempting to take over the world or infiltrate the minds of children with homophobic thoughts or do away with God or anything else. These two couples, and countless, more simply want to enjoy the same freedoms afforded to married, straight couples. They aren't attempting to dissolve the covenant of marriage. In fact, what they want is just the opposite. These, and couples like them, desire and value the covenant of marriage. Why do you think they fight so hard to be married? As hard as it may be for some to believe, it is NOT to spite conservative and fundamentalist Christians. Why must the straight community be so self-absorbed as to believe LGBTQ struggles for same-sex marriage is somehow about them or a target on their straight marriages? Is it not enough straight couples can readily marry? Why must the straight community begrudge a gay or lesbian couple so much they would do everything in their power to hinder their desire to marry and vehemently hate them in the process? If you are opposed to same-sex marriage, then simply don't marry someone of the same sex! To be certain, there is **nothing** Christ-like about the kind of prejudicial behavior denying another human being finding and marrying a person with whom they cannot live without. This Christ-less behavior needs to stop, NOW.

Chapter 7 Notes

1. *The Bible and Homosexual Practice: Texts and Hermeneutics* (Nashville: Abingdon, 2001) Robert Gagnon, page 488
2. Evangelical-Catholic coalition addresses same sex "marriage, The Alabama Baptist, Feb. 5, 2015, Volume 180, No. 6, page 5, Baptist Press.
3. Ibid.
4. Ibid.
5. *Genesis 2:7, 18-24; Holy Bible (New International Version) pages 7-8*
6. Plato's Dialogue, *"The Symposium"*: *"On Platonic Love and The Myth of the Androgyne"*. 02/06/2014 by Aquileana
7. Vines Complete Expository Dictionary of Old and New Testament Words, Vine, Unger, White, page 83.
8. Mark 10:8 (NIV)
9. Gay "Marriage "ruling threatens Alabama's ban, The Alabama Baptist,
10. Feb. 5, 2015, Volume 180, No. 6, page 5, Neisha Roberts.

11. Genesis 1:28 (NIV)

CHAPTER 8
EXHIBIT H: IN AND OUT

As a pastor, it was my responsibility to shepherd Christ's flock; feed them, lead them, protect them and attempt to create a climate toward spiritual maturity. Might I add, none of that happened by my own doing. It was only as I was fed, led, protected and immersed in a climate conducive to the Spirit of Christ that I could ever endeavor God's will for my life as His under-shepherd. Yet, that has been and is still, my calling. It is not an easy calling. People look to me for answers to some of life's most difficult questions. They want to know about life's meaning and their specific purpose for existence. They want to know about forgiveness; how to receive it when they have committed unforgivable actions and how to share it when unforgivable actions have been committed against them. They want to know about the mysteries of life, which includes the miraculous as well as the tragic. They want to know about love and how it grows and when it's appropriate and how much is needed and how much is to be shared. No, it's not always easy to pastor a flock or to attempt to proclaim, *"Thus saith the Lord!"*

One of the most difficult aspects of pastoring is being totally honest with God, one's congregation and one's self. What I mean is this; as a pastor, I want to hear the heart of God speaking to me and feel confident His Spirit is leading so I can usher His truth in His love to His congregation. I desire to do this without my own reservations or prejudices. Integrity is such an important part of who I am and want to be. If I can do nothing else, I can be honest: with God, with myself, with my family and with my congregation. I struggle to ensure it is God I represent and not just my own ideologies, opinions or agendas. Furthermore, I want to be free to share God's Word without peer pressure, whether it is from the community, the denomination or from the congregation, pressing me to hand over to them the blessing of God or the judgment of God, without the truth of God. Over the years of ministry, I have noticed pastors who, because of the fears of rejection or turmoil or job loss or whatever, either dodge certain issues and doctrines or simply go along with their church's stated traditions, creeds or doctrines, whether or not they agree. This is one reason I have been pecking away on this computer of mine. That is why I have been reading every piece of literature I can snap up on this subject of which I am now writing. That is why I have been going back to God's Word and immersing myself to either reaffirm what I have always been taught to believe or to honestly admit I have been wrong in my beliefs about homosexuality. I have been wrong.

Can I expect the Southern Baptist congregation, of which I was a part for eleven years, much less my denomination, to agree with my newfound stance on this subject? Do I really believe evangelical Christians will read this heartfelt plea and, in great masses, repent? Not hardly. But, my sincere desire and prayer is, even if everyone else refuses to listen, YOU will hear; not my words or my heart, but His. As hard as it is for you to wrap your head around all of this, God actually gives you and me grace and space to accomplish this monumental task. As active and reflective listeners, Holy Spirit speaks to our hearts and allows us to see, perhaps for the first time, that which has been so muddied in our minds. I would have never believed in a million years I would ever write a book defending same-sex attraction much less same-sex marriage. But God has lifted the blinders covering my eyes preventing me from imagining He could work in and through a community of people in ways I never thought possible. God has allowed me to discover truth I never knew existed, nor would I have ever known, if not for Addison.

I'm sure well meaning people have prayed for our family, believing Addison's "coming out" was a curse. But, in reality, it has been a great blessing God has shared with us all; not only because Addison is happier now living the truth as a gay young man rather than living the lie as a straight one. And, even much more so because God has changed all of our hearts to be more loving ... like Jesus.

Let me say this again: God actually gives you and me grace and space to accomplish this monumental task. The Apostle Paul writes, *"Accept the one whose faith is weak, without quarreling over disputable matters. One person's faith allows them to eat anything, but another, whose faith is weak, eats only vegetables. The one who eats everything must not treat with contempt the one who does not, and the one who does not eat everything must not judge the one who does, for God has accepted them. Who are you to judge someone else's servant? To their own master, servants stand or fall. And they will stand, for the Lord is able to make them stand."[1]*

There was a huge debate in the early church over foods considered kosher. The Jewish believers had grown up being taught the Jewish food laws and they carried that belief with them into Christianity. On the other hand, Gentile believers had no prior experience with the food laws practiced by the Jewish community and had no problem eating whatever tasted good to them. In addition, the Gentiles had no problem purchasing and consuming foods that might have been first presented as sacrifices to the various gods worshipped in their communities. So, when these mutual believers in Christ started worshipping and fellowshipping together, there were some immediate confrontations over the food being consumed. The more conservative Jewish Christians were passing judgment on the more liberal Gentile believers because they were not following the long-held traditions passed along in Scripture that ensured an outward sign of godliness. On the other hand, the liberal Gentile believers were scoffing at the more conservative Jewish believers for getting bent out of shape over nothing.

What God suggests, through the counsel of Apostle Paul, is for the people to find their common ground in the grace of Jesus Christ and set their differences aside. God says not to judge those whom you disapprove. God also says not to despise or make light of the ones who are judgmental. Rather, we are to value our unity in

Christ Jesus and love one another above all differences, trusting Christ to care for His own servants. We desperately need to realize it is the Lord who *"is able to make them stand."* It is God's grace in Christ who, in fact, empowers every single one of us to stand in our faith; not by our works at all! Neither is it our place to "watchdog" everyone's world; just our own! Why is it so many Christians can only see others in terms of "In" or "Out?" And, for that matter, why do we somehow believe God has given us the job of policing everyone else? I came across a letter that speaks to this point. For the sake of privacy, I have replaced direct references to the church and to the individuals named in the letter with the symbol, xxxxx. Nevertheless, the letter's intent is loud and clear.

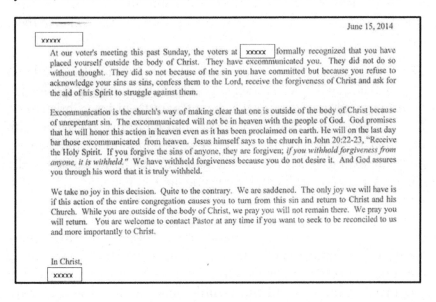

June 15, 2014

xxxxx

At our voter's meeting this past Sunday, the voters at [xxxxx] formally recognized that you have placed yourself outside the body of Christ. They have excommunicated you. They did not do so without thought. They did so not because of the sin you have committed but because you refuse to acknowledge your sins as sins, confess them to the Lord, receive the forgiveness of Christ and ask for the aid of his Spirit to struggle against them.

Excommunication is the church's way of making clear that one is outside of the body of Christ because of unrepentant sin. The excommunicated will not be in heaven with the people of God. God promises that he will honor this action in heaven even as it has been proclaimed on earth. He will on the last day bar those excommunicated from heaven. Jesus himself says to the church in John 20:22-23, "Receive the Holy Spirit. If you forgive the sins of anyone, they are forgiven; *if you withhold forgiveness from anyone, it is withheld."* We have withheld forgiveness because you do not desire it. And God assures you through his word that it is truly withheld.

We take no joy in this decision. Quite to the contrary. We are saddened. The only joy we will have is if this action of the entire congregation causes you to turn from this sin and return to Christ and his Church. While you are outside of the body of Christ, we pray you will not remain there. We pray you will return. You are welcome to contact Pastor at any time if you want to seek to be reconciled to us and more importantly to Christ.

In Christ,

xxxxx

Wow! I had no idea the Heavenly Father subcontracted the responsibility of admitting people through the gates of Heaven to church business meetings in churches across America. But, after a hint of sarcasm, the reality sets in this is not an isolated incident. Whether or not a formal letter is written, churches across the nation are sending THIS message. What's worse, this congregation probably considers itself a loving and accepting fellowship of believers.

"Our day" came on Sunday, May 24th, 2015. After over a year of back-and-forth cold-war tactics, I finally stepped down from the Southern Baptist congregation I had loved and pastored for over eleven years. The overwhelming majority hated to see our family go. But, as we prayed, there really wasn't any other unselfish option. To be sure, had our family remained, the day would have come when the church would have split. Like the mother in the Bible story, as found in 1 Kings 3:16-28, who would rather surrender her child than see him hacked in two, I could not watch a group of church members break the church in two over their extreme prejudice and insistance, somehow, our son was sinning simply because he had same-sex attraction. The real problem, however, wasn't that our son was gay; rather, the true issue was their pastor refused to join in with their determination of condemning his son. The unspoken breach of trust grew like a cancer and I knew the outcome would ultimately destroy the church. But, God had changed my heart and I could do no other.

I wonder how many other families are leaving the church for the very same reason. I wonder how many families feel isolated and rejected by the very ones who once called them brothers and sisters in Christ. I wonder. I can't help but believe today's traditional church is missing a huge opportunity, as the body of Christ, to minister to the LGBTQ communities and their families. Consider the following story: Jesus once met a Samaritan woman beside a well. He broke multiple rules, certainly considered taboo for a Jewish rabbi, by carrying on a conversation with this particular woman. According to Jewish law and tradition, it was wrong for Jesus to talk with a Samaritan. It was wrong for Jesus to speak to a woman. It was wrong for Jesus to ask to drink from the woman's cup. It was wrong for Him to suggest she could worship in a way that exceeded the temple in Jerusalem. It was wrong for Him to claim to be Messiah. Yet, Jesus loved this woman and had great compassion for her even if it meant being wrong by traditional standards.

His disciples happened upon the conversation and could hardly believe their ears or eyes! Although saying nothing, they were shocked at Jesus' actions. Rather than judging or shunning the woman, Jesus demonstrated compassion and unconditional love. The disciples were probably shocked all the more (although they shouldn't have been) when the woman returned, bringing with her a crowd of other Samaritan friends and acquaintances. She was so moved by Jesus she wanted her friends to meet Him, too. Upon their return, Jesus turned to His disciples and said, *"Don't you have a saying, 'It's still four months until harvest?' I tell you, open your eyes and look at the fields! They are ripe for harvest."*[2]

I submit to you, here and now, the gay, lesbian, bisexual, transgender and queer people are modern-day Samaritans. Does the gay community see the love and compassion of Christ in you or do they see the judgmental heart of the disciples? How many churches are offering love and support to the LGBTQ community? Oh, I know; I can hear evangelical and Catholic churches, alike, responding with, "How can we endorse sin?" So, let me ask THIS question; just how many of these same congregations are offering real and consistent support to the parents of gay and lesbian children

> **I submit to you, here and now, that gay, lesbian, bisexual, transgender and queer people are modern-day Samaritans. Does the gay community see the love and compassion of Christ in you? Or, do they see the judgmental heart of the disciples?**

or family members? Surely, the parents aren't sinning. Surely, they must be hurting! Yet, what I have observed over many years is churches from my own denomination are desirous to assist with just about any and every cause EXCEPT homosexuality. We help the hungry. We help the depressed. We help the drug addict. We help the alcoholic. We help the financially bankrupt. We help the adulterer. We help the sick. We help the aging. We even help the porn addict (so long as he or she is acting "normal" by looking at pictures or videos of someone from the opposite sex.) But, I cannot remember ever hearing about a Southern Baptist church openly offering *real* support for the homosexual community and their families. Oh, I am fully aware we preach, teach and offer "recovery" and "ex-gay" programs for homosexuals who want to try to "change back" to a heterosexual mind-set.

Like the letter sent to excommunicate the man from his church and inform him he was going to hell, we will certainly consider welcoming them back into the fold if and when they modify their behavior. But, I haven't seen any literature or programs or ministries designed to assist with the anxieties, concerns, fears and realities that come with being gay or being a family member of the same. To the contrary, The Southern Baptist Convention Executive Committee recently excommunicated an entire congregation, New Heart Community Church of La Mirada, California, because they chose not to judge homosexuality but, rather, to simply love and minister to all people including those in the LGBTQ community. In a statement made to The Baptist News, Executive Committee president Frank Page said, "This action does not reflect a lack of love for homosexuals…But when you love someone, you tell them the truth about their actions. By its action on behalf of the convention, the Executive Committee is telling New Heart its failure to condemn homosexuality breaks the heart of God."[3] I don't know about God's heart breaking but what I do know is there are countless families whose hearts are broken every day because they and their children are being ostracized by churches across America who claim to love like their Savior, Jesus Christ … unless you're gay.

Even in the case of my own family, the church just wanted to sweep it all under the rug and act like none of it ever happened. After I assured them Addison wouldn't bring up the subject at church and I wouldn't teach contrary to Baptist doctrine as long as I remained their pastor, they just smiled and went silent. Even if they were convinced my son was living in sin, they surely knew my wife and I were hurting. Surely, they knew we were transitioning. Just because it wasn't being openly discussed at church it didn't mean we weren't dealing with it at home. Granted, I asked the deacons not to share our son's private life in public if they were not going to allow him to discuss it, himself. But, we never said we didn't desire their love, support, prayers or help.

Did we ever receive a card, a call or a visit? Yes, oh yes we did, at first. We received one card reassuring me I would surely be allowed to keep my ministry if I handled the situation discreetly by not saying too much to the deacon body. Yes, I received a call. A deacon representative called to make sure I was writing a response letter and sending it to the deacon body in a timely fashion. Yes, I received a visit. Two deacons drove to our home and relayed to me the deacon body wasn't going to ask me to resign if conditions were met. One even had the nerve to say how "all of this has been traumatic on the youth group." Are you kidding me; traumatic on the youth group? What about the trauma my son had been enduring and wrestling with for years? This one call, one card and one visit were smothered in, "We're praying for you." "We're thinking about you." "We're sorry this is happening to your family." Yet, it was obvious there was an agenda and it didn't appear ministering to their pastor's family was it.

On the other hand, a few within the ranks of church leadership also dished out back-handed slaps from time to time. Most were directed at me, as certain deacons and other leaders became more uneasy with their pastor's family. I received anonymous letters imploring me to "preach the Law of God" and not so much about God's grace. I was within earshot several times, intentionally being allowed to eavesdrop into conversations about celebrity preachers they had heard on Christian radio, condemning the "gay lifestyle." As time rocked on, our family began to feel as if more and more rocks were being thrown. Most were from the shadows, but not always. One Wednesday evening following a weekly Bible study, I was confronted by two deacons. Representing the entire deacon body, they wanted to talk with me in private. After stepping into my office and sitting down, one bluntly asked, "Why were you wearing "gay" shoes?" I laughed out loud; they weren't laughing. "What are you talking about?" I responded. "You know." said one raising his voice, "the ones that were on Facebook."

I create folk art and participate in art shows all across the Southeast. I've been doing this since 2012, long before Addison came out. To better portray myself as an artist, I enjoy wearing tie-dye shirts and a red, white and blue Fedora. I also wear leather shoes I've painted. I was at a particular art show and my wife snapped a photo of my "art shoes" and put them on her Facebook page. The shoes were painted with several different colors. Also on the top of each shoe was a large heart, striped with primary colors. On the sides of each shoe were the painted words, "Love God/Love People."

I wasn't aware at the time, but some members and deacons had been monitoring all of our family's social media sites, to uncover our "gayness." Apparently, they felt they had caught the pastor in an indiscretion when they spotted the shoes. Immediately, the assumption was the shoes were "gay" because, after all, the stripes in the hearts matched an LGBTQ rainbow. "So," they asked, "Why were you wearing those gay shoes?" I told them they weren't intended to be "gay" but, from that day forward, they could rest assured I would openly refer to them as my gay shoes. I attempted to joke they had just come out of the closet but they weren't laughing. These men were serious. After several failed attempts to explain how ridiculous it was for them to be so upset about my shoes, I finally had heard enough. I stood up and told them I would wear those "gay shoes" anytime and anywhere I should so choose. Needless to say, the meeting was over and I was going home. Grabbing my extra-large Styrofoam cup, which contained leftover soft drink from an earlier visit to my favorite fast-food taco dive, I couldn't help but laugh when I noticed the logo on the cup was a giant cactus and primary color stripes (rainbow) behind it. Huh, I guess the tacos were gay, too!

The truth I've witnessed is local congregations prefer not to be associated with gays or their families. Churches, for the most part, are uninformed and, sadly, unconcerned about the needs, hurts and apprehensions of this obviously neglected community. From first-hand experiences, I have even witnessed some congregations dodging funerals, as well. Because of a friendship with a family who served as volunteers in a local AIDS awareness group, I have been called upon several times to conduct funerals for AIDS patients who have died. In each one of these cases, the deceased or their family members were members of local churches in the community. However, after being "outed", they were either asked to leave or simply ignored until they became inactive. Their families were also ignored until, likewise, they moved on. So, because they were inactive, the churches in these specific situations were obviously scarce when they were needed the most. It is troubling churches would not show Christ's compassion to minister to gays and their families, even in death. What many churches are good at doing; however, is teaching, "Homosexuality is sin!" They also claim to be good at teaching grace. From what the gay community reports, I'm not so sure the grace Jesus lives, teaches and dispenses is the same flavor of grace being taught by most local churches today.

Without further fanfare, I would like to now enter Exhibit H. The following historical evidence demonstrates how Christians, in the name of God and His Truth, have deeply hurt the cause of Christ. The following embarrassments have resulted from Catholic and Protestant believers clinging to preconceived notions and misinterpretations of Bible passages. I submit to you a small but weighty excerpt of the Christian Hall of Shame:

A noted casualty to Christian dogma was Nicolaus Copernicus, a native of Poland, who was born in AD 1473. Copernicus, a scientist, mathematician and philosopher, became famous by introducing heliocentrism; the theory the Sun, not the Earth, was at the centre of what we now know as the solar system. Both Martin Luther and John Calvin, arguably two of the most influential Christians in history since the early church, openly and vehemently criticized Copernicus as a heretic. Both solidly held to a theory introduced by Ptolemy (AD 90 – AD 168), some 1500 years earlier, the Earth was at the center of the universe. Christians readily accepted this theory and taught it as fact, basing their belief on Joshua 10:12–14 and the many passages referring to the sun's rising or setting. Copernicus was reviled as one spreading heresy and fought his entire life to save his good name and reputation.[4]

An even more famous scientist, Galileo Galilei, born in Pisa, Italy in 1564, actually faced the much-feared Roman Inquisition in 1615 for supporting Copernicus and his theory of heliocentrism, and for advancing the theory with the idea Earth is in a constant state of motion. Galileo, considered the Father of Modern Science, was convicted in court for teaching theories contrary to Scripture and advocating books that had been previously banned.[5] Galileo, considered a heretic by Christians, was forced to live out the remainder of his life under house arrest.

In addition to individuals who have felt the crushing judgment of dogma, there are also people groups who, likewise, have been deeply scarred, both physically and emotionally. Take slavery in America, for example. Slavery is certainly frowned upon in our day and age as one of the most horrible atrocities ever allowed in our United States of America. There are probably no respected denominations, churches or individual Christian leaders alive today who would argue otherwise. Yet, only 150 years ago, most all of today's denominations embraced slavery as a divine right, granted by God, Himself. Christian church leaders cited chapter and verse, defending slavery and justifying their actions by standing on the Word of God. In fact, a new Baptist denomination was born when white Baptists in the South withdrew fellowship from their northern counterparts on May 10, 1845, forming the Southern Baptist Convention in order to better defend the South's practice of and dependency upon black slavery.[6] In 1856, an Alabama Baptist labeled slavery "as much an institution of Heaven as marriage."[7]

In hindsight, we see these examples proving Bible-believing Christians landed on the wrong side of the equation. Their being wrong had nothing to do with either their zeal for God or their sincerity to be obedient to God. Rather, it was their misinterpretation of Scripture and/or the misunderstanding Scripture application might result in a different interpretation due to contextual differences from the original historical context. The world is not the center of the universe. The Earth is in constant motion. Slavery is wrong on all counts. Any one of these three statements would have probably landed me in jail years ago and would have certainly black-balled me from the mainstream of society. Yet, today we readily accept these statements as fact.

Now, fast forward from the days of Copernicus, Galileo and American slavery to Alan Turing, a London native, born June 23, 1912. Turing studied and later taught mathematics at Cambridge University. During World War II, Turing led the British cryptanalytic department for the English government. He played a vital role in deciphering the messages encrypted by the German Enigma machine, which provided vital intelligence for the Allies. After the war, Turing turned his thoughts to the development of a machine that would logically process information; the computer. But, because his colleagues didn't have confidence in computer technology, Turing lost his opportunity to develop the first digital computer.

In 1951, Turing was celebrated as a war hero and awarded one of England's highest honours; a fellow of the Royal Society. In 1952, however, Turing was arrested and tried for homosexuality, which was then considered a crime. Citing the Bible, the court convicted Turing and gave him the choice of incarceration or chemical castration. To avoid prison, Turing accepted hormonal injections so he might continue to be free to do on-going research in the area of artificial intelligence. What Turing didn't count on, however, was because of the great hatred and prejudice against him; his security clearance was revoked, literally locking him out of his own laboratory. Heartbroken, defeated and physically scarred for life, Turing committed suicide on June 7, 1954.[8]

There is no shortage of zeal on the part of the local church. There is no shortage of desire for believers to be obedient to God. On the other hand, there is no shortage of fingers pointing out another's sin. As Christians, we have been wrong in the past. It is my strong conviction we are wrong now. And, speaking of other hands, I must come clean and admit I am left-handed. My first grade school teacher forced me to write with my right hand, which I still sloppily do today. However, I am a lefty in most every other sense of the word. You know what that means don't you? Should I tell you? No. I would rather you go look it up on the Internet, yourself. See how else the church has acted in the past to yet another subset of people. Google search "the church and left-handed people." Read for yourself how Christians in the past and, some even today, view those who are left-handed. Some will probably say, "Aha! That's why this McQueen guy is defending all these gays and lesbians. He's left-handed." So, are you buying that, too? If so, I can't help you. But, if this left-handed garbage sounds a little far-fetched, perhaps you need to also reconsider before labelling and judging others by another trait of which people are born; like same-sex attraction, maybe. Yeah, that's the one.

Chapter 8 Notes

1. Romans 14:1-4 (NIV)
2. John 4:35 (NIV)
3. Southern Baptist Convention Kicks out LGBT Friendly Church For Breaking Heart of God, Scott Kaufman, September 24, 2014, Raw Story, US News
4. Luther, Calvin and Copernicus—A Reformed Approach To Science and Scripture, Ligonier Ministries, Keith Mathison, June 1, 2012
5. Isabelle Pantin (1999), "New Philosophy and Old Prejudices: Aspects of the Reception of Copernicanism in a Divided Europe", Stud. Hist. Phil. Sci. 30: 237–262
6. Baptists and the American Civil War, Bruce Gourley, "Yes,the Civil War was about Slavery" December 23, 2010
7. Wayne Flynt, Alabama Baptists in the Heart of Dixie, p. 108, Fire Ant Books, 2005
8. BBC History, 2014, Alan Turing

CHAPTER 9
EXHIBIT I: RIGHT AND WRONG

If a large majority of Christians who make up the church, are, in fact, assuming the wrong stance on the issue of homosexuality, how do we make it right? How do we turn this wayward, off-course ship in the right direction? On the other hand, what if the traditional church is already right and has, all along, been right? What if same-sex attraction is and always has been, in all cases, wrong? Even with the evidence presented throughout this book, it isn't easy convincing or being convinced. I'm sure there are some who, even now, are unscathed by the previous arguments. But, there is yet another witness I want to call to take the stand. There is another piece of the puzzle I want to enter into evidence. I'll call to the stand, Exhibit I: the testimony of Jesus.

What sets Christianity apart from any and every other world religion is Jesus Christ! His person and message are so unlike any other person and belief system in all of human history. While every other religion promotes a human behavior supposedly leading to god or a god-like state of being, Jesus attests He IS God and, through His behavior alone, all of mankind has the free gift to enter into relationship with the living God. Tragically, it is this very essence of Christ that is confused and lost in the shuffle of behavior modification.

> **So what, exactly, does Jesus have to say about homosexuality? {CRICKETS} That's right; nothing; absolutely nothing!**

Jesus Christ uniquely offers Himself to us. Augustine said, "I have read in Plato and

Cicero sayings that are wise and very beautiful; but I have never read in either of them: *'Come unto me all ye that labor and are heavy laden.'* [1] Of all the world religions, only Jesus offers a friendship with God. Every other religion is based on doing right. Each has their "rules" in which to follow; a list of do's and don'ts. But with Jesus, we find in Him the Way, the Truth and the Life! It is in relationship with Jesus through faith alone, not through behavior to please Him, we gain acceptance and access to God. I can't help but believe in Christ, alone, we find what is right.

So what, exactly, does Jesus have negatively to say about the controversial subject of homosexuality? {CRICKETS} That's right; nothing; absolutely nothing! However, Jesus did say plenty. For example, Jesus said, *"'Love the Lord your God with all your heart and with all your soul and with all your mind.' This is the first and greatest commandment. And the second is like it: 'Love your neighbor as yourself.' All the Law and the Prophets hang on these two commandments."* [2] In other words, loving God AND loving one's neighbor are inseparable. To engage in the one is to engage in the other. Conversely, to ignore the one is to ignore the other.

The problem for many is defining one's neighbor. Jesus chose to define "neighbor" to a Jewish audience as one of their most despised and bitter enemies: Samaritans. Isn't it ironic Jesus would depict for the Jewish people their "neighbor," whom they are supposed to love, as the very ones they loved to hate the most? Jesus' story of the Good Samaritan was an intentional opportunity to cut to the core of His Jewish audience by exposing the prejudice plaguing the religious community of that day. Listen to something else Jesus spoke: *"But love your enemies, do good to them, and lend to them without expecting to get anything back. Then your reward will be great, and you will be sons of the Most High, because He is kind to the ungrateful and wicked."* [3]

So, if we understand Jesus right, Christ followers are to love others, regardless of race, creed, sexual orientation or anything else that would, otherwise, divide. Then, as if that's not enough, Christ followers are to *"do good to them."* Is this what we are hearing

Jesus say? Are we to love and do good to those we consider "enemies?" Are we to love and do good to homosexuals, even if they are considered "enemies" to the church? And if Christians respond by saying, "They are not our enemies," then how much more should we love them and do good to them. Yet, do we extend love and goodness through our words and deeds to the LGBTQ community? Or, do we fight them at every turn, on every issue, at every venue and with every weapon at our disposal? Do we send both, verbal and non-verbal, messages telling them to stay away UNLESS they are either willing to pipe down or clean up? Do we dis-fellowship congregations of people who desire to love and minister to "whosoever" with no strings attached?

Regardless of one's theology, Christ emphatically says to *"love and do good"* toward all people. Isn't disobeying Jesus by refusing to love and do good toward others just as great a sin as all the charges levied toward the LGBTQ community? Consider these words of Christ: *"You have heard that it was said, 'Love your neighbor and hate your enemy.' But I tell you, love your enemies and pray for those who persecute you, that you may be children of your Father in Heaven. He causes His sun to rise on the evil and the good, and sends rain on the righteous and the unrighteous."*[4]

Honestly, I am ashamed to think I ignored, at best, and attacked, at worst, the LGBTQ community while serving Christ as one of His children and ministers. I ignorantly disobeyed God, believing I was somehow standing for righteousness while, actually, I was no better than a Pharisee, steeped in my own chosen brand of self-righteousness. In truth, I was the enemy.

The church has a difficult time being consistent in the way it administers grace. Hailing from a Southern Baptist background, I am well versed in the topic of grace. Baptists traditionally place a high value on "grace alone, by faith alone in Christ alone." For that matter, I still do. But, where many Christians and almost all Baptists would agree with the previous mantra, there is much confusion over behavior modification. Some outside Baptist circles would agree behavior changes are pre-requisite to salvation. Most Baptists, however, would argue they are not pre-requisites but, rather, evidence of salvation due to the subsequent indwelling of Holy Spirit. There is a problem, however, with this rationale. Just as Baptists argue with Armenian thinking individuals (people who believe one can fall from grace) about the line drawn in the sand concerning, "How much sin actually causes one to fall from grace?", the same question and logic could be posed to Baptists on this issue of grace and evidence: "How much behavior modification is needed to be evident grace has been dispensed and salvation is, in fact, valid?"

The truth is neither of these boundary lines can be adequately measured in a quantitative or qualitative way. It is impossible for any one of us to confidently declare, "This one is a Christian or that one is not," especially if the person claims faith in Christ. Yet, the church consistently makes these kinds of "judgment" calls every day. Take same-sex attraction, for example. I hear MANY who voice homosexuality and Christianity are incompatible because, to the straight Christian community, all same-sex attraction is considered a "lifestyle" sin and the practicing homosexual is obviously unrepentant. Therefore, he is either fallen from grace (Armenian view) or never saved in the first place (Calvinistic view). But consider this second example: The Baptist Faith and Message, which Southern Baptists strongly proclaim as their official stance on matters of faith and practice, states under Article Eighteen, FAMILY, the following: "Marriage is the uniting of one man and one woman in covenant commitment for a lifetime."[5] Notice the words, "**one** man and **one** woman" and "for a lifetime." Here are a few questions; how many churches across America are filled with divorcees? How many divorcees teach Sunday school classes? How many divorcees sing in choirs and on praise teams? How many divorcees work in the nursery or food pantry? How many divorcees lead the singing or preach the sermon? Are these people fallen from grace because of divorce? Or, were they ever saved? And, what if they remarried? Are their marriages valid? Are they not living in sin by remarrying, as a divorcee? What if they divorced one spouse to marry another with whom they had been cheating? Were they ever saved?

Almost half our society is touched by divorce. There once was a time when divorce was considered taboo especially in our church houses across America. There was a time when divorce might have meant excommunicating a person from fellowship in their local church. But, today, every other person has experienced divorce. Why doesn't the church treat the LGBTQ community the same way they do the divorcee? Why can a divorcee join the church but a lesbian can't? Why can a divorcee sing in the choir but a transgendered male has to stay away, altogether? Explain why a divorcee can preach the sermon while an openly gay young man can't even sit in the building to hear it?

While Jesus said nothing, not a word, nada, zilch about homosexuality, He spoke quite a mouthful concerning divorce. Mark 10:11-12 quotes Jesus as plainly saying: *"Anyone who divorces his wife and marries another woman commits adultery against her. And if she divorces her husband and marries another man, she commits adultery."* While Jesus was silent on same sex marriage, there is no question about what Jesus thought and taught concerning divorce and remarriage. My point is a majority of Christians simply give a "pass" to those behaviors they consider sins like their own while simultaneously condemning behaviors that aren't like their own. If Southern Baptist churches, alone, held divorcees to the same rigid moral standard to which they hold the LGBTQ community, the Southern Baptist denomination would shrink by almost half … and so would their church budgets!

Yet, the Baptist Faith and Message is clear on this point, just as it is on their point concerning homosexuality! The truth is crystal clear: Southern Baptists and other conservative and fundamentalist Christians hold a heavy prejudice over the LGBTQ community and insist they repent in order to be accepted in the church. On the other hand, when prospective heterosexual couples enter their churches they are welcomed, generally, without question. Are they questioned about previous marriages? Do church leaders check their credentials? Do they investigate as to whether their children were born in wed-lock? Of course not. Nor should they be questioned. That would be wrong. So, why is it right to act in a similar fashion toward the LGBTQ community? Is that not equally wrong? Is it not hypocritical to choose to condemn those with whom you, yourselves, are uncomfortable associating, regardless of what Scripture teaches? Are you not making judgment calls on certain groups of people simply because they are not a part of *your* majority? And, even if one suggests you are to hold another accountable for their failings, does Jesus not say, *"Do not judge, or you too will be judged. For in the same way you judge others, you will be judged, and with the measure you use, it will be measured to you. Why do you look at the speck of sawdust in your brother's eye and pay no attention to the plank in your own eye?"*[6] Again, an inconsistency in theological reasoning is clearly present at the LGBTQ community's expense.

Jesus taught, *"So in everything, do to others what you would have them do to you, for this sums up the Law and the Prophets."*[7] Jesus also modeled the same: it is called unconditional love. One of His most drastic measures was His inclusive meal practice of hanging out and eating with tax collectors and sinners. Tax collectors were considered traitors, a kind of lowlife who worked for the Roman government and preyed upon their own Jewish people for economic gain. The "sinners" were simply impure or "dirty" people. It included women, untouchables, the poor, prostitutes and the maimed. It is difficult for us, who live in a world in which we may take for granted an attitude of nondiscrimination, to appreciate the radical character of this inclusiveness in Jesus' time.

Sharing a meal with someone, anyone carried great significance in Jesus' social world that is also difficult for us to imagine. Rules surrounding meals were deeply embedded into their purity system. Jews were aware of the Levitical laws regulating, not only what might be eaten and how it should be prepared, but also with whom one might eat. No decent person would share a meal with an outcast. The meal, then, was a microcosm of their religious and social systems and one's standing therein. No one was expected to break the rules; but Jesus did.

"Jesus entered Jericho and was passing through. A man was there by the name of Zacchaeus; he was a chief tax collector and was

wealthy. He wanted to see who Jesus was, but being a short man he could not, because of the crowd. So he ran ahead and climbed a sycamore-fig tree to see Him, since Jesus was coming that way. When Jesus reached the spot, He looked up and said to him, 'Zacchaeus, come down immediately. I must stay at your house today.' So he came down at once and welcomed Him gladly. All the people saw this and began to mutter, 'He has gone to be a guest of a sinner.' But Zacchaeus stood up and said to the Lord, 'Look Lord! Here and now I give half of my possessions to the poor, and if I have cheated anybody out of anything, I will pay back four times the amount.' Jesus said to him, 'Today salvation has come to this house, because this man, too, is a son of Abraham. For the Son of Man came to seek and save what was lost.'"[8]

On, yet, another occasion, as described in Luke's Gospel, chapter 5:12-13; *"While Jesus was in one of the towns, a man came along who was covered with leprosy. When he saw Jesus, he fell with his face to the ground and begged Him, 'Lord, if you are willing, you can make me clean.' Jesus reached out His hand and touched the man. 'I am willing,' He said. 'Be clean!' And immediately the leprosy left him."*

Everyone knew, not only was it a huge health risk to touch a leprous person, it was also against the Levitical law. Jesus was incomprehensibly out of order to touch this man. Yet, it didn't concern Him one bit the religious hierarchy was gnashing their teeth. His thoughts were not focused on worrying over what others might think or, for that matter, what might happen physically to Him if He touched a diseased man. His only concern was to extend love and acceptance to an outcast of society and, thus, begin a relationship with a man otherwise being overlooked by the establishment.

Whether touching a leper's contagious skin or accepting an invitation to the home of a wee little man named Zachaeus, Jesus identifies with the underdog. He loves the outsider. Jesus has genuine love and compassion toward the marginalized. Make no mistake; the law of Jesus is to love everyone, regardless of race, creed or orientation. "God loves you just the way you are. If you think His love for you would be stronger if your faith were, you are wrong. If you think His love would be deeper if your thoughts were, wrong again. Don't confuse God's love with the love of people. The love of people often increases with performance and decreases with mistakes. Not so with God's love. He loves you right where you are." [9]

Furthermore, Jesus models the importance of humility. Philippians 2:6-8 reminds us that we are to imitate Jesus in the way we live in relationship with other human beings:

"Who, being in very nature God, did not consider equality with God something to be used to His own advantage; rather, He made Himself nothing by taking the very nature of a servant, being made in human likeness. And being found in appearance as a man, He humbled Himself by becoming obedient to death—even death on a cross!"

The phrase, *"made Himself nothing"* is translated from the Greek word, *Kenosis*, literally meaning "self-emptying." Jesus, who has every privilege and the ultimate pedigree, steps completely out of His superior status and becomes "a servant". Jesus empties Himself of all the privileges of heaven to rub elbows with the sinners on earth and, even, die at their hands. If Christians are to follow this example and practice incarnational living, that is, living like Jesus, how, then, should this translate for heterosexuals in the way they respond to their LGBTQ neighbors?

In her book, *Generous Spaciousness*, Wendy Vander Wall-Gritter identifies everyday privileges the heterosexual community enjoys as second nature while the LGBTQ community is left out in the cold, acutely aware their lives bring certain day-to-day struggles.

"The average heterosexual might commonly say:

- I can be pretty sure the people I encounter will be comfortable with my sexual orientation.
- If I pick up a magazine, watch television, or play music, I

can be certain my sexual orientation will be represented.

- When I talk about my heterosexuality, such as in a joke or talking about a significant relationship, I will not be accused of pushing my sexual orientation on others.
- I do not have to fear if my family or friends find out about my sexual orientation there will be economic, emotional, physical or psychological consequences.
- I did not grow up with games that attack my sexual orientation, such as "fag tag" or "smear the queer."
- I am not accused of being abused by my parents, warped, or psychologically confused because of my sexual orientation.
- I can go home from most meetings, classes and conversations without feeling excluded, fearful, attacked, isolated, outnumbered, unheard, held at a distance, stereotyped, or feared because of my sexual identity.
- I won't be asked to speak for everyone who is heterosexual.
- People won't ask why I made my choice of sexual orientation.
- People won't ask why I made my choice to be public about my sexual orientation.
- I won't have to defend my heterosexuality.
- I can easily find a faith community that will not exclude me for my being in a heterosexual relationship,
- I don't need to worry people will harass me because of my sexual orientation.
- I won't need to qualify my straight identity. My masculinity or femininity won't be challenged because of my sexual orientation.
- I won't be primarily or solely identified by my sexual identity.
- If I experience a negative encounter with others, I need not

ask whether it has sexual orientation overtones.

- I am guaranteed to find people of my sexual orientation represented in my workplace.
- I can walk in public with my significant other and not have people do a double take or stare.
- I can remain oblivious to the language and culture of sexual minority persons without feeling any penalty for such oblivion.
- I can go for months without being called "straight."
- People do not assume I have engaged in sex merely because of my sexual orientation.
- Nobody calls me "straight" with maliciousness.
- People can use terms describing my orientation and mean positive things (e.g. "straight as an arrow," "standing up straight" or "straightened out") instead of negative things (e.g., "Ewww, that's gay." or "Stop being so queer.").
- I am not asked to think about why I am straight.
- I can be open about my sexual orientation and not worry about losing my job, getting access to housing, reserving a room at a bed and breakfast, or receiving a critical response in a health crisis."[10]

As an average, straight male, I had never given thought I may be living a privileged life over an average LGBTQ person. And, even if I had known, there was a time when I would not have cared. In fact, I would have said it was their choice. But, if we as Christians are SERIOUS about living the life Jesus modeled, we must care. Our call to imitate Christ means the emptying of one's self. That includes status. That includes privilege. That includes our prejudices, too. Jesus was superior in every way. Yet, He mingled with the tax collectors and the lepers and the Samaritans and the wine drinkers and the gluttons and the women and the children and the...you get the picture. Jesus emptied Himself and, as Luke 7:34 describes, became *"a friend of sinners."*

Living as an incarnational Christian exposes the mark of a true believer, the fruits of the Spirit, which is the evidence of authentic faith. If a person claims to know the Lord, but has no love or compassion toward his fellow man, he or she needs to be reminded of 1 Corinthians 13:2 (NIV), where Paul writes, *"If I have the gift of prophecy and can fathom all mysteries and all knowledge, and if I have a faith that can move mountains, but have not love, I am nothing."* Jesus taught love and grace. He came to show us what's important and what's not. Scriptural knowledge, without love and humility, is worthless. It is a moot point. But, isn't it amazing Jesus said, *"A new command I give you: Love one another. As I have loved you, so you must love one another."[11]* Whatever else we might say or do one truth is certain: Jesus taught it is wrong for us to judge human beings and it is right for us to love human beings; period.

So, if Jesus had nothing negative to say about same sex attraction the question also needs to be asked; did Jesus have anything positive to say about it? The answer may just surprise you. While most Christians confidently assert God did not create people with same sex attraction, they somehow miss some essential words spoken by Jesus, Himself. In Matthew 19:4-6, Jesus addressed a question asked about whether divorce is permissible. The context of this passage is a dialogue between Jesus and the religious elite over the laws governing marriage and divorce. *"Jesus answered, 'Haven't you read' He replied, 'that at the beginning the Creator 'made them male and female,' and said, 'For this reason a man will leave his father and mother and be united to his wife, and the two will become one flesh'? So, they are no longer two, but one flesh. Therefore, what God has joined together, let no one separate.'"*

The irony is, while most Christians quickly conclude this conversation proves heterosexual marriage is the only valid form of romantic relationships; the next words out of Jesus' mouth seem to contradict those very conclusions. After the disciples are clearly shaken by Jesus' strict teaching on divorce, they suggest, as recorded in verse 10, *"it is better not to marry."* Then, Jesus responds by stating that NOT EVERYONE can follow the teaching Jesus just initiated. In other words, not everyone is cut out to marry women. For some, marrying a person of the opposite sex would be inappropriate. He puts it this way: *"Not everyone can accept this word, but only those to whom it has been given. For there are eunuchs who were born that way, and there are eunuchs who have been made eunuchs by others-- and there are those who choose to live like eunuchs for the sake of the kingdom of heaven. The one who can accept this should accept it."*[12]

There is no debating most people are created for heterosexual marriage. Jesus states those *"who can accept this should accept it."* That is the overwhelming majority of us. However, it is interesting to note Jesus does not stop with heterosexual attraction as being the only option. Jesus continues by identifying three specific groups of men, whom He calls eunuchs, who apparently "cannot accept this." They are simply not going to marry women … and Jesus KNOWS this about them. Furthermore, it is acceptable to Christ they are not attracted to women. So, who are these groups of men?

Jesus identifies three distinct and specific groups as those who are "born" eunuchs, those who are "made" eunuchs by others, and those who "choose" for the sake of Christ, to be eunuchs. Looking at these categories, it is obvious Jesus is referring to those who refuse marriage to better serve God, those who have been castrated and/or have injured testicles, and, finally, those who were "born that way." Two of the three groups are easy to distinguish. One group, however, pose a greater problem.

But, before we tackle the natural born eunuchs, let's clarify a myth; not all eunuchs are castrated. A closer look at this passage describes one group of men as clearly being castrated and/or having damaged or injured testicles. A second group, however, is not castrated at all but, rather, chooses to refrain from engaging in sexual relations with those of the opposite sex in order to focus on kingdom work more deliberately. This fact, alone establishes the term "eunuch" doesn't equate with castration; at least, not in Jesus' time. Therefore, arguing the men who were *"born that way"* were either born without testicles or had damaged testicles simply isn't plausible. On the other hand, to acknowledge some human beings have been created by God to follow a less common, but equally legitimate relationship path makes perfect sense and answers a lot of questions.

Opponents of same sex attraction will necessarily work to find ways to disprove this or, better yet, attempt to cover it over, altogether. Be honest: how many of you have ever heard a sermon on this text? If you examine this passage objectively, however, one can hardly deny a group of people who have absolutely no desire to marry someone of the opposite sex and, furthermore, were *"born that way"* can't be anything but gay and lesbians. Granted, if one concedes natural born eunuchs are, in fact, gays and lesbians, it is not necessarily an admission same sex marriage is acceptable. This acknowledgement, however, does reinforce the point Jesus recognized this subset of people as legitimate, acceptable and created by God. This, in itself, establishes reasonable doubt.

Chapter 9 Notes

1. Saint Augustine *Source unknown* 4th / 5th century AD, www.egs.edu/library/**augustine**-of.../**quotes**/
2. Matthew 22:37-40
3. Luke 6:35
4. Matthew 5:43-45
5. The Baptist Faith and Message, 2000. Article xviii, Family
6. Matthew 7:1-3
7. Matthew 7:12
8. Luke 19:1-10
9. Just Like Jesus, Max Lucado, W Publishing Group, 2003, pg. 3
10. Generous Spaciousness, Wendy Vander Wall-Gritter, Brazos Press, 2014, pg. 214-215
11. John 13:34
12. Matthew 19:11-12

CHAPTER 10
EXHIBIT J: HETEROSEXUALITY AND HOLINESS

As we have just focused on Jesus, it must be understood there is a monumental difference between acting like a Christian and acting like Christ. Holiness is so misunderstood. In religious circles, Christians are applauded for their actions by other church members. One is often considered holy by their rigid observance of the Law. One's unwillingness to bend or budge on "issues" welcomes an added sense of respect and awe from many Christian circles. For instance, in my home state of Alabama, the aforementioned former Alabama Supreme Court Judge, Roy T. Moore, is considered among many Alabamians as a stellar example of Christian holiness simply because of his unwavering stance on a number of issues, including the Ten Commandments, and now, same sex marriage. However, if and when someone acts like Jesus, not only might they not be applauded; they may just be crucified. Just ask Jesus. He paid the ultimate price simply being Himself. Jesus also warned His disciples they, too, would face trials for living their faith in a Christ-like manner. Like Jesus, all who live and love the way He lives and loves may never be understood; nor will the detractors be happy. You see, Jesus approaches people with grace and compassion while the naysayers equate holiness with the Old Testament Law.

This difference of perspective is, perhaps, most clearly evident on the battlefield of same-sex marriage. For instance, Crisis Magazine, a Catholic online publication, ran a story about Sweet Cakes by Melissa, a Gresham, Oregon based bakery that, in February of 2013, famously refused to make a wedding cake for a lesbian couple. On their business Facebook page, they also supposedly posted it wasn't the first time they had refused gay couples. While comments like those stirred Christians across the nation to applaud in support, the community of Gresham was not impressed. They began to picket and sign petitions, refusing to patronize the bakery. For that matter, the Oregon Bureau of Labor and Industry was equally unimpressed. The state bureau found substantial evidence the bakery unlawfully refused service to the couple and, in so doing, infringed on the couple's civil rights. The bakery maintained, throughout the investigation, being forced to serve the LGBTQ communities impinged on their religious freedoms.

Nevertheless, after six years and hundreds of cakes, candies and confections, the business closed its doors in August 2013. Melissa Klein, co-owner and namesake for the company, said in an interview, "The Bible tells us to flee from sin. I don't think making a cake for it helps." The Catholic publication went on to describe how the LGBTQ communities ruined the family business through their intense protests, boycotts and a storm of media attention. Aaron Klein, the husband and co-owner, stated in the interview for the article, "The LGBT attacks are the reason we are shutting down the shop. They have killed our business through mob tactics." His wife added: "I guess in my mind I thought we lived in a lot nicer of a world where everybody tolerated everybody."[1]

Did you catch that last statement? That is the precise spirit of anti-Christ to which I am referring. The shop owners, by refusing to bake a wedding cake are, in effect, discounting and demoralizing two women who happen to be in love. These Christian bakers, without blinking, stand in judgment of two women and, through their actions, are rejecting these women, discounting their mutual love and, are furthermore, labeling them as sinners. Yet, when the community voices its disdain for this kind of prejudiced behavior, in the name of Christ, no less, the storeowner has the audacity to say she "thought we lived in a lot nicer of a world where everybody tolerated everybody." I cannot believe what I'm reading! The question I want to ask is precisely this: "Where is the tolerance on the part of these shop keepers? Where is the tolerance

146

on the part of the Christian community that supports this kind of madness?" And, even more importantly, "Where is the love?" Where do these kinds of Christians get the idea it is only intolerance when they are on the short end of the stick? I am sorry to inform everyone but Christ calls for unconditional love! Where is the unconditional love when cakes aren't baked for couples who simply want to get married? Who gives Christians the right to disobey Christ's mandate to love? Who gives Christians the right to determine who is and who isn't worthy of a wedding cake or who deserves to be loved? How arrogant and self-righteous can one be?

Many years ago, a prophet by the name of Isaiah proclaimed how God was not amused with the self-righteous actions and attitudes prevalent among the Jewish people. God spoke through His prophet, as recorded in Isaiah 65:1-5: *"I revealed myself to those who did not ask for me; I was found by those who did not seek me. To a nation that did not call on my name, I said, 'Here am I, here am I.' All day long I have held out my hands to an obstinate people, who walk in ways not good, pursuing their own imaginations—a people who continually provoke me to my very face, offering sacrifices in gardens and burning incense on altars of brick; who sit among the graves and spend their nights keeping secret vigil; who eat the flesh of pigs, and whose pots hold broth of impure meat; who say, 'Keep away; don't come near me, for I am too sacred for you!' Such people are smoke in my nostrils, a fire that keeps burning all day."*

It sounds like those being called out are some really ungodly folk. But, if you breeze through this passage you might just miss the ungodly folk are, oddly enough, those who say, 'Keep away; don't come near me, for I am too sacred for you!' In other words, the sinners in question are self-righteous Jews. Apparently, their idea of holiness and God's were two different ideas. Unfortunately, this phenomenon is not just ancient history found on the pages of the Bible.

Upon my resignation from our church, my wife and I became quite popular on social media to some of the very people who had been so instrumental in our leaving. What is even more surprising is how some were suddenly going to miss us and had nothing but great things to say about us both. But, something was amiss. On our last Sunday, the church asked us to stand at the front of the sanctuary and say our good-byes as people came by to speak, shake our hands and hug our necks. In addition, the church gave a "going away" banquet for us on our last evening with the congregation. I was both amazed and appalled while several families (who were present in the room) refused to come shake our hands or acknowledge us at either of these last opportunities, were all-too-eager to post flattering messages on our church's social media page, stating how sad they were to see us leave and how they would surely miss their pastor's Bible teaching. While it was all-too-obvious to our family these few individuals had no intentions or desire of speaking to us again, it appeared equally clear they wanted to leave the impression they were genuinely going to miss us and were saddened by our leaving. My mind drifted to Isaiah and the people he addressed in the Old Testament book bearing his name. Like those people of old, there are just as many today who attempt to portray themselves as being holy, as if appearances mean anything. But, in reality, shouldn't there be at least some semblance of love, concern or compassion among those who would be holy? When God's people posture themselves to appear as holy, I can't help but believe His nostrils are smoking; then and now!

And, while we are on the topic of holiness, who ever said heterosexuality has ever been an objective of the Christian life? Isn't holiness and Christ-likeness the goal? Isn't our identity to be found in Christ Jesus? Why is it, then, everyone wants to identify people in terms of their sexual orientation? Granted, one's sexuality is part of a person's identity, but in Christ we find a truer identity: *"There is neither Jew nor Gentile, neither slave nor free, nor is there male and female, for you are all one in Christ Jesus."*[2] As Christ is our new identity, aren't we simply called to live holy lives, regardless of whether one has heterosexual or homosexual feelings? God said, *"Be holy, because I am holy."*[3] I don't recall reading anything about "being heterosexual, because I am

148

heterosexual." I ask you, member of the jury, to consider another piece of evidence I will now introduce as Exhibit J: a call to holiness.

Consider the following illustration: *"But Jesus went to the Mount of Olives. At dawn, He appeared again in the temple courts; where all the people gathered around Him, and He sat down to teach them. The teachers of the law and the Pharisees brought a woman caught in adultery. They made her stand before the group and said to Jesus, 'Teacher, this woman was caught in the act of adultery. In the Law Moses commanded us to stone such a woman. Now what do you say?'"* They were using this question as a trap, in order to have a basis for accusing Him. But Jesus bent down and started to write on the ground with His finger. When they kept on questioning Him, He straightened up and said to them, *'If any one of you is without sin, let him be the first to throw a stone at her.'* Again, He stooped down and wrote on the ground. At this, those who heard began to go away one at a time, the older ones first, until only Jesus was left, with the woman still standing there. Jesus straightened up and asked her, *'Woman, where are they? Has no one condemned you?' 'No one, sir,'* she said. *'Then neither do I condemn you,'* Jesus declared. *'Go now and leave your life of sin.'"*[4]

Was Jesus calling this lady to a life of heterosexuality? No! She was already practicing her heterosexuality, all too well. What she wasn't practicing was holiness. For that matter, neither were her accusers. Jesus exposed, while the woman had committed an obvious sin (sexual relations outside of marriage), her religious accusers had also committed no less a crime by judging hers. Jesus, then,

> **God said, *"Be holy, because I am holy."* I don't recall reading anything about "being heterosexual, because I am heterosexual."**

instructs the woman to *"Go now and leave your life of sin."* It is, in effect, a call to holiness. It isn't a call to live a perfect life. After all, if one could live a perfect life, there would be no need for Jesus, the perfect Savior. It isn't a call to be forgiven. She had just been forgiven by Jesus who chose not to condemn her. Nor is it a call to live a heterosexual life; she was already doing that pretty well on her own. No; this is a call to live a holy life. This woman, caught in adultery, was clearly not living a holy life. She was sleeping around with men. Yet, Jesus decided, rather than condemning her for her actions, He would redeem her personhood and free her to live a life of holiness. This was something the religious accusers were reluctant to embrace and, apparently, unable to fully comprehend. Their brand of holiness was all about following rules. But, what we see in Jesus is something quite different. In this snapshot of a messy life, Jesus models a holy life: love, compassion, forgiveness, reconciliation and faith. Through His words and actions, Jesus wraps this woman with hope. The religious accusers only wanted to give her death. Jesus could have judged the woman just as her accusers did. After all, Jesus is God in the flesh and is actually the only righteous one worthy to pronounce judgment on her. Yet, He didn't; Jesus restored the woman's life. It is in this picture of grace we discover the holiness of Christ and what it might look like when it is emitted from another person's life.

Holiness transcends religious behaviour. If following the Law of God equalled holiness, Jesus would not have chided the religious accusers. In fact, Jesus would have applauded their efforts and probably pitched in with a stone of His own. For that matter, holiness also transcends sinful behavior. This woman was sent away to live a life of holiness, not a life of rules and regulations. If she is merely sent away to mimic her religious accusers, who took up stones to cast, she is no better off than before. She would, in essence, only be exchanging one type of sinfulness for another. No, Christ is not sending her away to learn the finer art of behavior modification. Instead, He is freeing her to live a grace-filled and grace-giving life that looks like Jesus.

Holiness, in its purest form, is Jesus. Therefore, the life Jesus lives is the one we must emulate if we are to live holy lives. There is, according to God's Word, only one way we can accomplish holiness; namely, by allowing Christ into our lives. God explains when we trust in Christ by faith and accept the grace of His forgiveness and love, God places within us His Holy Spirit. Paul, the Apostle, wrote, *"I have been crucified with Christ and I no longer live, but Christ lives in me. The life I live in the body, I live by faith in the Son of God, who loved me and gave Himself for me. I do not set aside the grace of God, for if righteousness could be gained through the law, Christ died for nothing!"*[5] Paul's life of righteousness as a believer is the sole result of being Christ-filled. Paul claims no righteousness of his own. His obedience to the law adds nothing to his salvation. Rather, his righteousness (holiness) is merely a reflection of the righteousness (holiness) of Christ residing within Paul's internal being. Furthermore, the only way Paul (or any one of us) can live a holy life is as we surrender ourselves to Christ. Like the woman dragged into the street, we must depend on the grace and mercy of Christ to save us even while others would cast stones. We have nothing to offer but our brokenness. What a paradox it is that, only in our brokenness, Christ acknowledges and picks us up and empowers us by His Spirit to a life of holiness.

The Apostle also writes concerning the believer who has surrendered to Christ, *"You are not your own. You were bought at a price. Therefore honor God with your body."*[6] Jesus purchases us when we trust Him as our Lord and Savior. We literally give our lives to Him at the point of surrender. He buys us with His precious blood and then, forever, we belong to Him. Our response of salvation, then, should be our total commitment of life and body to the one who has saved us. Our salvation is not hinging on our actions. Rather, our actions are offerings of thanksgiving to the Lord, who has redeemed us totally on His own as a grace gift to us.

But, once again, this is where it gets sticky. What actions actually please God? How do we correctly demonstrate thanksgiving and praise? Is it by following a long list of rules? Is it by promising to live a heterosexual life? Let me call your attention to **Hebrews 13:15-16 (NIV)**: *"Through Jesus, therefore, let us continually* *offer to God a sacrifice of praise—the fruit of our lips that confess His name. And do not forget to do good and to share with others, for with such sacrifices God is pleased."* This passage is very similar to the mandate of Jesus to love the Lord God with our entire beings and to love our neighbors as ourselves. This phenomenon can only be realized as we surrender to the Holy Spirit and allow Him to work through us. A holy life, then, is allowing the Spirit of Christ to manifest through the fruit of the Spirit; that is, the outpouring of the indwelling Christ as a result of a surrendered life. *"But the fruit of the Spirit is love, joy, peace, forbearance, kindness, goodness, faithfulness, gentleness and self-control. Against such things there is no law."*[7]

Do you notice what's missing in this list? Did you say, "Heterosexuality?" If so, you are correct. A list of the Spiritual fruit of holiness and of a holy lifestyle does not include heterosexuality. What is included is love and joy. We also find peace and forbearance in the list. Then, there is kindness. Don't forget goodness and faithfulness and gentleness, either. And last of all, self-control must be mentioned. But, what isn't mentioned is one's sexuality. I repeat: the list of Spiritual fruit (evidences) of a Christ-changed life does NOT include heterosexuality. This idea that, in order to be holy, one must be heterosexual is simply not biblical. Yet, by their judgmental words and actions, many presume their being heterosexual is a clear sign of holiness, all its own.

Yet, these same heterosexual, conservative and fundamentalist Christians fail to exhibit the nine listed Spiritual fruit, at least toward the LGBTQ community. How does heterosexuality trump love ... or kindness ... or any of the other seven fruit? Aren't they falling short by attempting to steal the LGBTQ community's joy and peace? Aren't they falling short in the area of forbearance (patience), kindness and faithfulness toward the LGBTQ community, too? Aren't they also falling short in demonstrating the fruit of gentleness to the LGBTQ community? The only fruit they promote to the LGBTQ community is self-control; but not their own. Rather, they cry out for the LGBTQ community to practice the conservative and fundamentalist's version of self-control: namely, heterosexuality or, at the very least, celibacy.

The obvious prejudice was exposed a few years back when Andy Stanley, pastor of the mega-church, Northpoint Community Church in North Atlanta, told the following story in a CNN interview. Stanley remembered one particular Sunday when he was still an assistant pastor at First Baptist Church of Atlanta. Andy's father and senior pastor, Dr. Charles Stanley, was told a gay pride group was planning to march past his father's church at noon just as they would be letting out of worship. Leaders of the congregation, being warned in advance, dismissed church early to avoid contact with the group. But organizers of the march changed the schedule and started 30 minutes earlier.

Andy watched as First Baptist members filed out of the church and stared at the gay and lesbian marchers who streamed by the members who stood watching in shock. Just then, he noticed a Methodist church across the street whose members held out cups of water for marchers and signs saying, "Everybody welcome! Come worship with us!" The younger Stanley remembered thinking to himself, "We're the church that sings 'Just as I Am' after the sermon and here we are shunning this group of people because of a lifestyle we disagree with."[8] On that particular day, a congregation of Southern Baptists was clearly practicing their heterosexuality ... and their self-righteousness. What a shame they chose not to live out their Spiritual fruit. They left that for the Methodists across the street.

Chapter 10 Notes

1. Gay Persecution of Christians: The Latest Evidence, Crisis Magazine, Stephen Beale, October 10, 2013
2. Galatians 3:28
3. 1 Peter 1:16
4. John 8:1-11
5. Galatians 2:20-21

6. 1 Corinthians 6:20
7. Galatians 5:22-23
8. Two Preaching Giants and the 'Betrayal' that Tore Them Apart, John Blake, CNN, updated 1:40 PM EST, Mon November 19, 2012

CHAPTER 11
EXHIBIT K: PROUD AND PROTECTED

On September 17, 2014, John Pavlovitz swatted a hornet's nest. Over 4,000 people, mostly Christians from all denominations and walks of life, swarmed this former Methodist pastor from North Carolina for posting a blog defending and supporting gay rights. "I wrote the post because I've been in ministry for 18 years and have seen many LGBT people be mistreated and damaged by the Church, and with a lack of decency. I wanted to share a different sentiment from a Christian and pastor," says Pavlovitz.[1] His blog simply conveyed if his two children were to someday grow up and profess themselves as gay, he would keep four promises: first, everyone will know. In other words, he will not be ashamed of his children because they were gay; second, he will pray for them, not to be straight but, to be protected and blessed; third, he will love them no less than if they were straight, and; finally, he says if he has gay children, he will acknowledge they were born gay.

What is so damning about a dad, who happens to be a pastor, simply suggesting he will unconditionally love his children, regardless of their sexual orientations? What makes this so hard for Christians to understand? While conservative and fundamental Christians will quickly point to Scripture as the default reason they oppose homosexuality, I am finding another more honest and disturbing reason that may be an even greater deterrent to parents accepting their children who have exited the closet; namely, PRIDE. "What will the church think?"

Those five words are crippling. Parents are hesitant to ask

questions and seek honest answers in fear of what church leaders, friends and other family members might think or say. The fear of being labeled and ostracized sends parents deep into the closet from which their children are desperately trying to escape. While conservative Christian parents are chided for displaying anything other than "total resistance" to their LGBTQ child, the same watchful eye of the church turns its hypocritical head and overlooks the prideful spirit that so clearly surfaces from its membership when the good church boy or girl "comes out." As in the case with our own family, church leaders were embarrassed and afraid of the ripple effect it would cause the church. I must admit I, too, had those exact sentiments. I cannot begin to describe the initial embarrassment of telling our leadership Addison was gay or the fear of how family and friends would react. All of us were uneasy and unsure. Meanwhile, the son who dared take his stand was unfortunately, in some ways, relegated to a secondary issue. What quickly surfaced was not whether Addison was gay but, rather, how his parents would respond to their son being gay.

Two problems potentially surface in the church when one of their own comes out of the closet. The first problem is truth is discouraged from being sought. Pride quickly says, "The child, the friend, the spouse, etc. … is wrong, plain and simple. Shut it down and shut it up!" For example, I read a Facebook comment not long ago from a Christian man who responded to an article about a high-profiled transgender child who desires to be validated as a boy. He commented, "Sick. This kid and others like HER raised without a Bible don't have a chance." For this pompous man, and countless others, there is no reason to question. There is no reason to research. There is no reason to investigate; certainly, not the Bible. To question tradition's interpretation of Scripture is paramount to heresy. Instead, following the man's lead, a long list of other Christians chimed in with "Amen!", "Preach It!" and much, much worse.

But, who says this child has never been exposed to the Bible? And, regardless of this specific child and HIS parents, I've got some breaking news: "THIS" child is NOT the only transgender child on the planet. In fact, there are many who are coming out of conservative churches every day who have been exposed all their lives to the Bible. Deacon's sons are coming out as transgender; daughters of Sunday school teachers are coming out as lesbians; pastor's sons are coming out as gay or bi-sexual; trust me. Quite frankly, I find it offensive to suggest my wife or I did not expose our gay son to the Bible, Jesus, salvation, sin and all the rest. But, I can relate as to why parents of LGBTQ children go into hiding. The repercussions of peer pressure by other Christians can be overwhelming. Often, it is so strong parents become closed minded, even to the visible evidence they have witnessed in their children all their lives. It would have been so easy for me to quickly dismiss my son's declaration as a "sinful choice" except for the fact I have watched him all his life. Pride could have welled up in me and screamed, "NO!" I will not investigate this phenomenon that has occurred in our family. It would have been so easy to allow my pride to shut it all down and refuse to hear it, believe it or acknowledge it. And, that is precisely what so many Christians do; simply, sweep it under the rug. We refuse to take a second look at Scripture. Rather, parents are programmed to believe their children are possessed with a devil or, at least, intentionally choosing to rebel against God. By the time some parents finally come around to investigating and digging deeper, the church has usually already sent the family packing or worse, the child has ended his or her life. The damage is done.

Pride stifles truth and learning. Pride says, "You have already gotten all the answers. You need not search any further." Pride says, "Even if you do discover your previous beliefs are wrong, you can't acknowledge it because of what someone else might say or think about you." I believe many people are "right there" on this topic of affirming the LGBTQ community. I know moms and dads who are genuinely afraid to research, fearing if they find enlightening material to refute their longstanding traditions, they will face certain ridicule from their churches, their families and their peers.

When Addison first came out, my wife almost instantly began

researching and talking to whomever she could gain insight. One of the most helpful Internet sites for her was GCN, the Gay Christian Network. Jackie would go online and talk with gay Christians. There, she found a place to vent, ask questions and connect with people who were honest and caring. She turned there because she couldn't turn to her church friends. She turned there because the church proved, not only to be silent but, also ignorant and evasive on the subject. When Jackie did try talking to her Christian friends she was quickly "shot down" with the typical responses, reminding her how sinful homosexuality is and how sinful it is for her to even question or search for meaning.

I, on the other hand, refused to talk to anyone about it. I didn't want to discuss it with my son. After all, we had already talked. I knew he wasn't going to change (deep down, I knew he was born gay). I didn't want to discuss it with Jackie because I feared we would argue. And, I was too prideful to bring the topic up with anyone else. I certainly wasn't going to go online and ask a group of gay men about spiritual matters. After all, I was a Southern Baptist pastor with three earned degrees in Theology! There was no way I would entertain any insight from a so-called gay Christian website. I wasn't even sure one could be gay and a spiritually mature Christian, simultaneously. That's what pride will do to you. Pride keeps you in bondage and prevents you from listening and learning. I was in a "protective" mode; only, it wasn't my son I was attempting to protect. It was me.

A second problem that surfaces in the church when one of their own comes out of the closet is pride which squelches the potential for an, otherwise, nurturing and loving relationship. I'm sure some of you are, even now, wrestling with pride issues concerning a family member who has "come out." You are afraid of what others will think or say or do. You might even hide behind the excuse, "I'm just afraid for my_____." Actually, it may be you are most afraid for yourself and not your son or daughter or parent or sibling. That's pride. It's that very pride that will distance you from your loved one. You will be embarrassed to be seen with them in public. You will be embarrassed by their dress and demeanor. You will be embarrassed by their partners. You will scrutinize their thoughts and words and actions. That's pride. Don't think for a minute they don't notice. They feel the disconnect resulting from your pride. By avoiding your community friends and church family members, you may convince yourself you are somehow protecting your children. But, I believe we parents are simply attempting to protect ourselves.

While I was still on staff as our church's pastor, Jackie and I sat in bed one night discussing Addison and one of his friends; one of his gay friends ... that is. This friend invited Addison to attend a Sunday evening worship service. Addison asked and we agreed he could go with his friend to one of the Episcopal churches in town. The church is affirming so it was a non-issue as to whether they would be accepted. But, that's not what we were discussing. What WE were discussing was, "What if Addison wanted to invite his friend to worship with him at our Southern Baptist church? What would we say? What would everyone else say?" And, there you have it; pride. Our pride makes us uneasy and reluctant to embrace our son, OUR SON, the way we would under any other circumstances. We encouraged our son to invite friends to church ... and he did ... many times over the years. But, none of them were gay. So, when Addison came out, some had their "gay-alert" sirens definitely going off when he walked into the building. I can't imagine what might have happened if he had invited a male friend to sit with him during a worship service even if the other guy was straight as an arrow. In fact, I'm convinced some moms and dads discouraged their sons from sitting near or hanging out with Addison. Early on, the deacon body went so far as warning me to prevent Addison from acting or talking "gay" around any of our other students. They honestly feared Addison might have motives to influence them to "become gay," as they put it. It was their self-righteous pride that elicited such fear of having their children possibly being connected and/or exposed to our "leper gay" son.

Sadly, congregations across America are far too often unconcerned as to how their pride affects the LGBTQ child or his or her parents who happen to be church members. Rather, their rigid stance is, "We can't bend on the Scriptures!" and "We will not put our LGBTQ church members before Christ and the Bible." Although Christ tells us with clarity, from the Bible, to love others as we would love ourselves, many Christians focus only on the Scriptures, which supposedly denounce same-sex behavior. Yet, when Christians call people names and run them out of their churches and out of their homes and refuse to talk with them, eat with them, sit beside them or fellowship with them, are they not, in fact, bending the Scriptures and putting their own agendas before Christ?

A popular moniker among Christians is "WWJD: What Would Jesus Do?" Scripture demonstrates He would love the LGBTQ community with open arms. But not us; our pride doesn't allow for it. Conservative and fundamental Christians rally around a false pride, estimating themselves to be superior in knowledge, life and work. No wonder there is a mass exodus from the local churches in America. An Old Testament Proverb reads, *"Pride goes before destruction, a haughty spirit before a fall."*[2] I'm sure more than a few of you just equated the term "destruction" and those who "fall" to the LGBTQ community. You do realize, however, if those are your thoughts, that's your pride speaking. That's what pride does to us. It causes us to immediately assume it's the other guy who is broken or sinning or whatever.

Attempting to keep our pride in check for just a bit longer, allow me to humbly introduce the next piece of evidence for consideration, which I will refer to as Exhibit K: Christian Pride. In my research, I have met a number of parents; men and women, moms and dads, whose pride caused much damage to their families and themselves. The following testimonies are but a minute sampling of what I have discovered to be a widespread epidemic. While each of the following stories is written in their own words, some of the names have been changed to protect the identities and privacy of real families. I am very grateful for their candid conversation. May their words resonate in your heart, as they have in mine.

Jennifer's Story

It was the spring of 2008 when Aaron came out to me. He was 16. Aaron was a smart, compassionate, deep thinking young man. He was obedient, thoughtful, and kind. He was also depressed for much of his adolescence and early teen years. So much so, when my husband hinted at wanting to buy a handgun for home protection I said ABSOLUTELY NOT. I would not consent to bringing a gun home with my son who was obviously distressed this much. Since he was a little boy, I had been suspecting Aaron could be gay so I don't think I was actually surprised when he came out to me. But when he said the words, "I'm gay," it felt like my world came crashing down. Until then, if he hadn't said it to me then it wasn't true and I could go on making excuses for his lack of guy friends and his seemingly lack of interest in girls. I told myself he was just a late bloomer. Even though I suspected he might be ... I didn't want him to be. I didn't want it to be true for him; for our family. And, selfishly, I didn't want it to be true for me.

Fear was the driving emotion of the next couple of years. I was afraid. And the fear led to panic in the coming days, weeks and months. I cried more in those days than I had ever cried before. Sadly, I regret, Aaron saw way too many of my tears. I was crying out of fear and panic and although I tried to say the right words like, "I love you no matter what." and "This doesn't change anything." and "I will always be here for you." I also said many wrong words, too. I said, "Are you sure? Maybe you're just confused? I don't want you to date. Don't tell anyone in the family including your sister because I don't want your grandparents to find out. Can't you just try, one more time, to date a girl?" So, the love I tried to impart to him was overshadowed by lots of words I know made him feel broken and unworthy.

I so wish I had handled things better. I've had lots of time to reflect and to study and to talk to God. After years of asking hard questions, soul searching, and wrestling with my faith versus my child, I've come out of the closest myself in full and total support of this smart, compassionate, deep thinking, obedient, thoughtful, kind, gay young man. He's still the same person I've always loved. He always has been. Nothing has changed except MY own heart. I wish I could go back in time and have a do over. My background is Southern Baptist/conservative so the words, "I'm gay" well, they made me panic for many reasons.

One of the biggest reasons I panicked was the realization my son would never be able to marry. For me, the fact I have a husband who loves me, who wants the best for me, who has my back at all times, and who cares for me no matter what has always been one of the greatest blessings to me. We are a team. I do not have to walk through life alone because I have him; Ken Stringfellow. He is my person. When the Florida legislature put forth an amendment to the state's constitution, the amendment stated marriage was only to be allowed between one man and one woman. It also said the state would not recognize any other civil unions of any type. I remember standing in the voting booth that day staring at the ballot. The former me would have happily voted "Yes" without any reservation. After all, wasn't the Bible clear on the matter? But that was the former me. The me of that day stood there staring at the wording of the amendment. My child's future flashed before my eyes. And the future I saw was one of either a false life of trying to be something he was not OR a life of bleak aloneness.

My mind and my heart raced. Weren't we made to be in relationship with one another? Aren't we put on this earth to find love, to give love, to BE LOVE to one another? For me to prescribe a false life of pretending to feel something you don't/can't feel OR a life of aloneness to another person all while I sit comfy cozy in my happy marriage with the love of my life seemed wrong to me. So that day I voted NO on banning same sex marriage in the state of Florida. I remember thinking about my faith, my belief in God and His word, and my relationship with Jesus Christ, my Savior, my Redeemer. I remember knowing in my heart my child deserved to have a person. I remember believing in my soul God would never create him and then forsake him. And I remember knowing in the very center of my being Aaron hadn't done one single thing in his precious life to deserve a life sentence of being alone.

As of today, in the state where my family lives, BOTH of my children will be able to marry the person they love just like I did 26 years ago ... to have and to hold ... for richer and poorer ... for better, for worse ... in sickness and in health ... till death do us part. I know lots of people don't celebrate the decision the court made to strike down Florida's ban on same sex marriage. But, this mother celebrates! BOTH of my babies can have a person and for that I am so thankful.

David's Story

My Pharisee Tears...
They sting from the pride
The rolling down my cheeks effect is real
I am absorbed, self-absorbed
All the years of judgment, of self-righteousness
Throwing rocks at those I dislike, at least in my mind
Looking down my nose with disdain at tattoos, piercings and flamboyance
At those who are "different" from me
Never seeing the mirror of the Holy Spirit, showing me the arrogance and pride in my own self
Then my daughter, my precious Linda, who is such a miracle all unto herself ...
Has become one of them; the "them" I've so often put down and castigated in my mind.

You showed me God, I have crouched behind a wall of self-righteous attitudes
Thinking all those years I was pursuing you with all my heart Until Linda became one of them
And in Portland, at a conference which seemed to show me a brand new world
You were there Jesus, in more love and shimmering grace than I've seen in one place
And I cried; and cried; and cried
For the Pharisee I had BEEN

Until my Abba Father brought the same shimmering grace to me as He has to the "them" in Portland...

Jesus said to him, "Today salvation has come to this house, because this man, too, is a son of Abraham. For the Son of Man came to seek and to save the lost"

I was more lost than I thought

Now, after this Gay Christian Conference in Portland, I have more hope; my eyes are being opened

I am the "them" too! Linda and I are growing closer than ever before. Hope has come to our house.

Carol's Story

I grew up in a Southern Baptist church all of my life. My Dad was Sunday School Superintendent, my mother was active in everything there was to offer, and all four of us children were, too. My husband and I have been married 37 years, and we also raised our three children in the Southern Baptist faith. My husband was a deacon; I was the Baptist Young Women's President, taught the youth for years, and I TRULY believed in every "patented" answer we are given for the "whys" within Christianity.

The most hurtful and shameful teaching, in so many ways, has been I swallowed the beliefs about the "gay lifestyle" hook, line and sinker. I will grieve over that for the rest of my life because this belief surfaced while raising my own wonderful children. I would give anything to take a giant eraser and erase every careless remark and judgmental statement from their lives I personally made. Believing these teachings so fervently, I refused to allow the questions in my heart to bubble to the surface of my soul for so very long. I saw things in our son that may or may not lead one to think their child is gay, but since he isn't real effeminate, I kept telling myself not to stereotype. I even spoke with several Youth Ministers about my concerns and was always told to pray over him. This "bent" will go away because this is a "choice" and nobody is born this way. I also noticed even though these ministers were "called" to work with teenagers, they were very uncomfortable discussing most things to do with sexuality at all;

the one topic teens desperately want and need to discuss.

As time went on and our son entered college, I began to feel more and more uneasy about his lack of talking about or dating girls. He began to shut off from even talking to us and spent much of his time home from college in his room. This didn't make sense; we had always been close. Still, I didn't want to open this door, hoping it was possible for it to stay closed forever. I kept hearing those voices from my past, "This is a choice. This is a choice." I truly believed by opening this door, I would be a part of leading my son straight to hell. People do not understand this mentality unless they have grown up in a conservative church environment. One is surrounded by conservative theology through their emotional, social and spiritual relationships. It is all they know because they are taught "out there" in the "world," people are evil and lost.

Our son suffered greatly from this teaching. He continued through college to stay very depressed and began cutting and having suicidal thoughts. He also began to try and mask much of his pain with alcohol. I didn't learn of this until November 5th, 2012. After one attempt at trying to call to tell us, he ended the phone call. Then, about 20 minutes later, our phone rang again, and in one breathless sigh he said, "Mom and Dad, I'm gay." Our amazingly beautiful, precious son was 25 years old before he was able to share with his parents, who prided themselves on their Christian principles, he simply could not live this lie any longer. That will stay with me forever. Even though he has so graciously forgiven us, my dying breath will still contain the agony of those regrets. So much has happened since then, but the biggest difference is, during this past three years of truly educating ourselves on this topic, God has completely changed our thoughts surrounding a person's orientation.

We are reading everything we can get our hands on. The sad thing is when our son "came out" of the closet we felt the need to go "in." After about 6 months of getting our arms around this as a family, we slowly began to tell extended family and others. It was a catastrophe when we shared with our small group from church. We were never able to go back after that and it still breaks my heart into a million pieces. They were adamant about this being a sin and needing immediate repentance. There was to be no discussion about any other interpretations of Scripture period. I knew right then we couldn't go back.

My extended family loves our son and treats him like they always have but refuse to read any scientific articles or other interpretations of Scripture. This has been so hurtful because they can share all about their lives, but when I interject anything about what is going in the LGBT world, which I am fairly active in now, there is only silence. My husband and I could not buy into James Dobson's theory of absentee father and overbearing mom because we are truly neither of these people. My husband took Paul camping, hunting and even coached his t-ball team for years. I have never been described as being overbearing in my life.

I want to make it very clear God has never left my side during this journey. In fact, there have been the sweetest, most tender moments of my spiritual life these past three years. I wouldn't go back to who I was before Paul came out for anything in this world. I just love better now. My actions feel more Christ-like than ever before. God is so much bigger than I ever dreamed possible. I use my free time now trying to make a difference in this community — giving out "mom hugs," and trying my best to show who God really is through my own life and treatment of others. It gets better.

Pamela's Story

I am the Christian mom of a gay son, whom I love very much and my God does, too. It took Jordan nine years to "come out" and me, six years to "come out as a gay lover." As rumors fly, most of you probably already know about my Jordan, but you probably didn't hear it from me because I was "in the "closet" praying and crying and praying some more. I've learned the closet is a sad and lonely place to be and my greatest heartache is knowing my precious boy had to be in there so long without even his mom to comfort him.

166

Which brings me to why I feel the need to make this declaration at all, because it really isn't anybody's business, but it is something I can share that might save another child years of suffering, loneliness and self-loathing. It might even save a child's life and save parents a lot of guilt and remorse for the rest of their lives.

The Bible tells me homosexuality is wrong and I preached this to my children, thinking that would surely keep them on the "straight" and narrow. Anything that referenced homosexuality was used as a tool to emphasize my loathing so my children would not "choose" that lifestyle. In this regard, all I managed to do was wound my son so badly he could not trust my love for him enough to share his pain. I'm here to tell you shame does not keep someone from becoming gay because it is not something they have a choice in. It is not something we can change because, believe me, if shaming, crying, praying and pleading would have made my son straight, he surely would be straight by now. I beg you to teach your children to love themselves, and others, for the beautiful and unique gifts of God they are because that child of your heart may be gay. Please show them how to love more and judge less. Talk to them about your beliefs in a loving way and let them know you love them always and forever, No matter what ... and let God be the judge; just like it says in the Bible.

Jackie's Story

On April 8, 2014, my life was changed forever. That day marked the beginning of a painful journey my family would be forced to travel. I can honestly say it was a journey worth taking, though I certainly didn't start out feeling that way.

My husband was approaching his 10th anniversary of ministry as a Southern Baptist pastor of a local church. We were in the middle of revival services and he called me at work to ask me out for lunch. I always love a lunch date with my husband, but when he asked during such a busy week, I knew something was up. When I pressed him, he told me our youngest son, Addison, had told some kids in the youth group he is gay. When I heard those words, my heart sank. I felt true panic. I couldn't breathe. I was terrified.

Although it was a shock, I must admit it really came as no surprise. We had suspected this for most of Addison's life yet we dared not speak of it. But now it was real. The one thing I had dreaded and feared most for my son. He had spoken the words we would have never ever said ourselves. He said, "I'm gay." The news had already spread to other parents and church staff, leaving us no option to handle this privately as a family. We were forced to deal with it immediately, and there was much more to consider than just our son, even though he was, by far, most important. We were a Southern Baptist minister's family and I knew what that meant for us. Fear overtook me as I imagined what lay ahead for my family.

I used what little time I had that afternoon to research, "How to talk to your kid about being gay." I didn't find much, but I did come across these statistics. 40% of homeless youth are LGBT. 30% of gay youth attempt suicide near the age of 15. Almost half of gay and lesbian teens have attempted suicide more than once. Upon learning that, my mind raced back to when Addison was 14 years old. He went through the normal awkward teenager stage but it was more than that. He was angry and he seemed to hate everything about his life. One night, I caught him on his way upstairs to his bedroom carrying a zip-lock bag of pills. It was a mixture of Advil and Tylenol. His excuse was he wanted to keep medicine upstairs for convenience whenever he had a headache. The youth minister revealed to us shortly after, in a youth group meeting, Addison shared having suicidal thoughts.

Around that same time, he came to us wanting to be re-baptized. Addison said he just didn't feel like he had been saved before. We were very puzzled by this, but Scott counseled him and he prayed to receive Christ, followed by baptism. We watched him very closely during that time, and things eventually got better. But looking back, I realized what my precious son must have been going through years earlier and it scared me to death. That night, after an emotional wait, we finally had the opportunity to talk with Addison. We approached the conversation with an undeniable love for our son on one hand and our deeply imbedded conservative theology on the other. When we confronted him, Addison admitted to telling his friends. He had participated in an "honest hour" online where people can ask questions and you must answer honestly. Someone asked if he was gay and he simply said, "Yes". He did not intend to come out that way; it just happened.

I never will forget hearing Scott tell him how disappointed we were he had made this choice, and then, seeing the look on my son's face when he replied, "Dad, it's not a choice. Why would anyone choose this? If I could choose anything, I would choose not to be this way." He said he had prayed every night for years God would change him only to wake up the next morning still the same. He had always heard from us being gay is sinful. He heard his dad preach it from the pulpit and he heard me say it at home. We had unknowingly created in him such a fear of rejection he was too afraid to talk to us about it. Addison said he believed the Bible was true but he couldn't understand why God would say it's wrong and still create him gay. It was in that moment, as I sat there with my own heart breaking for him, I began to wonder the same thing.

Scott ended the conversation by making a deal with Addison. They both agreed to make it a matter of serious prayer and seek God's direction. Scott told him if they both did that he was convinced God would change one of them. I began praying, too. I desperately wanted to pray for my son not to be gay but, instead, I just prayed for answers. I had so many questions. Could it be my son really was born gay? If so, why would God's word clearly condemn homosexuality if it's not a choice? Why would God give us a gay son, knowing it meant the "death penalty" for a Southern Baptist minister? We couldn't reject our son, but were we wrong to accept him? How could anything good come from this? It felt like a curse.

For the next several days, well, actually weeks, I grieved. It took a conscious effort to even breathe as I merely went through the motions of my daily routine. I finally came to terms with the fact this was real. It was not going away. I grieved the loss of my hopes and dreams I had for my son; the dream one day he would marry one of those pretty girls he hung out with or the hope of him giving me grandchildren. I looked back at my son's life and wondered where I went wrong. What could I have done differently? Did I mother him too closely? I guess I had a full-blown pity party. Then one day I realized this wasn't really about me. It wasn't about me at all. My son was gay. What did this mean for him? It meant he would have to face prejudice throughout his entire life. Prejudice from people just like me who saw this as a sinful choice; a prejudice that could cost him family, friendships, employment, and basic civil rights. A prejudice that could leave him exiled from the church, and even worse, could cause him to leave his faith behind. This was my son; my son, MY SON! And then suddenly, I felt myself go quickly from "poor pitiful me" to "protective Mama Bear!" I went from "Oh my God my son is gay!" to, "Yeah, my son is gay, what have you got to say about THAT?" That's when I realized God was changing me.

Meanwhile, my husband was devoting every spare minute he had to research, desperately searching for answers to reconcile our faith with our reality. He plowed through the Hebrew and Greek, researched Biblical culture, and read every book he could find on the subject. The more he read, the more he began to understand the scripture like he never had before. God was changing him too. I remembered the deal Scott made with Addison that night in our bedroom, and I realized it wasn't our son God wanted to change; it was us.

I wish I could say everything was easy from that point on, but actually, that's when things began to get worse. Not only Scott's job, but also his career was hanging by a thread. We knew if he left the church because of this, no other Southern Baptist Church would want him. What would happen to our family? Would we have to sell our house? How would we pay the bills? We hoped for the best, but tried to prepare ourselves for the worst. Scott began looking for other job opportunities, but with no success. Ministry was the only thing Scott knew and he had poured his heart into nothing else for all those years. We feared for our family's future, but we wanted to honor God with our actions. I knew it would be difficult to hold back words as our family went under attack, but Scott and I made a conscious decision to treat the church with the same grace we desired for our family. We were convinced God would protect us somehow if we simply trusted Him.

People were beginning to gossip in the church. Imagine that! Scott tackled it head on, meeting with the deacons to address all their concerns. He shared deeply from his heart. He told them he was studying to find answers and he didn't know how it would affect his theology. He assured them, if and when he found himself in conflict with SBC doctrine, he would resign. The deacons said they were in 100% support of Scott, but they had some conditions. They wanted him to take three weeks off "to deal with our family crisis." (Our family was just fine; the only crisis was with them.) They also wanted assurance Addison wouldn't try to "sway" any of the other young people to become gay and prohibited him from talking about himself or doing anything "gay" on church property. And they wanted Scott to address the church when he returned, announcing to everyone our son is gay, but he did not support Addison's decision and firmly held to his beliefs according to Southern Baptist doctrine.

Scott did take a couple of weeks off. He honestly needed the break. He used that time to continue his research on everything he could get his hands on. We also continued to pray for guidance on how to handle conflict with the church. Our son was our main priority but we loved our church and we desperately wanted to protect it. Scott and the deacon body ultimately decided against making a church-wide announcement. Nothing more was said for nearly a year concerning an announcement, but I couldn't help but wonder why there was so much confusion when literally all our son did was go to school and come home to a few chores and homework every day. He wasn't "doing" anything.

As time went on, however, the tension only grew as rumors were spread, private meetings were held, Scott's sermons were picked apart, our parenting was criticized, and our family was put under the microscope like never before. Adults were even stalking Addison on social media, forcing him to close his Facebook account. We pulled him out of the youth group his senior year to protect him from the adult youth leaders whom we no longer trusted to care for his best interests. I was the Women's Ministry Leader and very involved with the ladies of the church, who knew of our situation began avoiding me like a plague. I lost a best friend in the church who just couldn't support me through this. Another close friend asked me, "Does he think he can still be a Christian now that he's decided to be gay?" One of the ladies suggested my son had a disease and she was sorry we didn't know about it soon enough to get him help. Another said, "I just want you to know I love your boys AND Addison." (We have three sons.)

Those words hurt me deeply, but what hurt most was the silence from the staff and leadership of the church, who knew our family was hurting. It seemed they did nothing to minister to us. Maybe they just didn't know how. I realized the majority of members were not even aware of the issue and we tried very hard to keep it that way. But, I felt so completely alone and isolated. It was a struggle to continue, putting on my smile week after week, as if nothing was wrong. As much as we tried to protect him, Addison became aware some of the adults didn't want him to be there. I'll never forget him saying to me, "Mom, if they don't want me at church, I can just stay home and Dad can have church with me there." I told my son, "The day you stay home I'll be staying home with you!" My heart was broken and there was absolutely no one who could understand.

Friendships were lost, but God was so gracious. I prayed for people I could talk to, people who had been where we were. I was randomly searching the Internet one day and landed on *The Gay Christian Network (GCN)*. There I found a wonderful support group of Christian people, but not like the Christians I was surrounded by at church. These people knew what it was like to be judged by other Christians and exiled from their churches. These people were GAY Christians, and they became my new best friends. They were patient and understanding even though I initially saw them as sinners. They traveled my journey with me, treating me with such love and compassion as they watched God change me right before their eyes.

Another lifesaver for me was a private Facebook group of moms I found. You name it; these moms have been through it, from being outcast from their churches, losing their jobs, having their spouse leave, being disowned by family, and some even losing their gay child to suicide. I've cried with these women and they have cried with me. Although I may never meet most of them in person, they are my true friends.

In addition, God blessed us with a few couples who stood by us and loved our family through the fire. I realize the courage it took to support us and the cost to them was great. Scott and I desperately needed them when others chose to judge or distance themselves from us, and I'm so thankful for their continued friendship.

With Addison's permission, we told our family about his news early on. His brothers said they had known all along and they both agreed he is their brother and they will love him no matter what. Aaron, his oldest brother, said, "If anyone gives Addison a hard time about it, they'll only do it once!" It made me happy to know his brothers had his back. My sister offered her shoulder for me to cry on and I used it often. That's what sisters are for, and I'm thankful she was willing to listen objectively, give sound advice, and simply love our family. Scott agonized over telling his mom, but when he finally did, she said, "Well I could've told you that young man was gay years ago but it wasn't for me to say!" My mother was supportive, as well, although I'm not sure either mom really understands what it means to be gay. They both think Addison could change his mind someday and they're probably holding onto the hope that a pretty girl might turn his head.

As time went on, God continued to reconstruct our faith. One day Scott said to me, "I've changed and I don't think the church can handle me anymore." He had come to the place where he could no longer continue to pastor the church with integrity. It wasn't even about our son anymore. My husband was not the same person he had been a year earlier, and there was no going back. He's always been one to follow God's call even when it didn't make sense on paper. In May of 2015, he met with our personnel team leader to share his plans to resign, without another job waiting. Our prayer for the past year had been for God to show us if and when to close that door. Now we had to pray for Him to open a new one, quickly. God answered that prayer when someone from Hospice of West Alabama contacted Scott, informing him about a chaplain's position opening and suggested he submit a resume.

God rewarded my husband's faith by providing a fulfilling job where he could minister to families and make a difference. Although this position created a substantial pay cut, we knew it was God's answer to our specific prayer for provision. He announced his resignation to the church and was able to leave under the best of circumstances; yet, it was by far the hardest thing we've ever done in ministry. We've left churches before, but this move was different from all the others. Not only were we leaving an eleven year pastorate, we came to grips with the truth that we were also leaving our denomination behind. Thirty-one years of ministry as we had known it was now over. We considered attempting to find a new church home, but for me personally, the risk is just too great. I will never subject my family and, particularly, my gay son, to the kind of abuse we endured at our former church. If the church family we loved and gave so much of ourselves to for eleven years were not willing to support us, we realized a new church, with no connection to us, would never fully accept our family. We've come to accept we are no longer Southern Baptists. We're just Jesus followers. And, I must say, it feels good.

We've been accused of compromising our beliefs to accommodate our son but nothing could be further from the truth. I believe God gifted us with a gay son and used him to bring about much needed change. Sometimes it takes something huge to get us to reconsider our lifelong interpretation of God's Word. Our son's life was important enough to search for the truth. And it was in our search we discovered having a gay son was not the problem, but rather, the means to finding the solution.

Our journey has been difficult to say the least. But God showed His grace to our family by offering protection, provision, and now healing. What once seemed like a curse has turned into the biggest blessing of my life! I have changed and I would never want to go back to the way I was before. I am learning more and more every day what it means to REALLY love people like Jesus. I'm learning to lay judgment aside, to show grace and understanding, and to walk a few steps in another's shoes. I've taught Addison all his life to love everyone, to never put himself above another person. But in the last year, I've learned more from him than I could have ever been taught. I'm so proud of him. My son is brave, loving, smart, funny, creative, sensitive, caring, so handsome, and, oh yeah, he's GAY. His two straight brothers are pretty amazing young men, too.

One of my friends from GCN sent me these words that I hang on to: "There is a difference between acting like a Christian and acting like Jesus. When you act like a Christian everyone at church will praise you and reward you. Heaven help the Christian who starts acting like Jesus. When believers act like Jesus there is a price to pay. You won't be understood and the church won't be very happy. But the end result is a relationship with the living God that is real, and honest and loving. It is full of grace."

These days my focus is pretty simple. I just want to act like Jesus.

Tammie's Story

It's been almost 23 years since I had my last child. He came two weeks early, ready to make his mark on the world and on me. When the Doctor handed him to me, I had this crazy, fleeting thought come out of nowhere; he's gay. I had given birth to three other children before him, and that thought had never entered my mind. I had no idea where it came from or why, so I buried it just as quickly as I'd had it. I remember our first Sunday back to Church after he was born, our Preacher took him from my arms, stood in front of our small congregation, and dedicated him to God. I was a proud Mother. I still am.

I was born and raised in Church and had studied the Bible quite a bit. In fact, I had become a little stubborn and arrogant about it. I

175

sadly remember one time when my children were very small, I pulled into my local bank and they had a big banner hanging out front that read, "We support the United Way." I had just recently read an article in Time magazine about the United Way pulling their support from The Boy Scouts because the Boy Scouts would not allow gays. So, I, in my self-righteous Christian arrogance, let the poor little Teller know just how wrong it was they would support United Way. I am now mortified when I think back about that. Nonetheless, by the time Matt was four, there was not a doubt in my mind my sweet boy was gay. He wasn't feminine, didn't play with dolls, or do any of the things one might associate with being gay, but somehow I knew and I was scared to death. It wasn't something I could say out loud, or talk to anyone about, so I did everything I could think of to "ungay" him to make him normal. I prayed day and night begging God to not let any of my children grow up to be gay. I couldn't specifically say Matt's name in my prayers, because that would be like admitting it. Even though I knew I still couldn't say it out loud not even in prayer. We went to church on Sundays, and like my other children, he was baptized. I did everything and anything I could think of to make him straight, and I certainly never missed a chance to tell him being gay was a choice, a very bad, sinful, choice.

When Matt was 15 I found some notes in his room written between he and his friends that confirmed my worst fear, he's gay. I lost my mind. When he came home from school that day I showed him what I'd found. It's a blur, but I remember crying and screaming at him. The worst part was telling him he was going to hell. At one point, I asked him if he had ever been sexually molested. I was grasping at straws, I figured there had to be a reason he wanted to be gay and if he had been molested, a good therapist could fix that, fix what I couldn't. He was never molested, so there went that theory. My heart was shattered in a million pieces. I thought I was having a nervous breakdown. I had to stay off Facebook during all of this because it was the same time the Chick Fil A fiasco was going on. Then, shortly after that, it was the Duck Dynasty posts. I couldn't handle it. All I saw when people were posting these things on Facebook were signs that said, "Hey Tammie, I hate your son, he's a faggot." So I would start crying and just go to bed.

There were days I couldn't get out of bed. I couldn't function. With my religious background, this was a one-way ticket to hell. How does a Mother live with that? So I would just lie in bed and sob. I was so angry at God. My life had never been a picnic, but this?! This was a deal breaker. This was God hitting below the belt, if there even was a God. I wasn't sure anymore. This was faith shattering. One day while lying in bed sobbing, I jumped up like a crazy woman and started screaming at Satan to leave my babies the hell alone, to pick on me. I could handle it, they could not!

Then I started screaming at God. "All of these years I've been doing everything in my power to make him straight, where have you been? Why haven't you helped me? How did those thousands of prayers escape you? Where have you been all these years when we needed you most?" Then I asked, "Why did you even give me this information when Matt was a baby if you weren't going to help me change him?" God spoke to me in that moment saying, "I didn't give you that information to change Matt. I gave you that information to change you."

I dropped to my knees. I didn't know where to go from there. I walked around like a zombie for a few weeks, and then I picked up my Bible. I of course knew the story of Sodom and Gomorrah and had read the few other scriptures about homosexuality but that was it. So I took it a bit further. I studied the original Greek/Hebrew texts of the Bible, and WOW. I learned not only what those scriptures actually meant, what the stories were actually about, but also that so many of the words used actually have a different meaning then how we know them to mean today. God opened my eyes and my very narrow-minded heart.

I look back now, and wish so much I would have started studying about this when Matt was little, when God first gave me those first few glimpses. There's so many things I would do differently. But, everything happens for a reason and this has turned out to be a wonderful, albeit very difficult part of my journey. Being gay isn't the one-way ticket to hell as I had been taught and as I had believed. My children, ALL of my children, are exactly who God lovingly made them to be and I couldn't be prouder. In the words of my friend Susan Cottrell, and I paraphrase, "I do not not support my gay child and his rights in spite of my faith. I support my gay child and his rights BECAUSE of my faith." [3]

Shirley's Story

People who have known me for many years wonder what happened. They think I am not the same person I was before. In a way they are correct. I am the same loving, caring person I have always been. I am the same strong Christian I have always been. What has changed is my understanding of what God calls sin.

I was brought up in a strict church although it was not as strict as others I have seen. One church I was in was so strict I would classify it as a cult. I didn't stay there long. Although I was taught certain things were sins, I always wondered why some sins seemed to be condemned by Christians more than others. In school, we were taught to think for ourselves and not just follow the crowd on stuff. Even in church, I learned to "try the spirits" to discern if they were of God or not. For this reason, I always questioned if what someone said from the pulpit was really what the Bible said or not.

Most of the time, I discovered it was indeed what the Bible taught; however, I was still struggling with what the church called sin that seemed to me may not actually be sin. This included divorce, people living together in a committed relationship, homosexuality, and other such sexual questions.

One day, about 5 years ago, a friend introduced me to the teachings of Martin Luther. I had known Luther was the spark for the Protestant movement but I had never been taught his beliefs on sexuality. The church steers clear of such matters. I read his thoughts on the subject and found it intriguing. So, I began to study the Scriptures about human sexuality.

For my study, I consulted Greek or Hebrew dictionaries to see what the original texts said and what the original words meant. During the course of my study, which took three years to complete, I discovered Sodom and Gomorrah were not destroyed because of homosexuality. This captured my attention. I continued to study and eventually came to the conclusion homosexuality was not a sin.

At this time, I was still in my Southern Baptist Church. My daughter had a group of friends at school who had, at various times, come out as lesbian, bisexual, or transgender. I loved these kids very much. My daughter loved these kids, too. She came out in support of them. What I didn't know at the time is she was pansexual. I tried to get my daughter to not be so vocal about her support, especially at church, because these people would not like it. I, too, kept my mouth shut about being affirming, though I did start saying things like we needed to show love to the LBGT community if we wanted them to see the Christ we serve. I took a lot of ridicule from people who "loved the sinner but hated the sin." Since I didn't think it was a sin, I didn't agree, and their actions didn't seem loving to me. So, I continued to remain silent.

Then my daughter came out to me. Again, I encouraged her to remain silent. She did tell a small group of friends she thought she could trust, including one youth leader. She soon found out the youth leader told a pastor.

She began to get bullied by "friends" in the church and she even got bullied by some of the leadership. While traveling to a mission trip with other kids, one of the girls asked her about what groups she was in at church. She mentioned GSA. The girl asked what it was and she told her Gay Straight Alliance. Well, my daughter, unbeknown to me, had been told she was not allowed to discuss homosexuality on this trip. She attempted to change the subject but the girl kept asking questions. Also unknown to me or my daughter, the woman in the car had been told to report back to the youth pastor if my daughter talked about it.

Next thing you know, my daughter is being disciplined for talking about it. She tried to say she was just responding to a question and tried to change the subject and the adult woman called her a liar. She had to watch everything she said or did the rest of the week.

A year later, she still hasn't come out, as I wasn't letting her. Only her family and those few close friends knew she was more than affirming. It came time for the mission trip again and she was told she could not go. When I asked why, I was told she was being disciplined for disrespect. I called for a meeting to find out what was going on. It was very clear they were disguising punishing her for supporting gay rights and not for being disrespectful. They wanted her to follow a "discipleship plan" that included reading a book criticizing the "gay agenda" as well as reporting to a staff member about that book, another book, and sexuality. This was all while she was a senior studying for finals at high school.

We left the church that day and never looked back. That week, my daughter came out publicly. I came out as affirming publicly. A week later another daughter also came out publicly as pansexual. A dear friend seeing the attacks we were getting on Facebook from our fellow "Christians" let me know about a support group for moms like me. After joining that group, I began to feel sad for the way I had stifled my daughter and very burdened for the way the LBGT community was being treated.

Thanks to being in a group of loving mama bears, I have been able to openly support the LBGT community. I have joined Equality Virginia so I might be able to do more than just talk about it. My LBGT friends I have had for years always knew I loved them and did not condemn them, but now they have an ally, which is even better. I have always loved unconditionally, but I never knew loving unconditionally would help in dealing with some very unloving "fellow Christians."

I am so thankful to my Lord and Savior, Jesus Christ. I am thankful He saves from all our sins, including being judgmental. I am thankful I have learned the phrase "Gay Christian" is not an oxymoron. I am looking forward to many more years serving the

Lord and loving unconditionally.

Marlene's Story

I grew up as a missionary kid in Brazil and my family was very conservative, both spiritually and politically. I began to question many of the positions my family took as I matured, never wavering in my faith, but definitely feeling God's mercy and love were wider than I had been raised to believe. I began to question the church's position on homosexuality many years ago, as I met more and more LGBTQ people who were wonderful, caring, loving people, and who didn't fit the stereotype usually presented in Christian circles. You know, deviants, promiscuous, out to "recruit" our children. I began to learn more about the science of sexual orientation which completely put to rest any doubts in my mind that someone could be "turned gay" by mere persuasion or influence. After knowing LGBTQ people, I had long since seen the ridiculousness of the argument sexual orientation was a choice.

My daughter's coming out eight years ago led me on a spiritual journey to really understand what the Bible truly says about homosexuality. I started with my love for my daughter and worked with my love for God to find a place of peace and understanding. I spent two years reading, talking to Christian friends and pastors, spending time with LGBTQ people, praying, and trying to understand what the Bible really said about loving, monogamous same-sex relationships. I now have an equals sign (=) as a bumper sticker and a closet filled with rainbow t-shirts and buttons so I guess you could say I have resolved my questions and come out as the proud parent of a gay child.

Since that time, I have felt a strong sense of calling to work with other parents on a similar journey as mine. I helped to start a support group at my former church for parents of LGBTQ children, served as the co-chair of the Oakland/East Bay PFLAG chapter for two years, and am currently serving as a co-facilitator for a brand new satellite meeting for the Seattle PFLAG chapter. I also am involved in several private Facebook groups of Christian moms of LGBTQ children, serve as an admin for two of them, and I have served as a resource parent for the Marin Foundation. I am also advocating for full inclusion of LGBTQ Christians in my current church.

God has taken me out of my comfort zone and given me an exciting new adventure; all because I was given the gift of a gay daughter.

Liz's Story

When my son came out at age 19 he told me he had come to the conclusion the Bible did not condemn loving, committed same sex relationships. I fully expected to be able to prove him wrong. I was accustomed to "studying" scripture as I led women's ministry in church for many years and also wrote and taught women's Bible studies during that time. I knew what it meant to dig into original language and consider the historical context of the verses I was studying. I was shocked to find my son was right ... there was no clear condemnation of the kind of same sex relationship my son was talking about. None of the "clobber" verses were speaking about a loving, monogamous, healthy same sex relationship. My son had not forsaken God nor was he living some kind of lustful life. There was nothing in scripture that spoke of a same sex couple falling in love, marrying, building a life and a family together. Therefore, in light of insufficient evidence in scripture I had to ask myself: "How should I respond to something if scripture doesn't clearly condemn it?"

The only thing I could think is I needed to know if there was any evidence same sex relationships were hurting people in real life. I took time to meet and get to know same sex couples and families and I couldn't find evidence they were any different than opposite sex couples. The evidence I discovered was healthy same sex relationships had the same potential to be good and healthy and life giving opposite sex relationships had.

When I was going through all of this study, research, thought and prayer, Micah 6:8 became a focal point for me:

> *"He hath shewed thee, O man, what is good; and what doth the Lord require of thee, but to do justly, and to love mercy, and to walk humbly with thy God?"*

It was one of those verses I kept being drawn back to and became one of those verses that ended up being "written on my heart." The lack of evidence to condemn same sex relationships and Micah 6:8 led me to this: "If scripture doesn't clearly condemn it and there is no evidence it is harmful to anyone it would be unjust for me to condemn it and I know how God feels about injustice."

Shortly after I realized it was unjust to condemn same sex relationships due to insufficient evidence, I also began to understand good theology should produce good fruit. I knew Scripture says we (followers of Christ) will be known by our good fruit or good psychology. I knew the good news should produce life giving fruit and if my theology was producing depression, hopelessness, self-loathing and suicide I had to come to grips with the reality my theology must be wrong.

As I pondered the "good theology = good fruit/good psychology" principle, and began to connect with a lot of Christian LGBT people, I began to see a pattern. When LGBT people were connected to non-affirming faith communities they were typically very broken, desperate, hopeless, unhappy people and many times they were living out their brokenness in self-destructive ways. But when they were connected to affirming faith communities, they typically were a lot healthier and living much healthier lives. The evidence was clear and convicting.

I had to let go of the theology that was producing death (emotional death, spiritual death, relational death, physical death) and embrace theology producing healthy ideas, healthy choices, healthy living. Theology that was producing health, wholeness and life.

At some point, I realized I could no longer reconcile my Christian faith with the idea same sex relationships were sinful. The two just didn't go together. I became affirming because of my faith, not in spite of it. I support equal rights and protection of LGBT people not "even though" I'm a Christian or "in spite of" of being a Christian, but BECAUSE I'm a Christian.

I haven't had to compromise or choose – I have fully embraced my faith throughout this journey.

Chapter 11 Notes

1. Christian Post, Pastor John Pavlovitz's Blog Entry "If I have Gay Children, I'll Love Them" Sparks bate Among Christians, Sami K. Martin, October 1, 2014
2. Proverbs 16:18 (NIV)
3. Mama Bear Story Project #18, Tammie Janagan, Serendipitydodah.Wordpress.com/…/mama-bear-story-project,.The Mama Bear Story Project is a collection of portraits and autobiographical essays from members of Serendipitydodah for Moms – a private Facebook group for open minded Christian moms of LGBTQ kids.
4. Mama Bear Story Project #19, Shirley Carley
5. Mama Bear Story Project #14, Marlene Lund
6. Mama Bear Story Project #33, Liz Dyer

CHAPTER 12
EXHIBIT L: BEAUTY AND BEAST

In 1964, a new and different kind of sitcom came to American homes: The Munsters. The television satire depicted the home life of a blue-collar family of monsters. The characters included Herman (Frankenstein's monster) and his wife, Lily (vampiress), their son, Eddie (werewolf), Grandpa (vampire) and their niece, Marilyn, (human). One major reoccurring plot in the seventy-episode series was the Munster's embarrassing niece. You see, in their eyes Marilyn was a hideous beast. The family had come to tolerate her looks, loving her in spite of her appearance. The family was amazed anyone would want to befriend Marilyn, much less date her. Needless to say, there were many episodes where the family of monsters couldn't understand how or why their niece turned out as she did.

Two observations are clearly evident: Marilyn was, in fact, a beauty. That's the joke, the gag, and the irony. The Munsters were the monsters, only they couldn't recognize their own hideous selves. Concerning the LGBTQ community, much of the general public is missing the same point, unable to see themselves in the mirror of objectivity. Conservative and fundamentalist churches wonder how and why their nieces and nephews, sons and daughters, fathers and mothers turn out as they do; failing to see the joke is actually on them. While conservative Christians gawk at LGBTQ people as if they are monsters, the opposite is what the rest of the world sees. The joke, the gag, the irony is God sees the LGBTQ community as being something beautiful.

A second observation is the Munsters loved and accepted their niece, unconditionally. Although they recognized her differences, they celebrated her personhood and she was part of their family. Never did they treat her as a second-class family member. No, they didn't understand Marilyn. But, their lack of understanding did not disqualify their love for her as a niece and as a human being. For that matter, their entire community was different. From Herman's co-workers to the occasional guest in their home, the family of Munsters was genuinely accepting and affirming. How much different Christendom treats the LGBTQ.

Some conservative and fundamentalist churches will tolerate the LGBTQ families, but desperately want to lock away this particular family member. In fact, they want to lock her out of the house, altogether. Back in 2012, England's Prime Minister, David Cameron, promised the legalization of gay marriage in the U.K. by 2015, as he compared Church opposition with England's political conservatives who once 'locked out' gay people from the party. Cameron said the Church should not "be locking out people who are gay, or are bisexual or are transgender from being full members of that Church because many people with deeply held Christian views are also gay."[1] Cameron was true to his word as legislation by the Parliament of the United Kingdom was passed to allow same-sex marriage in England and Wales in July, 2013 and came into force on March 13, 2014. The first same-sex marriages took place on March 29, 2014 [2]

I am surprised by the number of people with whom I regularly speak who automatically assume a person cannot be both gay and Christian or, if somehow they manage to be Christian, they certainly are backslidden and out of fellowship with God. While it is a fact Americans who identify as LGBTQ are considerably less likely to be religious and/or affiliated with a particular denomination, even so, a 2014 Gallop poll revealed 53% of polled LGBT adults viewed themselves as moderate to highly religious. The results of the 2014 poll is based on over 104,000 Gallup daily tracking interviews conducted between January 2, 2014 and July 31, 2014, including 3,242 adults who identified themselves as lesbian, gay, bisexual, or transgender.[3] (SEE APPENDIX FOR COMPLETE CHART) The real issue is not so much about

LGBTQ believers desiring to attend church or to engage in meaningful worship; rather, it is about their finding a place where they can worship without condemnation from straight Christians. Let's be honest; who wants to attend a church where they are constantly being put down and rejected? Who wants to share in a Sunday school group when their "story" is dismissed as being unacceptable? Who wants to gather with others who openly avoid them and ignore them and their needs? Of course, the numbers are going to reflect a greater number of LGBTQ believers who are walking away from the church. But, it's not the Lord they feel they must avoid; it's His prejudiced fan club who are relentless, convinced everyone must look, act and talk just like them in order to be considered important to God.

An amazing event occurred in my home state of Alabama when, on January 23, 2015, U.S. District Court Judge Callie V. Granade ruled in favor of the freedom to marry, striking down Alabama's ban on same-sex couples from marrying. 4 After some back and forth political jockeying, Alabama counties actually began issuing same-sex marriage licenses on February, 9, 2015. Immediately following the initial ruling by Judge Granade, the Alabama Baptist Convention State Board of Missions issued the "The Christian Response Task Force Report." As a Southern Baptist pastor, I was given a copy to review and carry to our church leaders. The purpose of the four-page document was "designed to help autonomous Baptist churches think through vital issues and formulate their own internal policies."[5] While the document goes on to say it is not binding on local congregations which are entirely self-governing, I couldn't help but think back to my friend Danny Cortez and the speedy exit from Southern Baptist life ushered onto his entire congregation in 2014 because, in their self-governing, they chose not to agree with the traditional SBC stance on the issue of same-sex marriage.

The "Task Force" document that made its way to my desk contains suggestions to ensure Southern Baptist congregations can continue to "protect" its conservative biblical values. In other words; the church needs to brainstorm ways to keep the LGBTQ out.

Information about ways to modify the local church by-laws, making it virtually impossible to sanction same-sex marriages, is detailed. In addition, it is recommended any Southern Baptist minister who chooses to perform same-sex marriages be terminated. Also laid out in detail are strategies to discourage the LGBTQ community from joining an Alabama Southern Baptist Congregation. Under the heading, "III. Membership," the following options are presented:

1. When a person desiring membership, who is not well known by the pastor, comes forward during the invitation, it may be wise for the pastor to delay presenting him/her for church membership.

2. When a person desires church membership, they may be voted on by the church at the next business meeting. No one will be granted church membership at the end of a worship service.

3. When a person desires church membership, the individual is placed under watch care until there is adequate time to deal with the individual's decision and desire to join the church.

4. When a person desiring church membership comes forward during the invitation, the individual is directed to a spiritual counselor who will deal with the individual to ascertain his/her decision. Following the service, the pastor would meet with the prospective member and the spiritual counselor. Upon completion of this process, the prospective member may be voted upon later by the church regarding his/her membership.

5. When a person desires church membership, they are encouraged to attend a membership orientation class, during which time they are under watch care. The purpose of the orientation class is to assist the prospective member in understanding their commitment to Christ and the

church and to explain the church's doctrine, ministries, practices and values. Upon completion of the class they may be presented for membership. [6]

Also found in the document are strategies to discourage and prevent LGBTQ people from serving in the church, should it be discovered they are already members. It is stated; "One means of preventing such an individual from being in a leadership role is for the pastor to be involved in the nominating process. A pastor is often aware of information others may not know." [7] In other words, the church has the right to discriminate against the LGBTQ community and if the pastor knows any dirty laundry on one of the congregants, it is his duty to use it in such a way as to block them from active ministry. That means the pastor is being encouraged to share information, which may be confidential with the nominating committee, especially if the person in question is gay. Concerning attendance, the document does suggest church members welcome and encourage LGBTQ guests to attend. But, even then, the phrasing of the document makes light of the LGBTQ's motives for wanting to attend a Southern Baptist church, saying it is surely a "shock factor statement" for a person to say, "I am gay, and I am bringing my partner."[8]

How arrogant the Alabama Baptist Task Force is to believe for one minute the LGBTQ community REALLY want to be subjected to this blatant brand of prejudice and hate. What a deceitful plot for Southern Baptist leadership to encourage their congregations to appear to be welcoming to ALL people while, behind the scenes, promoting this kind of propaganda and expecting local congregations to willingly adopt these strategies for their own. The sad part is MANY CHURCHES ARE ACTUALLY ADOPTING THESE STRATEGIES.

As evangelical Christians, we are called to reach out to people with the hope of Christ. Even if you are somehow still holding onto the belief same-sex relationships is wrong, surely you must see how much more wrong and prejudiced it is to attempt to manipulate churches to propagate hate. These kinds of documents are not written to reach out to the LGBTQ population; they are only meant to deter. Why won't you, as conservative Baptists and other fundamentalist Christians, own your beliefs? If you do not want gays in your churches, BE HONEST and admit your sin of prejudice. Stop hiding behind a few verses with holier-than-thou scowls on your faces. But, I am afraid that won't happen. It would expose the blatant prejudice, would it not? It would proclaim to the community-at-large the motives are not as pure as the church would want the public to believe. But, let me assure you, LGBTQ people hear you loud and clear. Many well-meaning church members may not realize they are, in fact being manipulated to be dispensers of hate. But, this community of people, their families and their allies are leaving you; most with broken hearts.

The remaining portion of this chapter is filled with the words of men, women and young people who love the Lord with their whole hearts but who have had their hearts broken by the rejection of the Lord's people. My prayer is you will have ears to hear. I now submit for evidence, Exhibit L: stories from just a few of God's beautiful people.

Marcus' Story

"Greetings in Christ, my name is Marcus, a former missionary pastor in the PCA (Presbyterian Church in America). I will be fifty-two on my next birthday. At the age of 19, I became an evangelical Christian and continue to be quite evangelical and conservative in my Christian beliefs. But, as far as I can tell, I have always been gay even though for most of my life I badly did not want to be that way.

I am from a college town in South East Georgia called Statesboro. From as far back as I can remember, I have always been a bit different from most boys my age. I've generally always been masculine, but from the time I was a small child I always did relationships in a way that was not really "boy-like". From the very beginning, I related better with girls and women and still do in many ways. In addition, early on my voice inflection and some mannerisms would also give me away as being different from most boys.

It was in the sixth grade I began to be aware of anything sexual. I did not connect it as sexual, but it was. I started playing football (tried to), not because I liked it in itself, but because I liked being tackled by other boys. It was 100% about the physical contact with other boys.

It did not occur to me something was profoundly wrong until my first day in class in seventh grade. The PE teacher, who had just retired from playing baseball professionally, had the perfect baseball player body, wore tight jeans and tee shirts, and was what attracted me sexually, then and now. Pretty quickly, I realized I had a huge crush on my P.E. coach. Understand, at the time, I was quite sure was not how it was supposed to be and I desperately did not want to have a crush on my coach or any man for that matter; but I did.

From that point until my sixteenth birthday, I tried to make myself attracted to girls. I even got into my older brother's secret stash of playboy magazines to try and make myself attracted to those naked women. Then and now, naked women trigger a visceral repulsion in me. If ever there were a futile activity under the sun, making myself sexually attracted to women would be it. Nothing worked, but if a man ever entered into a picture, "Oh boy!"

Somewhere in my junior high years my dad decided he was going to cure me of my effeminate tendencies. Now, I made sure no one knew I liked boys, but while I never really discussed it with them, I think my parents had a pretty good idea. Anyway, one evening my dad called me into the den. He was cleaning his guns. My name was "boy" when my dad was not happy with me for some reason. When I walked into the room my dad said, "Boy, you sound and act like a faggot. Understand, if you turn out to be a faggot, I'm going to run you off from here with these guns."

That experience sparked in me an obsession with trying to always look, act and sound masculine. From that point on, I was always insecure about how I presented myself sexually. From junior high until my late forties I would spend hours practicing conversation to rid myself of any "gay lilt" in my voice. I was always dissatisfied

191

with the results, but when I did eventually come out, even other gay people said I flew under their "gaydar". My boyfriend now tells me he would have never known I was gay if I weren't out as gay.

At the age of fourteen, I tried to date a girl. On my sixteenth birthday, she and I went swimming in a private lake. Let's just say, she was well developed for a sixteen-year-old girl. When I first saw her in a two-piece bathing suit, my first and only thought was "Euw!" Mind you, I was not a Christian at the time, but I did not want to be gay. Who would in the Deep South in 1980? So, what I did was break up with her and try to shut my sexuality off, altogether. That became my mode of operation for most of my life.

In my college years, I remember attending my mother's church at First Methodist Statesboro, and the sermon was based on John 3:16-18. *"For God so loved the world that he gave his only begotten Son that whoever believes on him shall not perish but have everlasting life. God sent not his Son into the world not to condemn the world but to save the world. He who believes on Jesus shall not be condemned, but he who does not believe is condemned already because he does not believe."*

By the end of the sermon, I understood grace and embraced Jesus as my Lord and Savior. However, the problem was, I was still gay. I came to understand sanctification as a process, so I redoubled my efforts to perpetually put "gay" to death along with my flesh. By this time, I had long given up on women. I was just trying to be asexual. But no matter how hard I tried; I could never rid myself of attraction for men. And of course, as with all men I know, masturbation was always there and with masturbation, fantasizing about men. Try suppressing all sexual attraction and sexual release as a straight person, and you will get an idea of how hard it is for me to not be gay. Gay or straight, if you are a man with everything working normally, you can't make sexuality go away totally and completely. But that did not prevent me from trying.

In 1996, I felt the call to go to seminary. I eventually ended up in missions working in Canada among the plains Cree Indians. While in seminary, we had a ministry lunch with an adjunct professor who was also the senior pastor of one of the largest churches in the PCA. I raised the question, "How does a minister find a job in the PCA when they are called to celibacy?" The professor's only answer was "Get a life; get a wife!" (Pastorally and theologically, that reply was just wrong on so many levels!)

As a result I decided to try the dating thing again. Mind you, I had avoided any sort of romantic contact with anybody since becoming a Christian. Anyway, there was a young lady at the seminary who seemed "interested" so I asked her out on a date. She wanted it to be a movie night at her house. Being the romantically inexperienced guy that I was, I was totally unsuspicious of her plans. Anyway, we started watching the movie and she started snuggling up to me and putting her hands on me and stuff. Believe me, I'm totally immune to being seduced by a woman, but she gave it a good try. But I figured, "Okay, if I'm to ever do the marriage thing, I will have to learn to tolerate this kind of physical contact with a woman." Then next thing I knew she had me in an embrace with her tongue in my mouth and I nearly barfed. In my head I was saying: 'Nope! I can't do this, not today, not tomorrow and not ever.' Somehow I got home without throwing up on her and then made a point not to go on another date. That was the end of my "get a life; get a wife" project.

While in ministry, I generally avoided letting men get too close to me. I knew if I ever let the wrong guy get too close that would be the end of my ministry. Fortunately, I bond better as friends with women, so I was happy for my friends to be women. The problem with that was single women kept falling in love with me and married women's husbands viewed me as a potential threat. I realized, as a closeted gay minister, I could never let anyone really get close to me.

It was during this time the deaths started happening. First, my dad died on Easter, 2011. Then my brother died unexpectedly in September the same year. Mission to the World sent me home for a one year sabbatical after the second death. By the following summer my mother began to enter the final stages of Alzheimer's and it became clear she was going to go anytime. It was the realization I was about to be truly alone in the world, apart from my sister, that drove me out of the closet.

When I sent my resignation /coming out letter to Mission to the World and Western Canada Presbytery, I told them this: "My homosexuality was always like a caged tiger in my heart. In the cage with the tiger was a T-Rex egg (loneliness). When I turned forty that dang thing hatched and began to grow, and when I was sent home, the T-Rex began attacking the cage. The cage could have held the tiger forever if it had to but it can't hold the T-Rex." I had to come out and deal openly with my sexuality and boldly ask the questions I had been hiding for all this time.

The past several years as an "out" gay Christian has been crazy for me. It has been sexually, theologically and emotionally traumatic. It has made my old relationships with other conservative Christians very strained and strange. In the process, I was excommunicated out of the PCA. I have had to rethink everything I thought I knew about the Bible and my faith. In addition, mine was a cold turkey introduction to the gay community, which is a totally different planet from the one I was accustomed. Unfortunately, there are few resources out there to help us navigate life as LGBT people, especially as a gay evangelical.

The gay community is a product of the Church's rejection of it and the church's total lack of interest in having a redemptive influence on it. The conservative evangelical church and secular nihilism are co-equal accomplices of the lascivious nature of secular gay culture. The gay Christian is presented from both sides the all or nothing proposition of either totally denying internal biological reality or else all moral restraint is pointless and ultimately futile for the gay person. For much of evangelicalism, sexual nihilism is better than a committed lifelong exclusive marriage relationship. Does quietly burning with loneliness and desire for sex with men exhibit love, joy, peace, goodness, faithfulness, kindness and self-control better than a loving, exclusive, life-long gay marriage with one another? Don't shrug this question off with some spiritual sounding "pie in the sky" platitude that doesn't touch the real world of a gay person. This is the real world with all kinds of physical, biochemical and relational realities. Seriously, what are the real practical alternatives to gay marriage for gay people burning with lust and loneliness? What alternative to marriage did Paul offer to straight men who burned with lust and loneliness? Paul offered nothing. Marriage was it. Young men who don't have self-control should marry. That's it. In another passage, Paul said young widows who are tempted to be idol busybodies are to marry. So, what is there for people like me to do but press forward and try to make a Christian marriage work, even if it is with virtually no encouragement or help from the conservative, evangelical church or the secular gay community? God Bless.

Hannah's Story

I never acknowledged my attraction to the same sex throughout the course of my childhood because of the fear of hell that was instilled within me by my parents. I was a closeted, homophobic lesbian who wouldn't even entertain the thought that I may be a damnable sin of a human. It wasn't until my 21st year of life that I finally recognized my attraction to the same sex, admitted that I'm a lesbian who is in love, and eventually come to a place by God's grace, where I learned that I am still a devout Christian.

I fell in love with my partner, Darlene. We began our committed relationship on June 1st, 2013. Soon after we began our life's journey together, we started to seek the Lord and do unbiased research to find out what God expected of us. We studied the Word, in the original Hebrew and Greek, and realized three things; that Jesus never said a word about us in all His teachings, that the word "homosexual" was added to the Bible in the 1946 version and that what we thought were references to people like us was really revealed to be descriptions of others, including male prostitution and pedophilia. Along with these findings, we watched Matthew Vines first YouTube video, speaking to the church on the subject of homosexuality and biblical interpretations. Like us, Vines and his father went on a journey as conservative Christians, and found all the same things we were finding at the time. Darlene and I knew that we needed to come out to our church leaders at the

Calvary Chapel we were attending, but we wanted to be prepared for this big step and we needed to be able to come out on our own terms.

I started with two of the few "spiritual parents" I had trusted at the time, who were also my Bible study group leaders. At first, they agreed to meet with me once a week to explore the topic. But, once it became clear to me that the conversations were one sided and clear to them that I wasn't going to change, things exploded. They kicked me out of their study group and soon after, the male leader threatened to out my partner and me to the church leaders and went through with it. Darlene and I weren't given the chance to come out to the pastors as we planned to do. The first leader they went to was an associate pastor. He e-mailed us both about going in to meet with him to discuss our being gay and what that meant, in his eyes, for our faith and our place in the church. He wouldn't let us go in together. Instead, he asked us to come in separately. Under the guise of a private talk, he invited three other staff workers to sit in the meeting with us. It felt like a pastoral gang up. When it became clear that we were firm as lesbian women of faith, we were kicked out of the church. The news of our new status quickly started spreading in the church. I couldn't believe it. I wanted to take a step back and put off coming out any further for a later date, but because of all the mutual connections that my parents and I had within the church, I felt I needed to come out to my parents immediately. If they found out through the grapevine, it would have made matters worse.

My parents lost their minds when I came out. They began bullying, stalking and harassing me; primarily my Mom, who ended up helping the people I had trusted in the Calvary church, to out my partner and me. The church leaders and my mother felt it was their duty to do that because the leadership and the flock had to know. News of our coming out spread like wildfire. Messages and calls poured in, either in the form of an attack, or by a "concerned church family member" reaching out in Christ. We lost everyone we were close to there. I tried to return to the Liberty Baptist church where I grew up, but I was not welcomed there, either, and pushed out the same year. I had lost all the friends I thought I had, who meant the world to me. All of this happened the same year. I have never felt so alone in my life. I didn't have a church community, friends, or family as my entire immediate biological family rejected me. I didn't feel like I had a place in the world. The world I had known came crashing down. My partner and I were forced to rebuild our life together from the ground up. I did go through a period of time where I didn't want to be called a Christian and was feeling it was time to leave the faith. I thought there wasn't room for me at the table of God. I lost sight of the truth I had learned earlier, and I became angry and bitter. I thought I was done, but my partner spoke life into the situation, and helped me to recognize that none of things we were going through was God's fault, and that He was hurting and weeping with us. Darlene asked me to give one more church a chance. She had found a United Church of Christ (UCC) not too far away. I had my doubts, my skepticism and my anxieties going in. I wasn't sure that I would give this church a real chance until the pastor introduced us to Marsha. Marsha came out of the Calvary movement, and went through the same things in the church. Her story was almost completely parallel to mine. She was the first lesbian Christian we met who let us know that we are loved and that we could let our guards down. Both she the pastor told us that we were valued there. There was room for us at the table. I needed to hear this. Marsha joined us on our journey and became a very close, dear friend of ours. We also appreciated the pastor taking time out to meet with us to discuss God, homosexuality, and the Bible. He answered our questions, and welcomed us in the faith.

Today my faith is stronger than ever. My healing journey began at a U.C.C. Church and after rededicating my life to the Lord at the 2016 Gay Christian Network Conference, I started making big strides in my healing journey. My experiences broke me down, and built me back up to be the strong lesbian woman of faith that I am today. I am grateful for the things I have been through, despite how hard every part of it was for me. I am grateful for Darlene and our family on her side who are supportive, as well as the few supportive cousins I have on mine, for our chosen family, and all the new, wonderful friends we have who love who we are, and who celebrate our love. I have made it through the process of mourning my family, and letting them go, although my parents continue to stalk and harass me in their belief that they cannot give up on me and the hope they have that I will turn straight, and run back to them. I had to change my name to disassociate. Aside from that situation, my life is now beautiful.

Ryland's Story (As shared by his mother, Jennifer)

Growing up in the Bible belt, I regularly attended a church affiliated with the largest Protestant denomination in the United States. My father was a deacon and not only were we there every time the doors were open, we were literally the ones holding the key more often than not. That particular denomination openly frowns upon being gay and/or transgender. It wasn't until I was eighteen and moved to San Diego that I met any openly LGBTQ people. My world expanded as I saw and heard the pain they experienced as they felt so unaccepted being who they were and yet so uncomfortable being who they weren't. I never anticipated I would play a major role in showing a family member unconditional love and acceptance in this area, but looking back, I can see how God was preparing me for this unplanned role as an ally and advocate.

Fast-forward thirty-something years and here I am, the parent of an openly transgender teenager, Ryland, living back in the south, fighting the prejudices of many who reject us, using their religious beliefs as their justification.

As a toddler and preschooler, he had long hair and I enjoyed dressing him in adorable girl outfits. While we had every toy imaginable, he gravitated away from baby dolls and stereotypical girl toys, instead opting for trains, action toys and shows.

There was never an actual "announcement" per se, just a slow realization he wasn't just a girl being a tomboy, like his older sisters. He definitely behaved more like his older brothers, and, while I regularly scheduled play dates with girls, his friends were mostly male. When asked, he said it was because he liked the games the boys played and the toys they played with at school. He said playing mommies and babies and the games the girls played was boring.

When Ry verbalized his preference to choose his own clothing and expressed his desire to wear clothes from the boys' department we tried to find compromises by allowing him to wear mostly jeans and t-shirts. At the age of eight, after seeing how completely miserable he was wearing dresses, I promised him he was wearing his last dress, as a flower girl in a wedding. His haircuts slowly became shorter but still obviously feminine.

At that time Ry and I were attending a non-denominational church and while the children didn't seem to have a problem with his boyish ways, the adults were another story. Some of his Sunday school teachers told him he should be happy God made him a girl and he was "wrong to want to be a boy". I found myself feeling as if I needed to protect him, asking him not to say certain things at church, but feeling torn that, perhaps, he would see my protection as actually unsupportive of him. The same held true with relatives. Fearing confrontation, I didn't want them to know. I had a strong suspicion we would be ostracized and family gatherings with extended relatives would be awkward, at best.

As time passed, and Ry grew closer to puberty, his discomfort with his biologically assigned gender was becoming more pronounced. His older siblings began to express concern we were at a crossroads and needed to help him transition completely. I'm so thankful for them. I cannot imagine doing that alone, without their unwavering love and support. Most people would believe I had two choices: accept or reject, but in my heart the only choices were "when" and "how" to help him transition. My child needed me now more than ever and I was going to do whatever it took to help him on his journey to feel comfortable in his own body and life. This was all new territory for me and I know I made mistakes along the way. But accepting him and assisting in his transition is not one of them. If anything, I regret not doing it sooner.

It was very clear that to continue to discount Ry's need to be fully accepted as a boy would be to deny him a fundamental right to pursue happiness. And, at this point, I knew I would be denying my instincts as a mother to not do everything possible to assist him in as full a transition as possible. Statistics show fifty-eight percent of LGBTQ youth from unsupportive families attempt suicide compared to four percent from supportive families.

I've always been the type of parent, who believes in slowly allowing a child that there isn't a magical age they suddenly become adults to grow up, that there isn't a magical age they suddenly become adults. However, twelve became as natural an age as possible to finally allow him to change his name and go by male pronouns. I also let him choose his haircut and of course it was a style undeniably "male".

This was when his counselor, who, in sessions prior to this, had made it clear she was a Christian, faced us with our first opposition. The first session after his haircut, she pointed at his head and very angrily told me I was "inviting bullying". I watched as my child's joy at being allowed to be himself visibly changed to pain as he literally folded in on himself in his chair. I was too shocked and concerned about Ryland to say much at that time but I walked out of the office knowing I would fight anything and anyone to allow him to be himself and to transition fully. The counselor also treated Ryland as if what he had was a mental disorder when, in fact, it is dysphoria; something she should have been aware of as a professional.

We found another counselor who affirmed Ry and assured us our instincts were correct, and we should go to the school as soon as possible and ask for accommodations, which we did. We were told Ry is the first openly transgender person in the city school system, called a trailblazer by several people we've encountered. While I know for a fact there were quite a few teachers who struggled with understanding, we received nothing but support. The only accommodations we are still waiting for are gender-neutral bathrooms. Ry uses the faculty restroom and while this initially seemed like a good compromise, he has expressed it makes him feel more obviously different. But the bathroom issue could be an entire chapter in a book.

This necessitated a formal announcement to grandparents, aunts, uncles, cousins, etc. ... Ry was transgender; something that caused me nothing short of a panic attack. At the same time our state governor was focusing a large portion of his campaign on his opposition to gay marriage and, while I never actually saw it, I was told one of my close relatives was in a commercial with the governor. I received several emails and messages from other family members who wanted to let me know they cannot support us because we are sinning. A couple of relatives have expressed they are allies but based on the letters and messages sent to me, I still feel strongly, by taking Ry to family gatherings, I am putting him at risk of feeling rejected and am concerned he might be called by his former name or even ignored. I know that isn't true for everyone who would be there, but it's a risk I'm not willing to take at this time. He has such a big heart and I plan to protect it as much as possible as he faces so much from the outside world. Families should be a refuge. Holiday gatherings should be something to look forward to.

I fully believe God placed certain people in positions to walk alongside us during this journey. Before Ry's public transition, I became somewhat reclusive because I was tired of answering questions, facing opposition at every turn, and feeling the need to defend myself as a mother. We all care what people think of us and at home we felt safe and loved unconditionally. While church had always been a place to receive hope and love, it was no longer a safe place for us and, because I've always been a spiritual person, I felt a huge loss.

The worst part of it all for me was my other children saw firsthand how we were judged on social media. After I posted something regarding Ry's transition on my personal account, we received on onslaught of responses stating this was a sin; we were sinners and quite a few messages about hell. Around this time I also began hearing absolutely insane and very infuriating (to put it mildly and without expletives) beliefs of some people demons might actually be involved. Seriously?

This was far too much for me to hear, let alone absorb. I believe the only evil involved here is the evil judgment we all struggle with as we find satisfaction in pointing out how our "sins" pale in comparison to someone else's "sins". I completely understand how off-putting religion must be to the world when the very people who are walking around touting their Christianity can be the biggest hypocrites. It doesn't matter if we preface our judgmental comments with "I know I'm a sinner" or dip it in sugar and say something with a "Bless her heart." and "We should pray for him/her." attached at the beginning or the end. The most frequent comment we've heard has been "Love the sinner, hate the sin." Seriously? Hate the sin? If the perceived sin is a huge part of who someone is? Do people really believe we can choose who we are sexually attracted to? Does someone choose to be transgender because they think it's trendy? If so, they aren't transgender. It was a term we didn't even know existed. The above quoted statements do the most damage but are thoughtlessly echoed by people who are the most uneducated about LGBT people and their families.

Ry didn't see those posts and to this day doesn't know how strongly some people oppose our "allowing" him to be who he is. That sounds ridiculous. How can we allow someone to be who they are? And yet, I guess I was supposed to wrestle him into girls' clothing and slap a bow on his head. Plan his "retreat" to conversion therapy? Ry's most frequent question, when it comes to other people is, "Why does it matter that I'm transgender? Why can't people just accept me as I am?" This completely breaks my heart and admittedly, angers me. At one point I even wrote a mass email to my family and then an apology for being so blunt. I was told by several there was absolutely nothing to apologize for, my pain and plea for support was so obviously strong and to turn to family only seemed natural. One person said they forgive me and I am welcome at their house anytime. For some reason those responses make me feel as if I should enter through the back door, perhaps because they also tell me I am actively sinning. Another response was to plan a gathering, completely ignoring me and the message.

People can be cold, and so judgmental, but I had to stop focusing on those people. I will always treasure some very beautiful memories but I had to stop caring so much about them and continue focusing on the people that matter the most-my children.

With the help of my amazing children, their significant others and some incredible friends, I grew much stronger. I found a PFLAG group and a group for Ry at a center for LGBTQ youth. I found a lot of peace and spiritual growth in yoga and prayer but I basically gave up on finding a church I could connect with and feel safe attending with Ryland. Oddly, it was one of my self-proclaimed atheist friends who encouraged me to hold onto my faith, regardless of how so many in the "Christian" community were treating us.

Our search for an inclusive church that shares a similar belief system as ours is ongoing but I have found an amazing group of very loving Christians whose lives are a daily testimony to God's grace and love. Or, maybe they found us? Either way, for every relationship we've lost, for everyone who has turned their back on us or their nose up at us, I have gained many, many relationships with people who are nothing but accepting and supportive. They may not understand being transgender, quite honestly I don't, and can't, fully understand being gay or transgender, but neither can I understand many things in this world. It's simply not my place to judge others. It's our job as Christians to love and if that's where our focus is how can we possibly go wrong?

Robert's Story

I was born into an agnostic family, yet I had a deep longing to know God from an early age. When I was 5 years old my parents let me attend a local church, and I went alone because no one would go with me. I learned the basics about God in Sunday school and continued to attend a conservative evangelical church. By the time I was 13 I understood what it meant to be a Christian and how to accept Christ as my Lord and Savior. I had all the academic knowledge about salvation but due to some spiritual uncertainties in my life I waited another two years. When I was 15 years old I went with my church youth group to a Billy Graham Crusade. It was there the Holy Spirit moved in my life and I became a Christian. It was that day I asked Christ to come into my life permanently - regardless of what the future would hold. As it turns out I was the catalyst for others in my family becoming Christians as well.

The two year delay in accepting Christ was due to the fact I was trying to deal with the bewilderment of coming to grips with the reality I'm gay. I have known I was gay since I was six years old, but back then it was just that background type of knowing. I didn't have words for it, I just knew I saw the world very differently than other guys. When I hit puberty the reality of those background feelings became foreground feelings - just like any other normal adolescent coming into their orientation.

My un-chosen orientation made no sense to me in light of what Christians were saying about gay people. I had no one to talk to about any of this. I knew better than tell anyone at church or my family what I was feeling. So at age 15 I let myself come out of a cloud of confusion, start the process of accepting myself for who I was, and to become a Christian. I had a Quaker grandmother who taught me to honor my God-given humanity and respect myself as a Child of God. Other gay kids were not so lucky. I knew what other Christians were saying about people like me just did not seem to add up. I knew for certain I loved God with all my heart and I knew for certain that I was gay. That was a breakthrough for me.

When I was 17, I felt God calling me into ministry but, because I was honest about the fact I am gay, I was automatically disqualified by other Christians. I knew better than to even try to have a ministry at that time. I wanted to attend a Christian college and I was blessed to be able to do so. I attended a conservative Christian university and got a degree in Business. Not such a "spiritual" degree, but despite that, I was able to take New Testament Greek for my language credits and to study under some of the brightest Christian scholars in the country. I was totally immersed in a faith-based environment for four years. I loved it. It was the most wonderful time of my life. We had mandatory chapel three times a week and I sat at the feet of some of the most amazing Christians on Earth. I've had gay secular friends ask me, "Why in the world did you go to a Christian university?" and my easy response was, "Because I am a Christian."

I have come to understand we are each given a personal framework by God in which to dwell. That includes many things. We have no idea why some people are gay or left-handed or transgender. They just are. God in His wisdom did not create a bland world of sameness. The richness, color, and diversity of our God is represented in His creation. I am a part of God's wonderful, colorful, diverse nature just like everyone else is. God is multi-faceted and so are His people.

As Christians, it is up to us to integrate our faith into our lives. My deep and abiding Christian faith informs my sexual orientation. Just like a straight non-Christian lives a life quite different to a straight Christian, so it is for gay and transgender people. A gay person who is a Christian will have their lives informed by their faith. This seems so basic, so it comes as quite a surprise to Christians who think all gay people are "less than" other people or their sexual orientation specifically, for some reason, makes them broken. I don't believe because I have not experienced that to be true. I'm broken because I am human, not because I am gay.

Psychologists know sexual orientation is an inborn and natural part of a person's human attributes. Heterosexuality, bisexuality, homosexuality, and asexuality are simply characteristics of humans and other species in nature as well. It is not that the attributes of heterosexuality and asexuality are not sinful, and bisexuality and homosexuality are sinful, it is rather how we use our God given attributes responsibly to love others - and towards a person's spouse in particular. Everyone should act responsibly and we are all equal in this spiritual quest.

The thing that saddens me the most is some Christians attempt to automatically link the word "gay" with "sinful" or say you cannot call yourself a gay Christian. To me "gay" is simply a personal attribute like "black, Korean, or talented," not "alcoholic, glutton, or fornicator." When young gay Christians hear these misleading comparisons to sin, they start taking their lives because they have been falsely taught to hate themselves. What Christians should be encouraging LGBT Christians to do is to integrate their sexual orientation into their faith in a healthy way. They need to be responsible with their sexual orientation just like straight Christians.

Like people on both sides of this issue, I take the Bible very seriously and I am quite conservative. I hold a high view of Scripture. In the Bible I cannot see anywhere God commands us to "understand" others. Even if we don't like some people, we are commanded to love them. This is not so the other person will "feel loved" but rather because you yourself will be a better more Christ-like person if love and grace are practiced. When we extend grace and love to people whom we do not understand, we, ourselves are transformed. People like me who are different are placed in your presence by God so you can practice unconditional love. We are a test. We are not a problem that needs fixing but rather we are God's gift to you.

Despite being wounded by the church I have to put my personal sorrow and indignation aside and hold fast to Christ. I must personally hold on to the same Christ whose grace is not always extended to me by my Christian brothers and sisters. If I took it personally, I would have left my faith a long time ago. Why should you love others when they do not love you back? Why should I love my fellow Christians when they do not always love me back? It is because that is what Christ has commanded of us. We must extend love and grace if we are to be real biblical Christians. It is not an optional extra.

There are very few courses of action and ministry that can be taken by gay people in some churches today. Having said that, being gay has made me a better Christian because I had to get serious with the Gospel despite what others were wrongfully saying about me and others like me.

Other than the condemnation I have received from some Christians, I have never felt condemnation from the Holy Spirit about being gay. God continues to work in my life and convict on other matters like self-sufficiency and pride. I know the voice and working of the Holy Spirit in my life but there has been no condemnation at all from God on this matter. I am frightened for Christians who, in their own pride, try to become the Holy Spirit in my life. They contradict what the still small voice of God has already told me, which is: this is not a problem and you were created as you are for a purpose. What does God think of someone who tries to become the Holy Spirit in someone else's life? We as individuals must always listen to the voice of God in our lives above all others.

As a gay person I have some hopes, prayers, and wishes for the church. I wish the church would understand the Holy Spirit can and does speak directly to the hearts of gay Christians. LGBT Christians are not from another planet. We pray, and fast, and read the inspired Word of God just like other Christians do. As we do, God speaks directly to us just as we are.

I wish the church would realize not everyone has to agree on every topic to be in fellowship as Christians. We don't always agree on other topics either (like divorce, or methods of baptism) but we have an obligation to love each other. If the church treated this like a disputable matter (like eating meat offered to idols in the New Testament) we could move forward and learn to appreciate those honest differences without scaring each other so much. Many younger Christians are already there. We need to get on with the task of winning others to Christ.

Last, I wish the church would be aware GBT people do not expect the church to understand them. Unless you're gay or transgender yourself, it will be impossible to fully understand. And to everyone reading this: give yourself a break because no one is expecting this of you. What the church should do is LOVE gay and transgender people because that is what God has asked Christians to do for each other. He has even asked us to do that for our enemies.

My spiritual challenge is exactly the same as it is for straight Christians. I cannot bear false witness. I need to own who I am and know God, in His love, did not make a mistake when He created me or other LGBT people. When I do that I understand nothing can separate me from the love of God.

Kayleigh's Story

I've been in the church all my life. I was always the good child. Growing up, I hardly ever got in trouble, and when I did, it was usually for talking too much. I was raised in the Southern Baptist Church and came to know God at a very young age. If you were to ask me when I was saved, I'd have a hard time pinning it down. I literally can't remember a time before I knew God and Jesus. Growing up, we were never taught there was such a thing as gay, lesbian or transgendered people. I was the dorky little kid who got excited about Sunday school and begged my mom to send me to Royal Ambassador's (a church group for elementary aged boys), youth conferences and church camps.

In school, I was your typical nerd. My favorite class was always science. I asked my parents for a chemistry set when I was in elementary and I'd proudly show off little experiments to my mom, dad, grandparents and anyone who would watch. I had a perfect future laid out in front of me. I "knew" I was going to go to college, graduate, marry a girl, have kids and raise them in the church. I didn't really think much about gender back in those days. I was told I was a boy and I took that at face value.

My father was, and still is, the textbook definition of masculine stereotypes. He hunts, fishes, races cars, and works a blue-collar job. He made it very clear from my early age what he thought made a man; that men acted and looked a certain way and anything else was being a sissy. I was his firstborn son and, even though he never used the term, I knew he saw me as his masculine heir; even going so far as to name me after his father. I lucked out to an extent. My interests and hobbies tended to be mostly nerdy things like video games, band, and reading sci-fi/fantasy novels. These things were acceptable for a boy. My father grew up in the age of

NASA and engineers. He saw me as his smart son whom he was going to be able to brag about to all his friends. As long as he didn't take away my hobbies, or force me into sports, or raising livestock, I was content.

Things changed for me in high school. My freshman year, I started noticing girls. That was okay. I was supposed to, after all. And, as young boys are wont to do, I had fantasies. And, for the most part, they were normal enough. Only, there was a problem. When I would picture myself, it was always as a woman. Suddenly, gender mattered. Having been raised in the church, I thought this was some sort of perversion. I would try, by sheer force of will, to force the images of myself as a girl out of my head. But it didn't matter how hard I tried, the thoughts wouldn't go away. I would stay awake at night, sometimes until dawn, crying, praying, and begging God to take this away from me.

I alternated back and forth between asking God to make me a normal boy or to somehow magically turn me into a girl. By this time, I'd heard of people who got "sex changes", mystical surgeries that would somehow turn you into a woman. I knew I could never have that. After all, that was something reserved for the type of people you see on shows like Jerry Springer. I knew if I just prayed hard enough, and tried hard enough, I could be "normal." I was such a fool back then. There were so many things I "knew". By the time I was 16, my mom had a transgender coworker. She would come home and speak of her as though the idea of working alongside someone like that was scandalous and funny. She would call her things like "a her what was a him" and giggle. Once again, I "knew" I could never tell her my secret.

The thing is, human beings are fragile creatures; our minds no less so than our bodies. And, just like there's only so much physical pain, stress, work, and struggle a body can take before it starts to break down, enough nights clutching your pillow in tears with no answer begins to wear your heart thin. My prayers to God grew more desperate. I started bargaining. If God wouldn't make me into a girl, maybe he would just give me a realistic dream. Just one night where I would get to experience it and remember as I lived the rest of my life as a guy. Of course, that never happened, either. Throughout my whole youth, God remained silent on the issue. I've never in my life prayed so hard, so long and so many times over one specific thing as this, and yet it seemed like this was the only prayer God wouldn't answer; not even to just say "no".

Eventually, as the silence lingered, my desperation grew all the more. I found myself doing things I wasn't proud of. I started borrowing bras from my grandmother without telling her. I'd hide one in my room for a month or so, and then drop it in the hamper at her house while she wasn't looking. I'd wear the thing for a little while at a time. I would feel better but then I would feel horribly guilty. I'd beg God to forgive me and promise not to do it again. I meant that promise every time I made it, but I never managed to keep it for long, no matter how hard I tried. Then, when I was 17, I noticed she had a prescription for Premarin. I was too smart for my own good and figured out it was estrogen. So, for the first, and last time in my life, I stole something.

I took the Premarin off and on every couple days for the better part of a month. I had no idea how to dose it or how regularly I should be taking it. All I knew is I felt better when I did. Soon, my body started changing. I panicked at this point; partly because I was afraid someone would notice the fact my chest was a bit too perky for just being an overweight teenage boy and partly because I was terrified by the fact I liked the changes. I got rid of the rest of the pills and tried my hardest to forget I ever took them. This was the first of several false starts for me.

Things carried on as normal for the next few years. I graduated high school and enrolled in a little Baptist liberal arts college in deep, east Texas. College was largely fun and uneventful. I tried to forget I'd ever wanted to be a girl. I met a girl and threw myself into our relationship. I convinced myself I could love her enough to be a man and that our relationship would cure me. I told her I'd had a phase back in high school, but I was over it now. To this day, I can't figure out how I managed to make myself believe that.

We were married in a traditional ceremony; her in a white dress, and me in a sports coat and khakis. We said our "I do's" in a little country church in front of our family, just like any other straight, young couple. Six months into our marriage, I came to her with a confession. When she wasn't around, I'd been wearing her clothes. I tried my hardest not to, but I failed. She went away for a couple of days to clear her mind. I wasn't sure if she was going to come back and I wouldn't have blamed her if she had decided not to. But, she did. I cried and apologized and promised not to wear her things anymore. And, like all the other times, I somehow believed it when I did. Over the next several years, I went through several cycles of "relapsing" into what I had decided was cross-dressing. After each time, I'd renew my vow not to do it and try to put it away for a little while. I'd decided this was my thorn in the flesh. Like Paul, I was destined to strive with this. But, I couldn't keep it up forever, and the mental strain started to pile up.

By 2009, my wife was ready for divorce. Not, as you might think, because of the clothing thing, but for other reasons. The strain of forcing myself to try and be a guy had been building for years. The mental energy of holding it all in was wearing me out. I'd been bottling up my emotions for six years of marriage and it was starting to show. I'd disconnected emotionally. Not just from her, but from everyone. I'd grown angry and malcontent. Nothing around the house was ever done well enough, and if I said or did something that hurt her feelings then that was her problem. I became obsessed with "transformation fiction"; poorly written stories on the internet by amateur authors centering on science fiction or fantasy stories where a character was turned from one gender to the other. I would spend hours a day reading them. My wife had had enough. She gave me an ultimatum; either I go to therapy and get help for why I was acting this way or she was through.

After several months of therapy, I finally was able to admit I wanted to be a woman. At the time, I settled for living a partial life. I'd go to work and church as a guy but, occasionally on the weekends, I'd go out as a woman. I bought my own clothes so I wouldn't wear my wife's. I took the name Kayleigh for when I was dressed as a woman. I liked that it linked me to my mother's Scot and Irish roots. Things started getting a little better but something was still missing. It felt like a costume. I'd come home after an evening out and take off all the clothes and I saw a guy underneath. Dressing alone felt fake and hollow. Like trying to take a drink from a picture of a cup, or to eat a piece plastic fruit. Sure, it looked the same, but there was nothing there and it left me still hungry with a bad taste in my mouth.

That's when the decision to try hormones came. My therapist wrote a recommendation and I found a doctor who had experience with them. Only there was a problem. I'd been taught this whole thing was a sin. Here I was, at the age of 28. I'd been praying to God about this since I was 14; literally half my life. And yet, there was still no answer. So, I took the decision to the altar. We started going to the Methodist church not long after we got married and by this time we had been members at our local First United Methodist Church for several years.

I'll never forget that day. For 14 solid years, I'd pleaded with God for one of four different things over and over again. I'd begged Him to either cure me, make me a girl, give me a dream of life as a girl or, at very least, reassure me it was indeed a sin and I was right to keep fighting it. I never got an answer to a single one of those prayers. This day was different though. Communion has always been a very sacred time for me. It's often when I feel closest to God. I wanted to get this right. I didn't want mixed signals and I wanted to know whatever answer I got came from God. So, I thought what better place? If I was ever going to get the answer I sought, it would be in God's house at his holy table, surrounded by a church full of people praying faithfully and while I prayed myself. I knelt down at the altar and bared my soul before God. The minister handed me the elements. And I just held them while I prayed. And for the first time, I came before God and laid the real situation at his feet. I told God I wanted to transition. I wanted to start hormones and I needed to know if it was ok. I asked God to either give me peace to do so or conviction to not. And, for the first time in 14 years, God answered. I got an immediate overwhelming sense of peace.

I knew in that moment this was the right path for me. I also knew why God hadn't answered my prayers all those years. You see, I had been praying the wrong thing. I had been asking God for magic and lies; either magic to turn my body into a woman, magic to turn my brain into a man, or false reality of a dream, or a lie I needed to fight this. The minute I came to God and asked, "What would you have me do?" I got my answer. I took and ate. I took and drank and I got up from that altar a new woman in Christ; truly reconciled with God for the first time in over a decade.

I started taking hormone replacement therapy (HRT) that September. This time, there were no secrets though, no lies, no stealing, and no shame. Within a week I felt better. Within a month, my wife came to me and said everything had changed. Without realizing it, my entire demeanor and attitude had undergone a transition of its own. I was quieter, kinder, and gentler. I listened to her feelings and took them into consideration. I was slower to anger and quicker to apologize. And, most importantly, I was at peace. I literally forgot about the transformation fiction of which I had been so obsessed. I didn't even attempt to stop reading it; rather, one day I looked at my browser history and realized it had been several months since I'd read one of the stories.

On a whim, I decided to read one casually. Maybe I could just enjoy them for what they were. After all, I'd always liked science fiction and fantasy. And now, I'd know a little bit more of what the characters had gone through. It turns out I was wrong. I couldn't enjoy them anymore. From the first page it was suddenly obvious to me what most of these stories were. They were poorly written wish fulfillment fantasies. Like the dreams I had begged God for as a teen, these authors were trying to have the life they wished they had through their characters. I didn't even make it through a chapter before I got bored and put them away for good. I didn't need them anymore.

We decided to take it slow at first. We both hoped I wouldn't need to fully transition; that I could be happy living sometimes as male and sometimes as female; that hormones would give me the feeling of authenticity I lacked, and that would be enough. And, for a while, it worked. It seemed like a good solution at first. My wife was, and is, a straight woman. She got to keep her straight relationship, I got to express myself. I didn't have to come out to coworkers, or church members, and my family didn't need to know.

Eventually, though, as the hormones did their work, and I spent more and more time as Kayleigh, I learned something. In many ways, I was still in the closet. My job, family and church didn't know. As the female part of my life began to grow and thrive, the walls of the closet started to feel all too close. I could fill a whole book with stories of the first four years after starting hormones. In the end, though, I came to my wife and told her I needed to go full time. Leading a double life wasn't working anymore. So I transitioned in my job and we told our families. Our families handled it better than expected. My father-in-law doesn't agree with it but he's not mean about it. Most of my family has gotten used to it. The only one who had any real problem was my father. We haven't spoken in over a year but I still call him on holidays in hopes he will answer. As a concession to my wife, I left one day a week, reserved for "guy time." Sundays, I would dig out the guy clothes and pull my hair back to go to church.

That lasted all of six months. Church is supposed to be family. And it's supposed to be the place you go to be in fellowship with God and Christians. It's supposed to be the one place full of grace and truth in this world. And yet, it was the one place I wasn't being myself. I started growing distracted and sad in church. I felt a wedge growing between God and me. That mask I had worn all those years had grown old and ill fitting. Or maybe the mask was the same but the person underneath was shaped differently. Either way, church became a chore, for me.

We sat down and talked once more. We were both scared of being judged; I for being transgender; her for being in what would now look like a lesbian relationship. This was one of the hardest decisions my wife made. She said she didn't want to be the one separating me from God and, if going to Church as a guy was doing that, then I should go as Kayleigh. So, I talked with my pastor, and we set a date. Ash Wednesday of 2015 was the last day I stepped foot in a church dressed as a guy. The next Sunday, I showed up in a dress. Lent is traditionally seen as a time of fasting; of giving up something that distracts us and separates us from God. I guess you could say I gave up pants for lent. I occasionally chuckle to myself about that timing. Once again, authenticity made all the difference. That first Sunday, it felt like the very air was alive with God. I sang and smiled and danced that morning, praising God in total freedom.

I wish I could say the time since then has been perfect; that transition solved all of my problems and my life is a breeze these days. Of course, it hasn't. There've been quite a few twists turns and bumps in the road along the way. The process has been full of trials for both my wife and me as well as a trial in our relationship. Our church has been accepting in some ways but not in others. Nobody said anything nasty to us or suggested we leave. Methodists are too polite to do anything like that. But, I found out after the first day several members did approach our pastor expressing "concern" over me using the restroom. I was asked not to use the women's restrooms. It felt like a stab in the back; like they assume I might be some kind of predator just because I am transgender. I was asked to use the gender-neutral restroom next to the pastor's office. After the third time in a row I went to use the restroom and found it locked, they compromised on the single stall women's restroom in the education wing. It's served as a metaphor for my experience in the church. I'm accepted, but I'm not. I'm seen as not quite a woman even if nobody is rude enough to say so to my face.

These days I don't live a double life anymore. But, I do sometimes feel like I straddle two worlds. In LGBTQ circles, Christians are often seen as judgmental, hateful, and fighting to deny us our rights. In the Christian world, LGBTQ people are often seen as sexually immoral, tampering with God's creation, and trying to tear down the fabric of society. As a Christian, a lesbian, and a transgender woman, I find myself a bit of an outcast in both.

Pete's Story

I was about 12 years old when I started experiencing attraction to other boys but I was probably about 14 or 15 before I realized these were gay feelings. I never had attraction to girls at all but, trying to be normal, I dated a girl while I attended a university; but we never even kissed. When, perhaps hugely frustrated, she finally forced her tongue into my mouth and I thought it was the most disgusting thing ever. We then broke up because of the failed kiss. I felt like I could never kiss anyone but I've since learned, I just don't enjoy kissing girls.

Growing up, I was part of Presbyterian and Methodist churches. Sexuality was never mentioned, but, from 80's secular culture and occasional comments from my parents, I understood it was not acceptable to be gay.

My faith really came into bloom at the university I attended. I was part of a great Methodist church and a very active member of the university's Christian Union. The parent organization of the CU is extremely conservative. I didn't pay much attention when people from this organization told us Catholics were not Christians, but I did listen when they told us being gay was wrong and acting on it was a very serious sin. In response, I buried all sexual feelings and attractions. Occasionally, I would think about my attractions and remember the sheer horror that I was an abomination in the eyes of my CU friends; if they only knew.

Without any romantic entanglements to distract me, I worked hard and ended up studying for a PhD. When that came to an end I moved to the city for work. In the new town I didn't know anyone and soon became quite depressed. I felt a deep loneliness and a sense I didn't have a place in the world. I got involved in a local church and made some friends. Having a way to advance the Kingdom made me feel more like I had a place in the world but my life still felt sub-human.

After a few years, the isolation came back. I became pretty much the only person I knew without their own home, spouse, baby and wood burning stove. I was in a catch-22 where I couldn't fit into society's ideals but attempting to socialize with people who did was my only way out of loneliness.

For several years I considered suicide almost every day. I started tutoring a high school kid at church in physics. His parents wanted to pay me but, actually, I really valued the company and being involved in a family. It didn't last.

One summer, while all my friends were away, things came to a head and I started having medical problems. At the same time, the house I rented a room in was being sold and, like many other single people, I was worried about affording rent somewhere else and I couldn't afford a mortgage.

I realized I needed more support and could perhaps get this by letting people in. I selected 12 trusted people (some Christians, some not) and "came out" to them. Some were very supportive, others less so, but nobody rejected me.

I knew I could never tell my parents. It wasn't that I thought they would be angry or cut me off. It was I thought I'd really upset them. We generally got along as a family but I tried to create an independence for myself. I found visiting them emotionally difficult as everyone else in the family had a partner whom they love or, at least, had capacity to seek that kind of intimacy. I knew I could never have that and often just felt "in the way". My Mum would use most phone calls to ask why I wasn't finding myself a girlfriend.

During my time of crisis, I felt closer to God than I ever had before. It sometimes felt like He was just around the corner, just out of sight - that if I was quick, I might just see His back. I learned God is not constrained by man or his laws, He is unfathomably powerful and can do whatever He wants.

Then, things got worse. For a straight person this would have looked like parents riding to the rescue but, for a closeted gay guy, it was the ultimate nightmare: my parents bought the house I was living in and became my landlords. Now, not only were my friends, family and church dependent on my remaining closeted; but my home was as well.

A few months later, I was walking to church and thinking about how good it would be if I could come out to my parents. Following Gideon's example, I asked God if it would be safe for me to come out to my parents. If so, then could the prophet Daniel be mentioned in the sermon? I didn't think this was very likely to happen by chance since I knew we were beginning a series on the cross. However, the whole sermon was based on Daniel 7. Nobody gets a chance like that.

The hardest thing for most gay people is coming out to your parents because you don't know how they will react. You may lose your entire family in one moment. If your family is Christian then you actually expect them to reject you. So, given the chance nobody else gets, I wrote to them.

God is wonderfully compassionate to me as they have been completely fine and accepting. My mum has even encouraged me to find a boyfriend, although that is easier said than done.

Before I came out, I thought my church would speak out against affirming parents. In reality, the reverse has happened. My pastor has said I am welcome at church and I don't have to hold to their belief gay relationships are wrong. However, other leaders in the church have not made it so easy and I am not able to be as involved in some of the ministries as I once was.

Church is the only place I've experienced any problems at all. For straight people, it is where they can receive unashamed support through life's difficulties. But for gay people, it is too often the cause of those difficulties.

During this same period, I've been on a journey theologically. I could see how confused church teaching was: some said being gay was wrong; others said just gay sex was wrong. I even encountered teaching that said it was OK to be gay as long as you didn't tell anyone.

Regardless of their official teaching, most churches seemed to go for a knee jerk reaction against anything with the label "gay". I felt frustrated and yearned for better teaching. I knew from my own life the isolation of gay, closeted celibacy produced very bad spiritual fruit and ultimately could lead to suicide. Through prayer, Bible study and an understanding Jesus' interpretation of the law is correct, I no longer believe the "clobber" verses banning gay relationships.

Regardless of these verses, we know God is good and it is not good for man to be alone. Since coming out, I have discovered our need for relationship is not a weakness or indicating God is not enough for us, but a key aspect of the divine. All of humanity is created in the image of God, so all of humanity needs to live in relationship. Many churches, including my own, only allow gay people to be part of the community if they remain celibate, closing off the route for intimacy most straight people enjoy. However, through church culture, lack of understanding and bad teaching, these churches are also making it harder for gay people to find intimacy in other relationships, making it harder to reflect the image of God and ultimately removing humanity from people like me.

But, change is on the way.

AUTHOR: Indeed, it is. In fact, Pete sent me his story on the same day The Supreme Court ruled to legalize same-sex marriage in all fifty states. Change is definitely on the way.

Chapter 12 Notes

Dailymail.Com, I'll Legalize Gay Marriage by 2015, vows, Cameron:

PM Warns Opponents from the Church 'Not to lock People Out', Political Correspondent, July 26, 2012
http://www.dailymail.co.uk/news/article-2179032/Ill-legalise-gay-

marriage-2015-PM-Cameron-warns-opponents-Church-lock-people-out.html#ixzz3OrEAkygi

"Same-sex marriages now legal as first couples wed". BBC News. 29 March 2014.

LGBT Population Significantly Less Religious, Frank Newport,

www.gallop.com/poll/174788/lgbt-population, August 11, 2014 http://www.freedomtomarry.org/states/entry/c/alabamahttp://www.freedotomarry.org/states/entry/c/alabama

http://www.freedomtomarry.org/states/entry/c/alabamahttp://www.freedomtomarry.org/states/entry/c/alabama

5.The Christian Response Task Force Report, Alabama Baptist Convention State Board of Missions, February 2, 2015

Ibid, III. Membership

Ibid, IV. Leadership

Ibid, II. Attendance

CHAPTER THIRTEEN:
CLOSING ARGUMENTS

The Prosecution's Closing Remarks

Members of the Jury, to reiterate:

God does not create a person with homosexual desires (orientation), as homosexuality is unnatural and a choice; a choice the Bible declares as sin. All sin is offensive to God and will be judged if not forgiven.

God has made us male or female, according to His holy purposes. Adopting a transgender self-conception is inconsistent with God's plan and purpose for one's life. Male and female reproductive structures at one's birth is essential to defining and understanding one's self-conception.

The Bible never mentions same-sex behavior except in a negative way. In fact, every marriage relationship found in the Bible involves, specifically, male and female. A foundation to human identity and to the institution of marriage can only be understood in and through a biblical framework of one man and one woman.

Genesis 2 reveals God made Adam and Eve to complement each other in the bond of marriage. Human anatomy, itself, naturally reveals God's intended will, as it concerns sexuality.

The local church has the moral responsibility to teach its congregants the whole truth of God, pointing out the sin of homosexuality, as laid out in Scripture. The church should not and cannot turn a blind eye to that which the Bible clearly denounces as sin. Christians cannot be neutral on this subject or else they, themselves, would be sinning by remaining silent.

Therefore, all those who identify as lesbian, gay, bi-sexual, transgender or queer are charged with living outside the framework of God's intended plan and design for their lives. They are outside the will of God and are in need of forgiveness. True repentance is the only proper response to finding relationship and fellowship with God in Christ.

The Prosecution rests.

The Defense's Closing Remarks

A moment of clarity came to me when, maybe for the first time ever, I realized a large number of LGBTQ people, regardless of mine or anyone else's theology on the issue, are living authentic Christian lives. Over these past years since our son's revelation, I have met and talked extensively with many Christians who also happen to be gay, lesbian, bisexual or transgender. I have also talked with countless moms and dads who, likewise, have children who are gay or transgender. What has been made abundantly clear time and again is the spiritual fruit I have witnessed in the lives of these grace-giving people. That makes them my brothers and sisters in Christ, regardless of what I say, feel or believe.

I can criticize and vilify a concept or a dogma or a lifestyle that differs from my own. But, these concepts wear faces. Maybe you haven't had to sit and listen to the pain of weeping Christian parents who were shunned by their church family simply because they allowed their gay son with AIDS to come home to die; it's devastating! Maybe you haven't had a Christian friend cry in your presence and confide in you they are gay and scared to death. Maybe you haven't had a Christian son ask you if he was born with a birth defect or mental illness because he has to admit to himself he is gay. Maybe you haven't had a Christian child tell you, with no success at their bedtime prayers, they have, for years, pleaded with God to change them so they would see the opposite sex in the same way they see the same sex. Maybe you haven't had the chance to know a Southern Baptist pastor who once served in a neighboring community, one day, finally admit he was gay the whole time the church was thriving in numerical and financial growth. Maybe you haven't had to preach a graveside service over a Christian gay man who died from AIDS in his parent's home, whose last words from his death bed were simply: "I love the Lord. Pray for me." Maybe you haven't met a family who's been ostracized by their church, their parents and their siblings because their child is transgender. Maybe you haven't experienced any of these circumstances but I have lived each and every one and have talked with countless others who have witnessed these exact same scenarios.

We are not talking about an "issue" here– we're talking about real people. And, whether, any of us like it or not, these people ... ALL PEOPLE ... are created in the image and likeness of God. LGBTQ people have real feelings, hopes and dreams. Furthermore, these are people, many of whom love the Lord every bit as much as you or I could imagine. Years ago, there was another group of people who loved the Lord just that much. The only problem was they were considered "outsiders." Concerning one particular man, the story goes something like this: *"'Teacher,' said John, 'we saw someone driving out demons in your name and we told him to stop, because he was not one of us.' 'Do not stop him,' Jesus said. 'For no one who does a miracle in my name can in the next moment say anything bad about me, for whoever is not against us is for us. Truly I tell you, anyone who gives you a cup of water in My name because you belong to the Messiah will certainly not lose their reward.'"*[1]

Jesus had a passion for people and an unusual sensitivity to the poor and the ostracized. When His disciples would have discounted a man, simply because he wasn't like them or part of their specific group, Jesus was quick to bridge the gap. Jesus continually undermined the distinct boundaries between people so very prevalent in His day; in fact, He still does. Jesus welcomed everyone, even those who were treated like trash. On another occasion, *"When one of the Pharisees invited Jesus to have dinner with him, he went to the Pharisee's house and reclined at the table.*

A woman in that town who lived a sinful life learned Jesus was eating at the Pharisee's house so she went there with an alabaster jar of perfume. As she stood behind him at his feet weeping, she began to wet his feet with her tears. Then she wiped them with her hair, kissed them and poured perfume on them.

When the Pharisee who had invited him saw this, he said to himself, "If this man were a prophet, he would know who is touching him and what kind of woman she is—that she is a sinner." Jesus answered him, "Simon, I have something to tell you." "Tell me, teacher," he said. "Two people owed money to a certain money lender. One owed him five hundred denarii, and the other fifty. Neither of them had the money to pay him back, so he forgave the debts of both. Now which of them will love him more?" Simon replied, "I suppose the one who had the bigger debt forgiven." "You have judged correctly," Jesus said. Then he turned toward the woman and said to Simon, "Do you see this woman? I came into your house. You did not give me any water for my feet, but she wet my feet with her tears and wiped them with her hair. You did not give me a kiss, but this woman, from the time I entered, has not stopped kissing my feet. You did not put oil on my head, but she has poured perfume on my feet. Therefore, I tell you, her many sins have been forgiven—as her great love has shown. But whoever has been forgiven little loves little." Then Jesus said to her, "Your sins are forgiven." The other guests began to say among themselves, "Who is this who even forgives sins!" Jesus said to the woman, "Your faith has saved you; go in peace."[2]

Jesus not only did the unthinkable by allowing this woman to touch Him; He forgave her sins. To the amazement and anger of the Pharisees, Jesus engaged with the very ones the religious establishment considered outsiders and unclean. But, there's even more to this story. This woman's sins are forgiven, not because she followed protocol or made an abrupt change in her life but simply because she loved Jesus and approached Him in faith. She didn't change her behavior. She didn't change her appearance. She didn't change anything about herself. In fact, the only change that took place was that which Christ initiated in her life when He accepted her just as she knelt before Him. What's more, when she departed, her only mandate was to *"go in peace."*

We could go on and on examining case after case and person after person for whom Jesus demonstrated unconditional love. Jesus always loved FIRST. On the other hand, I cannot say the same about myself. There was a time when my actions more resembled Saul of Tarsus than Jesus. I have to admit if anyone were zealous about persecuting the LGBTQ community, that person would have been me. My entire life I was taught homosexuality is a sin. My entire life, I viewed it as being "unnatural." My entire life I held a prejudice in my heart and, at best, tolerated gay people in my presence. As a teenager, I made fun of kids I knew were gay and even participated, on occasion, calling them terrible names meant to be hurtful. As an adult, I felt uncomfortable in their presence. In churches where I pastored, I openly admitted I struggled with prejudice toward LGBTQ people.

What's worse, however, is I solemnly believed my stand against what I once called "abnormal behavior" was a valid, noble and biblical cause. I would quote the rhetoric; "Hate the sin, but love the sinner." But the grim truth is I didn't love any part of it ... sin, sinner or situation. What's more, the churches of which I was a part always agreed, applauded and endorsed the beliefs I propagated in my sermons and actions. For that matter, the denomination with which I associated, regularly cloaked their disdain for the LGBTQ community with rhetoric of love and a welcoming spirit, all the while strategizing ways to limit LGBTQ involvement in the church.

But having lived it now from both sides, I honestly believe at the core of it all is fear. People have a tendency to lash out at that which they fear. Most conservatives I know have never spoken to, much less, sat down to get to know an LGBTQ person. Some feel threatened and afraid their way of life is being challenged. Some are afraid their children will be converted by some mythical, "homosexual agenda." Some are afraid they will contract AIDS if they get too close to a gay person. Almost all are afraid of what they don't know or understand. Behind their righteous fear, many

Christians feel justified by a longstanding tradition of biblical interpretation to "correct" the LGBTQ community and save them from the pits of hell. "In C.S. Lewis' *Screwtape Letters*, Screwtape writes to Wormwood, "Hatred is often the compensation by which a frightened man reimburses himself for the miseries of fear. The more he fears, the more he will hate. Fear is played out as hatred and we see so much of it as bullying. The darkest fear of all, the fear that has the power not only to shape a life for death-dealing, but also to distort an entire community, is the fear that lurks beneath the pretense of power and privilege, the fear which crouches behind the doorways of prejudice and preys upon the least of these."[3]

Not too long ago, my wife, Jackie wrote a post for her Facebook page. Here's what she posted:

This post is going to upset some people. Some may unfriend me on Facebook or even write me off as a friend altogether. But I have reached the point I cannot take any more. I'm done.

I mean really done.

I have not gone off the deep end. I have simply made a choice and I am finally brave enough to share it. I have chosen to love people. I have made a drastic change in the way I want to treat people. I didn't realize how much change was necessary. I thought I already loved people. Everyone! But, the more deeply I dug into my heart, I realized there were things in there that didn't belong. Things like prejudice, judgment, pride and neglect. I had spent more time looking at the sin in other people's lives than I had spent seeing them JUST AS THEY ARE. All my life I have bought into the "love the sinner, hate the sin" rhetoric. I am finally realizing what Jesus actually taught was love the sinner and hate our own sin; to look at the plank in our own eye rather than the speck in our brothers'.

There are some things that are impossible to change about ourselves. I believe that more now than ever. But the way we treat people is definitely a choice. So, I choose to love. I will do my best to love all people. This means straight people, gay people, bi people, trans people, bi-racial people, people of all races and backgrounds, no matter what side of the tracks they are from. I will even love ignorant, close-minded people who judge me for loving people. I will strive every day to see people through the eyes of Jesus. I will let God be the judge and let the Holy Spirit do the convicting while I simply love.

I have heard some say the gay "lifestyle" is being shoved down their throats. I can only speak for myself but no one has tried to persuade me to be gay. No one has asked me to be transgender. Now that I think about it, no one has asked me to be anything other than who I am. None of my rights are being withheld. I'm able to worship wherever I choose. I haven't faced discrimination in the workplace. No one harasses me for being who I am. I can shop wherever I want and nobody has refused me cupcakes or pizza.

But our judgmental attitudes are constantly being shoved down the throats of people who are different. I don't understand why we spend so much time focusing on the personal lives of others most of whom we will never even meet. We make it our job to point out everyone else's sin as we interpret it. Some of us go as far as to disrespect them and pass judgment on them. Why do we feel the need to debate their sin when it doesn't concern us? Why can't we just let it lie?

My mother always taught me if I can't say something nice to say nothing at all. It's time to stop meddling in other peoples' business because lives are at stake here, people. Can you imagine living your entire life being told who you are and what you feel on the inside is wrong? That you're gross? Unworthy of acceptance? That you're an abomination? Or even worse, you can't go to Heaven? Do you have any idea what damage that can do to someone?

Did you know 40% of homeless youth are LGBTQ? That 30% of gay youth attempt suicide near the age of 15? Almost half of gay and lesbian teens have attempted suicide more than once? Is your opinion more valuable than their precious lives? They need to hear they are good enough and there is a wonderful and merciful Savior.

Jesus only gave us one job: Love God supremely and love others. When you really understand what it means to love others, you realize two things. 1) This includes everyone. I mean everyone. E-V-E-R-Y-O-N-E. 2) It requires personal sacrifice to put the needs of others before your own, laying personal beliefs aside in order to show them Jesus. Christians, we are the Christ they see. What are we showing them?

Please read this from my heart. I love my Facebook friends. But I use FB as a place to give and receive encouragement. I don't expect anyone to compromise his or her beliefs for the sake of my friendship. But it's not always about proving whose right or making your convictions known at the expense of damaging other people. Sometimes it's more important to show compassion and just leave things to God. I can no longer compromise my feelings by subjecting myself to all the negativity I've seen here from Christian friends. If this post offends you, please unfriend me. I've done a little unfriending myself lately, so it's okay. And try to remember, you never know when a situation may find its way into your own family and, when it does, you'll have absolutely no choice in the matter other than how you react to it. Will you choose to simply love?

Jackie

As I was reading my wife's post, I remembered a poem I wrote the year before that sums up how many Christians carry themselves with an air of arrogance and self-entitlement. I should know; there was a day when I was no different. It reads, as follows:

Go To Hell

> Who's to blame, can you really tell? Someone's guilty, go to hell.
> Point a finger, raise your nose; present a smug, strike your pose.
> Who's to blame, can you really tell? Someone's guilty, go to hell.
> Pass your judgment, keep the law; lift your gavel,

note their flaw.
Who's to blame, can you really tell? Someone's
guilty, go to hell.
Know the rule, place the blame; always another,
always the same.
Who's to blame, can you really tell? Someone's
guilty, go to hell.

Looking back, I see how wrong I was to harbor such hurtful feelings of prejudice and hatred. Even in the past, when I believed homosexuality was, in itself, a sin, I knew full well all sin separated us from God and there were no "big" sins and "little" sins. Nevertheless, I regrettably treated homosexuality different. I knew I shouldn't treat one sin differently, but I did. So did many, if not most, of my colleagues. So did the churches in our Southern Baptist associations.

The 2014 ruling by the Executive Board to dis-fellowship one of its cooperating churches for its stance to love and accept **LGBTQ people** and the 2015 National Convention's resolution to only recognize marriages between heterosexuals (which they refer to as the "biblical and traditional marriage") with disregard to the laws of our nation, clearly demonstrates they still do.

> **We should no longer sing *"Just As I Am"* if everyone is not welcomed into the Body of Christ, just as they are!**

And not only Baptists but most, if not all, evangelical and fundamentalist denominations continue to make villains of anyone engaged in same-sex relationships. This book is a plea to my brothers and sisters in Christ, who claim to love and follow Jesus, to lay down your stones and repent. My attitude, like many of yours, was once a parallel to that of the Pharisees and, even Jesus' disciples, who were bent on purging the outcasts from the community of believers. But, God's love and compassion flooded my spirit and overwhelmed me to the point of submission. God opened my eyes. I didn't

229

decide to turn "liberal." I haven't gone mad. I'm not filled with an evil spirit. God simply opened my eyes; period. My prayer is He will similarly speak to your heart through these written pages and open your eyes, too. I trust you will objectively allow God's Spirit to speak to you concerning the seven passages that, for so long, have been misused to intentionally bully millions of people for whom Christ died.

I pray you will pay close attention to the testimony of Jesus throughout this book and hear His heart and revisit His grace. The grace of Christ is abundant and freely dispensed to all those who consider themselves on the fringe. And now it is our place, as the body of Christ, to genuinely love and embrace the outcast, the downtrodden and the marginalized. We cannot, in good conscious, continue to claim to be Christ followers while discounting or ignoring fellow Christ followers who happen to be members of the **LGBTQ community**. We cannot truly claim to love with the compassion of Christ while picking and choosing whom we will accept into our congregations, whether our decisions are based on race, creed, gender or sexual orientation. We should no longer sing "Amazing Grace" if we are not fully participating in that grace with all people, including those who are transgender or those in same-sex relationships. We should no longer sing "Just As I Am" if everyone is not welcomed into the Body of Christ, just as they are. When churches and denominations refuse to love people like Jesus loves them but, rather, insist on debating theological differences of opinion, we lose sight of the very reason for which Jesus Christ died. On the other hand, theological debates make it much easier to throw stones.

One last passage of Scripture I want to bring to your attention is 3 John, verses 9-14. John pens: *"I wrote to the church, but Diotrephes, who loves to be first, will have nothing to do with us. So if I come, I will call attention to what he is doing, gossiping maliciously about us. Not satisfied with that, he refuses to welcome the brothers. He also stops those who want to do so and puts them out of the church. Dear friend, do not imitate what is evil but what is good. Anyone who does what is good is from God. Anyone who*

*does what is evil has not seen God. Demetrius is well spoken of by
everyone--and even by the truth itself. We also speak well of him,
and you know that our testimony is true. I have much to write you,
but I do not want to do so with pen and ink. I hope to see you soon,
and we will talk face to face. Peace to you. The friends here send
their greetings. Greet the friends there by name."*

Here, we find a tale of two church members. One is well spoken of
by everyone and God's truth bears evidence of the same. Known
by his peers as Demetrius, even the Apostle John, knows this man,
not only by his name but also as being a good and godly man. On
the other hand, Diotrephes is known to be a selfish man who insists
on having his way. He is neither kind nor gracious toward others.
He is a malicious gossip who (GET THIS) refuses to welcome
others into the church. "He also stops those who want to do so and
puts them out of the church." John calls this man "evil" and
discourages anyone from imitating this kind of man.

Let me ask you a question: Which of these two individuals most
reflect your thoughts and feelings toward anyone, straight or gay,
who would desire to enter the doors of the church building you
attend? Is EVERYONE welcome to enter, worship, join and
participate? Does it matter how they dress, the color of their skin,
the origin of their birth, the politics they prefer or the sexual
orientation to which they ascribe? Does it matter if they are
married and, if so, does it matter to whom?

If you have reservations about anyone actively participating in the
life of the local church, gay or straight, married or single, you are,
according to John the Apostle, imitating the evil of Diotrephes. If
you are condemning those who would welcome anyone and
everyone, you are acting out in the spirit of Diotrephes and, again,
John calls this evil. However, it is the welcoming and grace giving
spirit of Demetrius we should emulate as God's people. So, again I
beg the question: To whom do you most relate and reflect with
your life? Is there any question as to which of these two men most
reflect Christ?

Members of the jury, in light of the overwhelming evidence and testimonies presented on behalf of the defense, I submit the LGBTQ community is "Not Guilty" of any and all charges imposed by the conservative and fundamentalist churches, as it pertains to their sexual orientation or perceived gender. I remind you, if this were a court of law, all a defense lawyer must prove to sway a jury to find a "not guilty" verdict is to show there is a "reasonable doubt". It is not necessary they find conclusive evidence the defendant be absolutely "innocent." If a jury of one's peers determines a reasonable doubt exists, that same jury, if honest and objective, cannot, nor should they, convict.

Rather, the defense lawyer's only task is to introduce enough evidence exists to render a "not guilty" verdict. I respectfully propose that MORE than adequate evidence BEYOND a reasonable doubt has been duly presented. Therefore, I ask the Christian community to embrace LGBTQ people of faith as brothers and sisters in Christ. I ask the LGBTQ community be allowed full inclusion and membership in the local church of their choosing. I ask the LGBTQ community be allowed the same privileges in our local congregations, including the right to marry whomever they should so choose, with the blessings of the church. I call for all charges to be immediately and forever dropped so the love of Christ Jesus may be taken up and embraced in its place. I humbly and respectfully rest my case.

After objectively considering the evidence and listening to Holy Spirit speak to your heart to bring discernment from God, as a member of the jury, have you reached a verdict?

_____Guilty

_____Not Guilty

Chapter Thirteen Notes

1. Mark 9:38-41
2. Luke 7:36-50
3. Cynthia Jarvis, "The Shadow Side," The Christian Century, July 17-30,   2002, P. 19

ABOUT THE AUTHOR

Scott McQueen, a former Southern Baptist pastor, currently serves as a hospice chaplain. In addition, Scott is also an accomplished folk artist, participating in shows across the Southeast. Scott continues as a vocal advocate for the LGBTQ community and is also available for speaking engagements. He is a graduate of Samford University (B.A.), New Orleans Baptist Theological Seminary (M.Div) and Luther Rice Seminary (D.Min). Scott is married to Jackie, his wife of 34 years. Together they have three sons and a daughter-in-law. Scott is an ordained minister who lives in Northport, Alabama.

Thank you for purchasing *Reasonable Doubt: A Case for LGBTQ Inclusion in the Institutions of Marriage and Church.* For additional copies to share with friends, family members and others needing greater insight, you can order from Amazon, ask for it by name at your local bookstore or purchase signed copies by emailing pastorscott@minister.com .

Bulk orders are also available for larger groups. For bulk prices contact pastorscott@minister.com.

-God bless you in your search for Truth-

APPENDIX

RESOURCES

The following is a list of resources and materials that may be found useful as you continue research and study. This is far from an exhaustive list. These are simply resources I researched and found helpful to me.

ORGANIZATIONS
Gay Christian Network
www.gaychristian.net
(800)268-3688
Just as their name suggests, this site will quickly help acclimate you to LGBT Christians. There are chat groups, blogs, articles and other information.

Gay Church.Org
www.gaychurch.org
This site will provide helpful information about where to find an affirming denomination and/or local congregation. There is also a bookstore link and some helpful reading as it concerns LGBT and the Bible.

PFLAG.Org
www.pflag.org
PFLAG is the United States' largest organization uniting families and allies with people who are lesbian, gay, bisexual, transgender, or queer. PFLAG has nearly 400 chapters across the United States, with more than 200,000 members and supporters.

Human Rights Campaign
www.hrc.org
LGBTQ related articles, events and world news are all covered here. In addition, one can find ways to participate locally and nationally to make a difference.

CRISIS RESOURCES

National Suicide Prevention Lifeline
Free 24-hour hotline
800-273-TALK
    (8255)

The Trevor Project
Crisis and suicide prevention for LGBTQ youth
866-4-U-TREVOR
866-488-7386

Trans Lifeline
Hotline staffed by transgender people for transgender people
USA- (877)565-8860
CANADA- (877)330-6366

i Am Clinic
A professional counseling practice specifically devoted to the Christian LGBTQ community and their religious parents
www.iAmClinic.org
(303) 335-9210
899 Logan Street, Ste 309
Denver, CO 80203

BOOKS

Bible, Gender, Sexuality: Reframing the Church's Debate on Same-Sex Relationships by James V. Brownson

Walking The Bridgeless Canyon: Repairing the Breach Between

the Church and the LGBT Community by Kathy Baldock

A Letter to My Congregation by Ken Wilson

Torn: Rescuing the Gospel from the Gays-vs.-Christians Debate by Justin Lee

Changing Our Mind, second edition by David Gushee

Mom, I'm Gay: Loving Your LGBTQ Child Without Having to Sacrifice Your Faith by Susan Cottrell

Religiosity Among National Adults

By LGBT status and gender

	Highly religious	Moderately religious	Not religious
	%	%	%
NATIONAL ADULTS			
LGBT	24	29	47
Non-LGBT	41	29	30
MALE			
LGBT	25	26	49
Non-LGBT	36	28	35
FEMALE			
LGBT	24	31	46
Non-LGBT	45	30	25

January-July 2014

GALLUP

Made in the USA
Columbia, SC
19 May 2021